BOLLINGEN SE

HEINRICH ZIMMER

MYTHS AND SYMBOLS
IN INDIAN ART
AND CIVILIZATION

EDITED BY JOSEPH CAMPBELL

BOLLINGEN SERIES VI

PRINCETON UNIVERSITY PRESS

THIS VOLUME IS THE SIXTH IN A SERIES
OF BOOKS SPONSORED BY BOLLINGEN FOUNDATION

First Princeton / Bollingen paperback printing, 1972

Second printing, 1974

Eighth printing, for the Mythos edition, 1992

15   16   14

*Princeton University Press books are printed on acid-free paper,
and meet the guidelines for permanence and durability of the
Committee on Production Guidelines for Book Longevity of the
Council on Library Resources*

Library of Congress Catalogue Card No. 46-7144

ISBN 0-691-01778-6 (paperback edn.)

ISBN 0-691-09800-X (hardcover edn.)

Text designed by Stefan Salter

Printed in the United States of America

EDITOR'S FOREWORD

It was a great loss when Heinrich Zimmer (1890–1943) died suddenly of pneumonia, two years after his arrival in the United States. He was at the opening of what would certainly have been the most productive period of his career. Two bins of notes and papers remained to testify to his rapidly maturing projects. The lectures that he had been delivering at Columbia University were roughly typed and arranged for conversion into books; a volume on Hindu medicine was half completed; an introduction to the study of Sanskrit had been outlined; a popular work on mythology had been begun. Scraps of paper, scribbled in German, English, Sanskrit, and French, were sifted everywhere into the pages of his library and files, suggesting articles to be written, research work to be accomplished, even excursions to be made to specific localities in India after the close of the war. He had quickly adapted himself to the ways of his new country and was fired with an eagerness to make his contribution to its intellectual heritage. Hardly had he begun to find his stride, however, when, suddenly stricken, he passed from full career to his death within seven days.

The task of rescuing from oblivion as great a portion as possible of the abruptly interrupted labors was taken up immediately. MYTHS AND SYMBOLS IN INDIAN ART AND CIVILIZATION *is a reworking of the lecture course delivered at Columbia University the winter term of 1942. The typewritten notes had been supplemented in the classroom by impromptu amplifications and illustrated by a series of over two hundred lantern slides. Their transformation into a book demanded considerable recomposition, re-arrangement, abridgments and augmentation. Recollections of conversations with Dr. Zimmer supplied most of the materials for this reconstruction. Where such help was lacking, I turned to the authorities he most respected.*

Dr. Ananda K. Coomaraswamy very kindly supplied a number of supplementary notes to complete the work. His additions have been introduced in square brackets and initialed AKC; undoubtedly they would have met with the approval of Dr. Zimmer. I am indebted to Dr. Coomaraswamy, also, for the print of Figure 55, and for many indispensable emendations throughout the length of the text.

Since Dr. Zimmer had no need to fill his private papers with such annotations, credits, and references as are necessary to a published volume, a complicated task confronted the editor when it came to tracking down the sources of the numerous myths and illustrations. For valuable assistance I wish to thank Dr. Marguerite Block of Columbia University, who helped select, arrange, and identify the pictures, and who read an early draft of the manuscript; Mr. and Mrs. Nasli Heeramaneck, who enabled me to discover the sources of many of the photographs; Dr. David Friedman, formerly of the University of Leyden, whose suggestions guided me to the Sanskrit originals of several of the myths; and Mrs. Peter Geiger, who performed a large portion of the actual work of research, labored on the manuscript and proofs, and took charge of a cumbersome burden of details. Swami Nikhilananda opened his library and aided with advice. Mrs. Margaret Wing reviewed the last two drafts of the manuscript, prepared the index, and assisted with the proofs. Without the generous co-operation of these friends, the work would not have been accomplished.

J.C.

New York City, October 28, 1945

CONTENTS

VII

LIST OF PLATES*

---

* The sources for a number of Dr. Zimmer's photographs could not be ascertained. The Editor regrets that these have to be presented without due credit.

12. Vishnu's Boar Avatār (varāha avatāra) rescuing the Earth Goddess; colossal sandstone relief at Udayagiri, Gwalior, 440 A.D. (Burgess.) See p. 79.

13. Vishnu Avatār: The Deliverance of the Elephant King; relief in temple at Deogarh, IV–VI centuries A.D. (Burgess.) See p. 77.

14. Krishna (Vishnu) conquering the Serpent Prince, Kāliya; Rājput painting, Kāngrā, late XVIII century. (Metropolitan Museum of Art, New York.) See p. 85.

15. Padmā (the goddess "Lotus") with attendant elephants; decoration from ruined Stūpa at Bhārhut, II–I centuries B.C. See pp. 92, 103.

16. Winged Goddess; terracotta from Basārh, III century B.C. See p. 92.

17. Gangā (the goddess "Ganges"); black steatite image from Bengal (partial view), XII century A.D. (Rajshahi Museum; Photo Kramrisch.) See p. 110.

18. Padmapāni (the Bodhisattva "Lotus in Hand," or Avalokiteshvara); copper image from Nepāl, IX century A.D. (Museum of Fine Arts, Boston.) See p. 97.

19. Tree Goddess (vṛikṣa-devatā); from ruins of Stūpa-balustrade at Bharhut, II–I centuries B.C. (Indian Museum, Calcutta. Photo: India Office.) See pp. 69, 70.

20. Prajñāpāramitā; Java, c. 1225 A.D.; (Ethnographic Museum, Leyden: Photo, van Oest.) See p. 98.

21-23. Seals in steatite, showing animal forms and undeciphered inscriptions; from Mohenjo-Daro (Indus Civilization), 3000-2000 B.C. (Archaeological Survey of India.) See p. 94.

24. Nude Goddess, terracotta (height 4 inches); Mohenjo-Daro (Indus Civilization), 3000-2000 B.C. (Museum of Fine Arts, Boston.) See p. 96.

25. Stone Lingam from Mohenjo-Daro (Indus Civilization), 3000-2000 B.C. (Archaeological Survey of India.) See pp. 96, 126.

MYTHS AND SYMBOLS IN
INDIAN ART AND CIVILIZATION

CHAPTER ONE

ETERNITY AND TIME

I.

The Parade of Ants

INDRA slew the dragon, a giant titan that had been couching on the mountains in the limbless shape of a cloud serpent, holding the waters of heaven captive in its belly. The god flung his thunderbolt into the midst of the ungainly coils; the monster shattered like a stack of withered rushes. The waters burst free and streamed in ribbons across the land, to circulate once more through the body of the world.

This flood is the flood of life and belongs to all. It is the sap of field and forest, the blood coursing in the veins. The monster had appropriated the common benefit, massing his ambitious, selfish hulk between heaven and earth, but now was slain. The juices again were pouring. The titans were retreating to the underworlds; the gods were returning to the summit of the central mountain of the earth, there to reign from on high.

During the period of the supremacy of the dragon, the majestic mansions of the lofty city of the gods had cracked and crumbled. The first act of Indra was to rebuild them. All the divinities of the heavens were acclaiming him their savior. Greatly elated in his triumph and in the knowledge of his strength, he summoned Vishvakarman, the god of arts and crafts, and commanded him to erect such a palace as should befit the unequaled splendor of the king of the gods.

The miraculous genius, Vishvakarman, succeeded in constructing in a single year a shining residence, marvelous with palaces

3

and gardens, lakes and towers. But as the work progressed, the demands of Indra became even more exacting and his unfolding visions vaster. He required additional terraces and pavilions, more ponds, groves, and pleasure grounds. Whenever Indra arrived to appraise the work, he developed vision beyond vision of marvels remaining to be contrived. Presently the divine craftsman, brought to despair, decided to seek succor from above. He would turn to the demiurgic creator, Brahmā, the pristine embodiment of the Universal Spirit, who abides far above the troubled Olympian sphere of ambition, strife, and glory.

When Vishvakarman secretly resorted to the higher throne and presented his case, Brahmā comforted the petitioner. "You will soon be relieved of your burden," he said. "Go home in peace." Then, while Vishvakarman was hurrying down again to the city of Indra, Brahmā himself ascended to a still higher sphere. He came before Vishnu, the Supreme Being, of whom he himself, the Creator, was but an agent. In beatific silence Vishnu gave ear, and by a mere nod of the head let it be known that the request of Vishvakarman would be fulfilled.

Early next morning a brahmin boy, carrying the staff of a pilgrim, made his appearance at the gate of Indra, bidding the porter announce his visit to the king. The gate-man hurried to the master, and the master hastened to the entrance to welcome in person the auspicious guest. The boy was slender, some ten years old, radiant with the luster of wisdom. Indra discovered him amidst a cluster of enraptured, staring children. The boy greeted the host with a gentle glance of his dark and brilliant eyes. The king bowed to the holy child and the boy cheerfully gave his blessing. The two retired to the hall of Indra, where the god ceremoniously proffered welcome to his guest with oblations of honey, milk, and fruits, then said: "O Venerable Boy, tell me of the purpose of your coming."

The beautiful child replied with a voice that was as deep and soft as the slow thundering of auspicious rain clouds. "O King of

Gods, I have heard of the mighty palace you are building, and have come to refer to you the questions in my mind. How many years will it require to complete this rich and extensive residence? What further feats of engineering will Vishvakarman be expected to accomplish? O Highest of the Gods,"—the boy's luminous features moved with a gentle, scarcely perceptible smile—"no Indra before you has ever succeeded in completing such a palace as yours is to be."

Full of the wine of triumph, the king of the gods was entertained by this mere boy's pretension to a knowledge of Indras earlier than himself. With a fatherly smile he put the question: "Tell me, Child! Are they then so very many, the Indras and Vishvakarmans whom you have seen—or at least, whom you have heard of?"

The wonderful guest calmly nodded. "Yes, indeed, many have I seen." The voice was as warm and sweet as milk fresh from the cow, but the words sent a slow chill through Indra's veins. "My dear child," the boy continued, "I knew your father, Kashyapa, the Old Tortoise Man, lord and progenitor of all the creatures of the earth. And I knew your grandfather, Marīchi, Beam of Celestial Light, who was the son of Brahmā. Marīchi was begotten of the god Brahmā's pure spirit; his only wealth and glory were his sanctity and devotion. Also, I know Brahmā, brought forth by Vishnu from the lotus calix growing from Vishnu's navel. And Vishnu himself—the Supreme Being, supporting Brahmā in his creative endeavor—him too I know.

"O King of Gods, I have known the dreadful dissolution of the universe. I have seen all perish, again and again, at the end of every cycle. At that terrible time, every single atom dissolves into the primal, pure waters of eternity, whence originally all arose. Everything then goes back into the fathomless, wild infinity of the ocean, which is covered with utter darkness and is empty of every sign of animate being. Ah, who will count the universes that have passed away, or the creations that have risen afresh, again and again, from the formless abyss of the vast waters? Who will number the passing ages of the world, as they follow each other endlessly? And who will search through the wide infinities of space to count the universes side by side, each containing its Brahmā, its Vishnu, and its Shiva? Who will count the Indras in them all—those Indras side by side, who reign at once in all the innumerable worlds; those others who passed away before them; or even the Indras who succeed each other in any given line, ascending to godly kingship, one by one, and, one by one, passing away? King of Gods, there are among your servants certain who maintain that it may be possible to number the grains of sand on earth and the drops of rain that fall from the sky, but no one will ever number all those Indras. This is what the Knowers know.

"The life and kingship of an Indra endure seventy-one eons, and when twenty-eight Indras have expired, one Day and Night of Brahmā has elapsed. But the existence of one Brahmā, measured in such Brahmā Days and Nights, is only one hundred and eight years. Brahmā follows Brahmā; one sinks, the next arises; the endless series cannot be told. There is no end to the number of those Brahmās—to say nothing of Indras.

"But the universes side by side at any given moment, each harboring a Brahmā and an Indra: who will estimate the number of these? Beyond the farthest vision, crowding outer space, the universes come and go, an innumerable host. Like delicate boats they float on the fathomless, pure waters that form the body of Vishnu. Out of every hair-pore of that body a universe bubbles and breaks. Will you presume to count them? Will you number the gods in all those worlds—the worlds present and the worlds past?"

A procession of ants had made its appearance in the hall during the discourse of the boy. In military array, in a column four yards wide, the tribe paraded across the floor. The boy noted them, paused, and stared, then suddenly laughed with an aston-

6

ishing peal, but immediately subsided into a profoundly indrawn and thoughtful silence.

"Why do you laugh?" stammered Indra. "Who are you, mysterious being, under this deceiving guise of a boy?" The proud king's throat and lips had gone dry, and his voice continually broke. "Who are you, Ocean of Virtues, enshrouded in deluding mist?"

The magnificent boy resumed: "I laughed because of the ants. The reason is not to be told. Do not ask me to disclose it. The seed of woe and the fruit of wisdom are enclosed within this secret. It is the secret that smites with an ax the tree of worldly vanity, hews away its roots, and scatters its crown. This secret is a lamp to those groping in ignorance. This secret lies buried in the wisdom of the ages, and is rarely revealed even to saints. This secret is the living air of those ascetics who renounce and transcend mortal existence; but worldlings, deluded by desire and pride, it destroys."

The boy smiled and sank into silence. Indra regarded him, unable to move. "O Son of a Brahmin," the king pleaded presently, with a new and visible humility, "I do not know who you are. You would seem to be Wisdom Incarnate. Reveal to me this secret of the ages, this light that dispels the dark."

Thus requested to teach, the boy opened to the god the hidden wisdom. "I saw the ants, O Indra, filing in long parade. Each was once an Indra. Like you, each by virtue of pious deeds once ascended to the rank of a king of gods. But now, through many rebirths, each has become again an ant. This army is an army of former Indras.

"Piety and high deeds elevate the inhabitants of the world to the glorious realm of the celestial mansions, or to the higher domains of Brahmā and Shiva and to the highest sphere of Vishnu; but wicked acts sink them into the worlds beneath, into pits of pain and sorrow, involving reincarnation among birds and vermin, or out of the wombs of pigs and animals of the wild,

7

or among trees, or among insects. It is by deeds that one merits happiness or anguish, and becomes a master or a serf. It is by deeds that one attains to the rank of a king or brahmin, or of some god, or of an Indra or a Brahmā. And through deeds again, one contracts disease, acquires beauty and deformity, or is reborn in the condition of a monster.

"This is the whole substance of the secret. This wisdom is the ferry to beatitude across the ocean of hell.

"Life in the cycle of the countless rebirths is like a vision in a dream. The gods on high, the mute trees and the stones, are alike apparitions in this phantasy. But Death administers the law of time. Ordained by time, Death is the master of all. Perishable as bubbles are the good and the evil of the beings of the dream. In unending cycles the good and evil alternate. Hence, the wise are attached to neither, neither the evil nor the good. The wise are not attached to anything at all."

The boy concluded the appalling lesson and quietly regarded his host. The king of gods, for all his celestial splendor, had been reduced in his own regard to insignificance. Meanwhile, another amazing apparition had entered the hall.

The newcomer had the appearance of a kind of hermit. His head was piled with matted hair; he wore a black deerskin around his loins; on his forehead was painted a white mark; his head was shaded by a paltry parasol of grass; and a quaint, circular cluster of hair grew on his chest: it was intact at the circumference, but from the center many of the hairs, it seemed, had disappeared. This saintly figure strode directly to Indra and the boy, squatted between them on the floor, and there remained, motionless as a rock. The kingly Indra, somewhat recovering his hostly role, bowed and paid obeisance, offering sour milk with honey and other refreshments; then he inquired, falteringly but reverently, after the welfare of the stern guest, and bade him welcome. Whereupon the boy addressed the holy man, asking the very questions Indra himself would have proposed.

"Whence do you come, O Holy Man? What is your name and what brings you to this place? Where is your present home, and what is the meaning of this grass parasol? What is the portent of that circular hair-tuft on your chest: why is it dense at the circumference but at the center almost bare? Be kind enough, O Holy Man, to answer, in brief, these questions. I am anxious to understand."

Patiently the old saint smiled, and slowly began his reply. "I am a brahmin. Hairy is my name. And I have come here to behold Indra. Since I know that I am short-lived, I have decided to possess no home, to build no house, and neither to marry nor to seek a livelihood. I exist by begging alms. To shield myself from sun and rain I carry over my head this parasol of grass.

"As to the circle of hair on my chest, it is a source of grief to the children of the world. Nevertheless, it teaches wisdom. With the fall of an Indra, one hair drops. That is why, in the center all the hairs have gone. When the other half of the period allotted to the present Brahmā will have expired, I myself shall die. O Brahmin Boy, it follows that I am somewhat short of days; what, therefore, is the use of a wife and a son, or of a house?

"Each flicker of the eyelids of the great Vishnu registers the passing of a Brahmā. Everything below that sphere of Brahmā is as insubstantial as a cloud taking shape and again dissolving. That is why I devote myself exclusively to meditating on the incomparable lotus-feet of highest Vishnu. Faith in Vishnu is more than the bliss of redemption; for every joy, even the heavenly, is as fragile as a dream, and only interferes with the one-pointedness of our faith in Him Supreme.

"Shiva, the peace-bestowing, the highest spiritual guide, taught me this wonderful wisdom. I do not crave to experience the various blissful forms of redemption: to share the highest god's supernal mansions and enjoy his eternal presence, or to be like him in body and apparel, or to become a part of his august substance, or even to be absorbed wholly in his ineffable essence."

9

Abruptly, the holy man ceased and immediately vanished. It had been the god Shiva himself; he had now returned to his supramundane abode. Simultaneously, the brahmin boy, who had been Vishnu, disappeared as well. The king was alone, baffled and amazed.

The king, Indra, pondered; and the events seemed to him to have been a dream. But he no longer felt any desire to magnify his heavenly splendor or to go on with the construction of his palace. He summoned Vishvakarman. Graciously greeting the craftsman with honeyed words, he heaped on him jewels and precious gifts, then with a sumptuous celebration sent him home.

The king, Indra, now desired redemption. He had acquired wisdom, and wished only to be free. He entrusted the pomp and burden of his office to his son, and prepared to retire to the hermit life of the wilderness. Whereupon his beautiful and passionate queen, Shachi, was overcome with grief.

Weeping, in sorrow and utter despair, Shachi resorted to Indra's ingenious house-priest and spiritual advisor, the Lord of Magic Wisdom, Brihaspati. Bowing at his feet, she implored him to divert her husband's mind from its stern resolve. The resourceful counselor of the gods, who by his spells and devices had helped the heavenly powers wrest the government of the universe from the hands of their titan rivals, listened thoughtfully to the complaint of the voluptuous, disconsolate goddess, and knowingly nodded assent. With a wizard's smile, he took her hand and conducted her to the presence of her spouse. In the role, then, of spiritual teacher, he discoursed sagely on the virtues of the spiritual life, but on the virtues also, of the secular. He gave to each its due. Very skillfully he developed his theme. The royal pupil was persuaded to relent in his extreme resolve. The queen was restored to radiant joy.

This Lord of Magic Wisdom, Brihaspati, once had composed a treatise on government, in order to teach Indra how to rule the world. He now issued a second work, a treatise on the polity and stratagems of married love. Demonstrating the sweet art of wooing ever anew, and of enchaining the beloved with enduring bonds, this priceless book established on sound foundations the married life of the reunited pair.

Thus concludes the marvelous story of how the king of gods was humiliated in his boundless pride, cured of an excessive ambition, and through wisdom, both spiritual and secular, brought to a knowledge of his proper role in the wheeling play of unending life.*

2.

The Wheel of Rebirth

INDIA'S treasure of myths and symbols is immense. In the teeming texts and multitudinous architectural monuments eloquent details so abound that, though scholars since the end of the eighteenth century have been editing, translating, and interpreting, it is by no means an infrequent experience to come across tales hitherto unnoticed or unknown, images undeciphered, expressive features not yet understood, esthetic and philosophical values uninterpreted. From the second millennium B.C., the Indian traditions have been handed on in unbroken continuity. Since the transmission has been mainly oral, there is left to us only an imperfect record of the long and rich development: certain periods, long and fruitful, are barely documented; much has been irretrievably lost. Nevertheless, though tens of thousands of pages remain in manuscript still waiting to be edited, the great works already published in printed Western and Indian editions are so many that no individual may hope to cover them in a lifetime.

This inheritance is both prodigious and fragmentary, and yet

---

* *Brahmavaivarta Purāṇa*, Kṛiṣṇa-janma Khaṇḍa, 47. 50-161.

11

homogeneous to such a degree that it is possible to present the main features in a simple, consistent outline. We shall be able to review in the present volume, and in some measure to fathom, the major areas and problems, the dominant symbols and most significant features of the abundant world of Hindu myth. Questions of methodology and interpretation, which will inevitably arise as the exotic forms unfold their amazing secrets, we shall deal with as they come. They cannot be coped with at the outset; for we are not yet familiar with the personages, the style, the sequences of events, the basic conceptions and scales of value of this tradition so utterly different from our own. It would not do to seek to constrain the Oriental conceptions into the delimiting frames familiar to the West. Their profound strangeness must be permitted to expose to us the unconscious limitations of our own approach to the enigmas of existence and of man.

The wonderful story of the Parade of Ants opens before us an unfamiliar spectacle of space and throbs with an alien pulse of time. Notions of space and time are commonly taken for granted within the pale of a given tradition and civilization. Their validity is seldom discussed or questioned, even by people who sharply disagree on social, political, and moral issues. They appear to be inevitable, colorless and unimportant; for we move through and are carried on by them, as the fish by water. We are contained within and caught by them, unaware of their specific character, because our knowledge does not reach beyond them. Hence, the time and space conceptions of India will at first seem to us of the West unsound and bizarre. The fundamentals of the Western view are so close to our eyes that they escape our criticism. They are of the texture of our experience and reactions. We are prone, therefore, to take them for granted as fundamental to human experience in general, and as constituting an integral part of reality.

The astounding story of the re-education of the proud and successful Indra plays with visions of cosmic cycles—eons following each other in the endlessness of time, eons contemporaneous in the infinitudes of space—such as could hardly be said to enter into the sociological and psychological thinking of the West. In "timeless" India these extensive diastoles give the life-rhythm of all thought. The wheel of birth and death, the round of emanation, fruition, dissolution, and re-emanation, is a commonplace of popular speech as well as a fundamental theme of philosophy, myth and symbol, religion, politics and art. It is understood as applying not only to the life of the individual, but to the history of society and the course of the cosmos. Every moment of existence is measured and judged against the backdrop of this pleroma.

According to the mythologies of Hinduism, each world cycle is subdivided into four yugas or world ages. These are comparable to the four ages of the Greco-Roman tradition, and, like the latter, decline in moral excellence as the round proceeds. The Classical ages took their names from the metals, Gold, Silver, Brass, and Iron, the Hindu from the four throws of the Indian dice game, Krita, Tretā, Dvāpara, and Kali. In both cases the appellations suggest the relative virtues of the periods, as they succeed each other in a slow, irreversible procession.

Krita is the perfect participle of the verb *kri*, to do; it means, literally, "done, made, accomplished, perfect." This is the dice-throw that wins the jackpot, the total gain. According to the Indian conception, the idea of total, or totality, is associated with the number four. "Four square" signifies "totality." Anything complete and self-contained is conceived as possessing all of its four "quarters" (*pāda*). It is established firmly on its "four legs" (*catuḥ-pāda*). Thus, Krita Yuga, the first of the ages, is the perfect, or "four-quartered," yuga. Dharma, the moral order of the world (which is in virtual existence before the beginning, but then becomes manifest in the spheres, energies, and beings of the world), is during this period firm on its four legs, like a sacred cow; one hundred percent, or four quarters, effective as an all-pervading structural element in the organism of the universe. During this yuga men and women are born virtuous. They devote their lives to the fulfillment of the duties and tasks divinely ordained by Dharma.* The brahmins are established in saintliness. Kings and feudal chiefs act according to the ideals of truly royal conduct. The peasants and townsfolk are devoted to husbandry and the crafts. The lower, servile classes abide lawfully in submission. People even of the lowest extraction observe the holy order of life.

As the life-process of the world-organism gains momentum, however, order loses ground. Holy Dharma vanishes quarter by quarter, while its converse gains the field. Tretā Yuga is therefore named after the dice-cast of the three. Tretā is the triad or triplet; three of the quarters. Etymologically, the word is related to the Latin *trēs*, Greek *treîs*, English *three*. During Tretā Yuga, the universal body, as well as the body of human society, is sustained by only three fourths of its total virtue. The modes of life proper to the four castes have begun to lapse into decay. Duties are no longer the spontaneous laws of human action, but have to be learned.

Dvāpara Yuga is the age of the dangerous balance between imperfection and perfection, darkness and light. Its name is derived from *dvi, dvā, dvau,* meaning "two" (compare the Latin *duo,* French *deux,* English *deuce,* Greek *dúo,* Russian *dva*). This is the dice-cast of the duad. During Dvāpara Yuga, only two of the four quarters of Dharma are still effective in the manifest world; the others have been irrecoverably lost. The cow of ethical order, instead of firmly standing on four legs, or resting safely

---

* [Dharma: *Lex aeterna,* ideal or absolute Justice or Righteousness, Greek δικαιοσύνη as in Plato and Luke 12.31; the proportionate part of this Justice, which pertains to an individual, is his 'own-justice' (*sva-dharma*), the vocation, social function, or duty as determined for him by his own nature.—AKC.]

EDITOR'S NOTE: Dr. Ananda K. Coomaraswamy has kindly supplied a number of explanatory notes to supplement the material left by Dr. Zimmer. These are introduced in square brackets, and initialled AKC.

14

on three, now balances on two. Destroyed is the ideal, semidivine status of society. Lost is the knowledge of the revealed hierarchy of values. No longer does the perfection of the spiritual order energize human and universal life. All human beings, brahmins and kings as well as tradespeople and servants, blinded by passion and eager for earthly possessions, grow mean and acquisitive and averse to the fulfilment of such sacred duties as require self-denial. True saintliness, to be achieved only through devotional observances, vows, fasting and ascetic practices, becomes extinct.

Finally, Kali Yuga, the dark age, miserably subsists on twenty-five percent of the full strength of Dharma. Egoistic, devouring, blind and reckless elements now are triumphant and rule the day. *Kali* means the worst of anything; also, "strife, quarrel, dissension, war, battle" (being related to *kal-aha*, "strife, quarrel"). In the dice-play, kali is the losing throw. During the Kali Yuga, man and his world are at their very worst. The moral and social degradation is characterized in a passage of the Vishnu Purāna: * "When society reaches a stage, where property confers rank, wealth becomes the only source of virtue, passion the sole bond of union between husband and wife, falsehood the source of success in life, sex the only means of enjoyment, and when outer trappings are confused with inner religion . . ."—then we are in the Kali Yuga, the world of today. This age, in the present cycle, is computed as having begun, Friday, February 18, 3102 B.C.

Deficiency of Dharma accounts for the short duration of the Kali Yuga, which is, namely, 432,000 years. The preceding Tretā Yuga, strong with double the amount of moral substance, is described as surviving twice as long, 864,000. Correspondingly, Dvāpara Yuga, provided with three of the four quarters of Dharma, endures the length of three Kali units, 1,296,000 years; and Krita Yuga, the period of Dharma "four square,"

---

* A classic source of Hindu mythology and tradition, dating from the first millennium of our era. Translated by H. H. Wilson, London, 1840. The above text is a condensation of a long descriptive passage in Book IV, Chapter 24.

1,728,000. The grand total is thus 4,320,000 years, ten times the duration of one Kali Yuga. This complete cycle is called Mahā-Yuga, "The Great Yuga."

One thousand mahāyugas—4,320,000,000 years of human reckoning—constitute a single day of Brahmā, a single kalpa. In terms of the reckoning of the gods (who are below Brahmā, but above men) this period comprises twelve thousand heavenly years. Such a day begins with creation or evolution (*sṛṣṭi*), the emanation of a universe out of divine, transcendent, unmanifested Substance, and terminates with dissolution and re-absorption (*pralaya*), mergence back into the Absolute. The world spheres together with all the beings contained in them disappear at the end of the day of Brahmā, and during the ensuing night persist only as the latent germ of a necessity for re-manifestation. The night of Brahmā is as long as the day.

Every kalpa is subdivided also into fourteen manvantaras, or Manu-intervals,* each comprising seventy-one and a fraction mahāyugas and terminating with a deluge.† The intervals are named from Manu, the Hindu counterpart of Noah, the hero who escapes the flood. The present period is called the Interval of Manu Vaivasvata, "Manu the Son of the Radiating One," "Manu the Son of the Sun God Vivasvant." ‡ This is the seventh

---

* In Sanskrit, *u* before a vowel becomes *v;* therefore *manu-antara* ("Manu-interval") becomes *manvantara.*

† 71 × 14 = 994, leaving 6 mahāyugas to be accounted for. The adjustment is effected as follows. The first of the fourteen manvantaras is regarded as preceded by a dawn the length of one krita yuga (i.e., 0.4 mahāyuga), and every manvantara as followed by a twilight of equal length. 0.4 × 15 = 6. 994 + 6 = 1000 mahāyugas, or one kalpa. This complicated calculation seems to have been introduced in order to co-ordinate two originally separate systems, the one based on a chronology of wheeling mahāyugas, the other on a tradition of periodic universal floods.

‡ Each manvantara is named from its special manifestation of the flood hero. Vaivasvata Manu, the progenitor of the present race of mankind, was rescued from the deluge by the fish incarnation of Vishnu. His father was the Sun God Vivasvant.

Vivasvant is a Vedic name of the Sun God. In the Zoroastrian tradition of Persia the same name occurs as a patronymic of the first mortal, Yima, who in Sanskrit is called Yama. The flood hero and the first mortal are finally two versions of the same primordial being.

manvantara of the present day of Brahmā, seven more being due to pass before the day comes to its close. And this present day is termed Varāha Kalpa, "The Kalpa of the Boar"; for it is during this day that Vishnu becomes incarnated in the figure of a boar. This is the first day of the fifty-first year in the lifetime of "our" Brahmā. It will end—after seven deluges more—at the next dissolution.

The progress and decline of every kalpa is marked by mythological events that recur similarly, again and again, in magnificent, slowly and relentlessly rotating cycles. The victories of the gods, by which they become established in authority over their respective spheres of the universe; the interludes of defeat, downfall, and devastation, when they are overcome by the titans or antigods—who are their stepbrothers, ever alert to overthrow them; the avatārs * or incarnations of Vishnu, the Supreme Being, when he assumes an animal or human form, in order to appear in the world as its savior and deliver the gods: these marvels, singular and breath-taking though they must seem when they come to pass, are but unchanging links in an ever-revolving chain. They are typical moments in an unvariable process, and this process is the continuous history of the world organism. They constitute the standard schedule of a day of Brahmā.

At the dawn of each kalpa, Brahmā re-emerges from a lotus that has stemmed and blossomed out of the navel of Vishnu. During the first Manu-interval of the present Varāha Kalpa, Vishnu descended as a boar to rescue the freshly created Earth from the bottom of the sea, whither she had been ravished by a demon of the abyss. In the fourth interval or manvantara, he rescued a great elephant king from a sea monster. In the sixth occurred the cosmic event known as the Churning of the Milky Ocean: the gods and titans, contending for world dominion, concluded a temporary truce, in order to extract the Elixir of

---

* Avatāra, "descent," from the root tṛī, "to pass across or over, to sail across," plus the prefix ava-, "down."

Immortality from the Universal Sea. During the present mahā-yuga of the seventh manvantara the events described in the two great Indian epics are considered to have occurred. Those recounted in the *Rāmāyaṇa* are assigned to the Tretā Age of the present cycle, those in the *Mahābhārata* to the Dvāpara.

It should be observed that the traditional texts allude only very seldom to the fact that the mythological events which they are describing and extolling take place again and again, recurring every four billion three hundred and twenty million years, i.e., once every kalpa. That is because, from the viewpoint of the short-lived human individual such a prodigious circumstance may be temporarily disregarded. But it cannot be totally and finally dismissed; for the short-lived individual, in the round of his transmigrations, remains involved, somehow, somewhere, under one mask or another, throughout the whole course of the protracted span. In one of the Purānic * accounts of the deeds of Vishnu in his Boar Incarnation or Avatār, occurs a casual reference to the cyclic recurrence of the great moments of myth. The Boar, carrying on his arm the goddess Earth whom he is in the act of rescuing from the depths of the sea, passingly remarks to her:

> *"Every time I carry you this way . . ."*

For the Western mind, which believes in single, epoch-making, historical events (such as, for instance, the coming of Christ, or the emergence of certain decisive sets of ideals, or the long development of invention during the course of man's mastery of nature) this casual comment of the ageless god has a gently minimizing, annihilating effect. It vetoes conceptions of value that

---

* The Purānas are sacred books of mythological and epic lore supposed to have been compiled by the legendary sage and poet Vyāsa. There are eighteen Purānas (*purāṇa,* "ancient, legendary") and associated with each a number of Secondary Purānas (*upapurāṇa*). Among the latter are reckoned the great epics, *Rāmāyaṇa* and *Mahābhārata.*

are intrinsic to our estimation of man, his life, his destiny and task.

From the human standpoint the lifetime of a Brahmā seems to be very lengthy; nevertheless it is limited. It endures for only one hundred Brahmā years of Brahmā days and nights, and concludes with a great, or universal, dissolution. Then vanish not only the visible spheres of the three worlds (earth, heaven and the space between), but all spheres of being whatsoever, even those of the highest worlds. All become resolved into the divine, primeval Substance. A state of total re-absorption then prevails for another Brahmā century, after which the entire cycle of 311,-040,000,000,000 human years begins anew.

3.

The Wisdom of Life

IT is easy for us to forget that our strictly linear, evolutionary idea of time (apparently substantiated by geology, paleontology, and the history of civilization) is something peculiar to modern man. Even the Greeks of the day of Plato and Aristotle, who were much nearer than the Hindus to our ways of thought and feeling and to our actual tradition, did not share it. Indeed, Saint Augustine seems to have been the first to conceive of this modern idea of time. His conception established itself only gradually in opposition to the notion formerly current.

The Augustinian Society has published a paper by Erich Frank,* in which it is pointed out that both Aristotle and Plato believed that every art and science had many times developed to its apogee and then perished. "These philosophers," writes

---

* E. Frank, *Saint Augustine and Greek Thought* (The Augustinian Society, Cambridge, Mass., 1942, obtainable from The Harvard Cooperative Society), see pp. 9-10.

Frank, "believed that even their own ideas were only the rediscovery of thoughts which had been known to the philosophers of previous periods." This belief corresponds precisely to the Indian tradition of a perennial philosophy, an ageless wisdom revealed and re-revealed, restored, lost, and again restored through the cycles of the ages. "Human life," Frank declares, "to Augustine was not merely a process of nature. It was a unique, unrepeatable phenomenon; it had an individual history in which everything that happened was new and had never been before. Such a conception of history was unknown to the Greek philosophers. The Greeks had great historians who investigated and described the history of their times; but . . . the history of the universe they considered as a natural process in which everything recurred in periodical circles, so that nothing really new ever happened." This is precisely the idea of time underlying Hindu mythology and life. The history of the universe in its periodic passage from evolution to dissolution is conceived as a biological process of gradual and relentless deterioration, disintegration, and decay. Only after everything has run its course into total annihilation and been then re-incubated in the boundlessness of the timeless cosmic night, does the universe reappear in perfection, pristine, beautiful, and reborn. Whereupon, immediately, with the first tick of time, the irreversible process begins anew. The perfection of life, the human capacity to apprehend and assimilate ideals of highest saintliness and selfless purity—in other words the divine quality or energy of Dharma—is in a continuous decline. And during the process the strangest histories take place; yet nothing that has not, in the endless wheelings of the eons, happened many, many times before.

This vast time-consciousness, transcending the brief span of the individual, even the racial biography, is the time-consciousness of Nature herself. Nature knows, not centuries, but ages—geological, astronomical ages—and stands, furthermore, beyond them. Swarming egos are her children, but the species is her con-

20

cern; and world ages are her shortest span for the various species that she puts forth and permits, finally, to die (like the dinosaurs, the mammoths, and the giant birds). India—as Life brooding on itself—thinks of the problem of time in periods comparable to those of our astronomy, geology, and paleontology. India thinks of time and of herself, that is to say, in biological terms, terms of the species, not of the ephemeral ego. The latter *becomes* old: the former *is* old, and therewith eternally young.

We of the West on the other hand, regard world history as a biography of mankind, and in particular of Occidental Man, whom we estimate to be the most consequential member of the family. Biography is that form of seeing and representing which concentrates on the unique, the induplicable, in any portion of existence, and then brings out the sense-and-direction-giving traits. We think of egos, individuals, lives, not of Life. Our will is not to culminate in our human institutions the universal play of nature, but to evaluate, to set ourselves against the play, with an egocentric tenacity. As yet our physical and biological sciences —which, of course, are comparatively young—have not affected the general tenor of our traditional humanism. So little, indeed, are we aware of their possible philosophical implications (aside from the lesson of "progress" which we like to derive from their account of evolution) that when we encounter something of their kind in the mythological eons of the Hindus, we are left, emotionally, absolutely cold. We are unable, we are not prepared, to fill the monstrous yugas with life significance. Our conception of the long geological ages that preceded the human habitation of the planet and are promised to succeed it, and our astronomical figures for the description of outer space and the passages of the stars, may in some measure have prepared us to conceive of the mathematical reaches of the vision; but we can scarcely feel their pertinence to a practical philosophy of human life.

It was consequently a great experience for me, when, while reading one of the Purānas, I chanced upon the brilliant, anonymous myth recounted at the opening of the present chapter. Suddenly the empty sheaves of numbers were filled with the dynamism of life. They became alive with philosophical value and symbolic significance. So vivid was the statement, so powerful the impact, that the story did not have to be dissected for its meaning. The lesson was plain to see.

The two great gods, Vishnu and Shiva, instruct the human hearers of the myth by teaching Indra, king of the Olympians. The Wonderful Boy, solving riddles and pouring out wisdom from his childish lips, is an archetypal figure, common to fairy tales of all ages and many traditions. He is an aspect of the Boy Hero, who solves the riddle of the Sphinx and rids the world of monsters. Likewise an archetypal figure is the Old Wise Man, beyond ambitions and the illusions of ego, treasuring and imparting the wisdom that sets free, shattering the bondage of possessions, the bondage of suffering and desire.

But the wisdom taught in this myth would have been incomplete had the last word been that of the infinity of space and time. The vision of the countless universes bubbling into existence side by side, and the lesson of the unending series of Indras and Brahmās, would have annihilated every value of individual existence. Between this boundless, breath-taking vision and the opposite problem of the limited role of the short-lived individual, this myth effected the re-establishment of a balance. Brihaspati, the high priest and spiritual guide of the gods, who is Hindu wisdom incarnate, teaches Indra (i.e., ourself, the individual confused) how to grant to each sphere its due. We are taught to recognize the divine, the impersonal sphere of eternity, revolving ever and agelessly through time. But we are also taught to esteem the transient sphere of the duties and pleasures of individual existence, which is as real and as vital to the living man, as a dream to the sleeping soul.

CHAPTER TWO

THE MYTHOLOGY OF VISHNU

1.

Vishnu's Māyā

THE vision of endless repetition and aimless reproduction mini-
mized and finally annihilated the victorious Indra's naïve conception of himself and of the permanence of his might. His ever-
growing building projects were to have provided the appropriate
setting for a self-confident, natural, and dignified ego-concept.
But as the cycles of the vision expanded, levels of consciousness
opened in which millenniums dwindled to moments, eons to
days. The limited constitution of man, and of such lower gods
as himself, lost substantiality. The burdens and delights, possessions and bereavements of the ego, the whole content and the
work of the human lifetime, dissolved into unreality. All that
had appeared to him as important only the moment before, now
was seen as no more than a fleeting phantasm, born and gone,
intangible as a flash of lightning.

The transformation was effected by a shift in Indra's point of
view. With the enlargement of the perspective every aspect of
life shifted value. It was as though the mountains—permanent
when considered from the standpoint of our brief human span
of some seven decades—should be beheld, all at once, from
the perspective of as many millenniums. They would rise and
fall like waves. The permanent would be seen as fluid. Great
goals would melt before the eyes. Every experience of value
would be suddenly transmuted; the mind would be hard put to

23

reorient itself, and the emotions to discover solid ground.*

The Hindu mind associates such ideas as "transitory, ever-changing, elusive, ever-returning," with "unreality," and conversely, "imperishable, changeless, steadfast, and eternal," with "the real." As long as the experiences and sensations that stream through the consciousness of an individual remain untouched by any widening, devaluating vision, the perishable creatures that appear and vanish in the unending cycle of life (samsāra, the round of rebirth) are regarded by him as utterly real. But the moment their fleeting character is discerned, they come to seem almost unreal—an illusion or mirage, a deception of the senses, the dubious figment of a too restricted, ego-centered consciousness. When understood and experienced in this manner, the world is Māyā-maya, "of the stuff of Māyā." Māyā is "art": that by which an artifact, an appearance, is produced.†

The noun māyā is related etymologically to "measure." It is formed from the root mā, which means "to measure or lay out (as, for instance, the ground plan of a building, or the outlines of a figure); to produce, shape, or create; to display." Māyā is the measuring out, or creation, or display of forms; māyā is any illusion, trick, artifice, deceit, jugglery, sorcery, or work of witchcraft; an illusory image or apparition, phantasm, deception of the sight; māyā is also any diplomatic trick or political artifice designed to deceive. The māyā of the gods is their power to assume diverse shapes by displaying at will various aspects of their

---

* The usual word in Sanskrit for "it is" is "it becomes" (bhavati). Asti ("it is") tends to be confined more to logical formulations (for example, tat tvam asi, "that thou art; thou art that"). Comparably, the Sanskrit term for "world or universe" is jagat, a modification of the root gam, "to go, to move"; jagat connotes "that which moves, the transitory, the ever-changing."

† [Māyā is precisely the maker's power or art, "Magic" in Jacob Boehme's sense: "It is a mother in all three worlds, and makes each thing after the model of that thing's will. It is not the understanding, but it is a creatrix according to the understanding, and lends itself to good or to evil . . . from eternity a ground and support of all things . . . In sum: Magic is the activity in the Will-spirit." (Sex Puncta Mystica, V.—AKC.]

24

subtle essence. But the gods are themselves the productions of a greater *māyā*: the spontaneous self-transformation of an originally undifferentiated, all-generating divine Substance. And this greater *māyā* produces, not the gods alone, but the universe in which they operate. All the universes co-existing in space and succeeding each other in time, the planes of being and the creatures of those planes whether natural or supernatural, are manifestations from an inexhaustible, original and eternal well of being, and are made manifest by a play of *māyā*. In the period of non-manifestation, the interlude of the cosmic night, *māyā* ceases to operate and the display dissolves.

Māyā is Existence: both the world of which we are aware, and ourselves who are contained in the growing and dissolving environment, growing and dissolving in our turn. At the same time, Māyā is the supreme power that generates and animates the display: the dynamic aspect of the universal Substance. Thus it is at once, effect (the cosmic flux), and cause (the creative power). In the latter regard it is known as Shakti, "Cosmic Energy." The noun *śakti* is from the root *śak*, signifying "to be able, to be possible." *Śakti* is "power, ability, capacity, faculty, strength, energy, prowess; regal power; the power of composition, poetic power, genius; the power or signification of a word or term; the power inherent in cause to produce its necessary effect; an iron spear, lance, pike, dart; a sword"; *śakti* is the female organ; *śakti* is the active power of a deity and is regarded, mythologically, as his goddess-consort and queen.

Māyā-Shakti is personified as the world-protecting, feminine, maternal side of the Ultimate Being, and as such, stands for the spontaneous, loving acceptance of life's tangible reality. Enduring the suffering, sacrifice, death and bereavements that attend all experience of the transitory, she affirms, she is, she represents and enjoys, the delirium of the manifested forms. She is the creative joy of life: herself the beauty, the marvel, the enticement and seduction of the living world. She instils into us—and she is, herself—surrender to the changing aspects of existence. Māyā-Shakti is Eve, "The Eternal Feminine," *das Ewig-Weibliche;* she who ate, and tempted her consort to eat, and was herself the apple. From the point of view of the masculine principle of the Spirit (which is in quest of the enduring, eternally valid, and absolutely divine) she is the pre-eminent enigma.

Now the character of Māyā-Shakti-Devī (*devī* = "goddess") is multifariously ambiguous. Having mothered the universe and the individual (macro- and microcosm) as correlative manifestations of the divine, Māyā then immediately muffles consciousness within the wrappings of her perishable production. The ego is entrapped in a web, a queer cocoon. "All this around me," and "my own existence"—experience without and experience within—are the warp and woof of the subtle fabric. Enthralled by ourselves and the effects of our environment, regarding the bafflements of Māyā as utterly real, we endure an endless ordeal of blandishment, desire and death; whereas, from a standpoint just beyond our ken (that represented in the perennial esoteric tradition and known to the illimited, supra-individual consciousness of ascetic, yogic experience) Māyā—the world, the life, the ego, to which we cling—is as fugitive and evanescent as cloud and mist.

The aim of Indian thought has always been to learn the secret of the entanglement, and, if possible, to cut through into a reality outside and beneath the emotional and intellectual convolutions that enwrap our conscious being. Such was the effort to which Indra was allured, when his eyes were opened by the apparitions and teaching of the divine Child and the millennial Sage.

The Waters of Existence

HINDU mythology treats of the riddle of Māyā graphically, in a pictorial script that renders accessible to the common mind the philosophical implications of the puzzle. The tales have been handed down in a great tradition of oral communication; they appear today in many variants. A vast number of these variants have become fixed in literary renderings; others continue in the fluid form of unwritten folklore.

The story is told of a semi-divine ascetic, Nārada, who once demanded directly of the Supreme Being to be taught the secret of his Māyā. This Nārada, in the mythology of Hinduism, is a favorite model of the devotee on the "path of devotion" (*bhakti-mārga*).* In response to his prolonged and fervent austerity, Vishnu had appeared to him in his hermitage, and granted the fulfilment of a wish. When he humbly expressed his profound desire, the god instructed him, not with words, but by subjecting him to a harrowing adventure. The literary version of the tale comes to us in the Matsya Purāna, a Sanskrit compilation

---

* The earliest classic document of *bhakti-mārga*, this whole-hearted humble surrender to the infinite grace of the Divine Being, is the *Bhagavad Gītā*. The paths or techniques (*mārga*) followed during earlier ages, when Dharma was more effective in the universe and in man, become in the Kali Yuga no longer suited to human need. *Karma-mārga*, the path of ritual and vocational activity, and *jñāna-mārga*, intuitive realization of the divine and its identity with man's innermost self, yield then to the techniques of *bhakti-mārga*, the path of fervent devotion. The devotee humbles himself with pious love before the personification of the divine, as represented in Vishnu, principally in the incarnations or *avatāras*, Krishna and Rāma.

[*Bhakti* is literally "participation," "share"; the *bhakta*, one who gives his share, in this case to the deity; and this giving, especially of oneself, implies love—as in Mīrā Bāī's well-known lines:

> "I gave in full, weighed to the utmost grain,
> My love, my life, my soul, my all."
> —AKC.]

that assumed its present form during the classical period of medieval Hinduism, approximately in the fourth century A.D. It is presented as recounted by a saint named Vyāsa.

A group of holy men had gathered around the venerable hermit, Vyāsa, in his forest-solitude. "You understand the divine eternal order," they had said to him, "therefore, unveil to us the secret of Vishnu's Māyā."

"Who can comprehend the Māyā of the Highest God, except himself? Vishnu's Māyā lays its spell on us all. Vishnu's Māyā is our collective dream. I can only recite to you a tale, coming down from the days of yore, of how this Māyā in a specific, singularly instructive instance worked its effect."

The visitors were eager to hear. Vyāsa began:

"Once upon a time, there lived a young prince, Kāmadamana, 'Tamer of Desires,' who, conducting himself in accordance with the spirit of his name, spent his life practicing the sternest of ascetic austerities. But his father, wishing him to marry, addressed him on a certain occasion in the following words: 'Kāmadamana, my son, what is the matter with you? Why do you not take to yourself a wife? Marriage brings the fulfilment of all of a man's desires and the attainment of perfect happiness. Women are the very root of happiness and well-being. Therefore, go, my dear son, and marry.'

"The youth remained silent, out of respect for his father. But when the king then insisted and repeatedly urged him, Kāmadamana replied, 'Dear father, I adhere to the line of conduct designated by my name. The divine power of Vishnu, which sustains and holds enmeshed both ourselves and everything in the world, has been revealed to me.'

"The royal father paused only a moment to reconsider the case, and then adroitly shifted his argument from the appeal of personal pleasure to that of duty. A man should marry, he declared, to beget offspring—so that his ancestral spirits in the realm of the fathers should not lack the food-offerings of descendants and decline into indescribable misery and despair.

" 'My dear parent,' said the youth, 'I have passed through lives by the thousand. I have suffered death and old age many hundreds of times. I have known union with wives, and bereavement. I have existed as grass and as shrubs, as creepers and as trees. I have moved among cattle and the beasts of prey. Many hundreds of times have I been a brahmin, a woman, a man. I have shared in the bliss of Shiva's celestial mansions; I have lived among the immortals. Indeed, there is no variety even of superhuman being whose form I have not more than once assumed: I have been a demon, a goblin, a guardian of the earthly treasures; I have been a spirit of the river-waters; I have been a celestial damsel; I have been also a king among the demon-serpents. Every time the cosmos dissolved to be re-absorbed in the formless essence of the Divine, I vanished too; and when the universe then evolved again, I too re-entered into existence, to live through another series of rebirths. Again and again have I fallen victim to the delusion of existence—and ever through the taking of a wife.

" 'Let me recount to you,' the youth continued, 'something that occurred to me during my next to last incarnation. My name during that existence was Sutapas, "Whose Austerities Are Good"; I was an ascetic. And my fervent devotion to Vishnu, the Lord of the Universe, won for me his grace. Delighted by my fulfilment of many vows, he appeared before my bodily eyes, seated on Garuda, the celestial bird. "I grant to you a boon," he said. "Whatever you wish, it shall be yours."

" 'To the Lord of the Universe I made reply: "If you are pleased with me, let me comprehend your Māyā."

" ' "What should you do with a comprehension of my Māyā?" the god responded. "I will grant, rather, abundance of life, fulfilment of your social duties and tasks, all riches, health, and pleasure, and heroic sons."

29

" ' "That," said I, "and precisely that, is what I desire to be rid of and to pass beyond."

" 'The god went on: "No one can comprehend my Māyā. No one has ever comprehended it. There will never be anyone capable of penetrating to its secret. Long, long ago, there lived a godlike holy seer, Nārada by name, and he was a direct son of the god Brahmā himself, full of fervent devotion to me. Like you, he merited my grace, and I appeared before him, just as I am appearing now to you. I granted him a boon, and he uttered the wish that you have uttered. Then, though I warned him not to inquire further into the secret of my Māyā, he insisted, just like you. And I said to him: 'Plunge into yonder water, and you shall experience the secret of my Māyā.' Nārada dived into the pond. He emerged again—in the shape of a girl.

" ' "Nārada stepped out of the water as Sushilā, 'The Virtuous One,' the daughter of the king of Benares. And presently, when she was in the prime of her youth, her father bestowed her in marriage on the son of the neighboring king of Vidarbha. The holy seer and ascetic, in the form of a girl, fully experienced the delights of love. In due time, then, the old king of Vidarbha died, and Sushilā's husband succeeded to the throne. The beautiful queen had many sons and grandsons, and was incomparably happy.

" ' "However, in the long course of time, a feud broke out between Sushilā's husband and her father, and this developed presently into a furious war. In a single mighty battle many of her sons and grandsons, her father, and her husband all were slain. And when she learned of the holocaust she proceeded in sorrow from the capital to the battlefield, there to lift a solemn lament. And she ordered a gigantic funeral pyre and placed upon it the dead bodies of her relatives, her brothers, sons, nephews, and grandsons, and then, side by side, the bodies of her husband and her father. With her own hand she laid torch to the pyre, and when the flames were mounting cried aloud, 'My son, my son!'

30

and when the flames were roaring, threw herself into the conflagration. The blaze became immediately cool and clear; the pyre became a pond. And amidst the waters Sushila found herself—but again as the holy Nārada. And the god Vishnu, holding the saint by the hand, was leading him out of the crystal pool.

" ' "After the god and the saint had come to the shore, Vishnu asked with an equivocal smile: 'Who is this son whose death you are bewailing?' Nārada stood confounded and ashamed. The god continued: 'This is the semblance of my Māyā, woeful, somber, accursed. Not the lotus-born Brahmā, nor any other of the gods, Indra, nor even Shiva, can fathom its depthless depth. Why or how should *you* know this inscrutable?'

" ' "Nārada prayed that he should be granted perfect faith and devotion, and the grace to remember this experience for all time to come. Furthermore, he asked that the pond into which he had entered, as into a source of initiation, should become a holy place of pilgrimage, its water—thanks to the everlasting secret presence therein of the god who had entered to lead forth the saint from the magic depth—endowed with the power to wash away all sin. Vishnu granted the pious wishes and forthwith, on the instant, disappeared, withdrawing to his cosmic abode in the Milky Ocean."

" 'I have told you this tale,' concluded Vishnu, before he withdrew likewise from the ascetic, Sutapas, 'in order to teach you that the secret of my Māyā is inscrutable and not to be known. If you so desire, you too may plunge into the water, and you will know why this is so.'

"Whereupon Sutapas (or Prince Kāmadamana in his next to last incarnation) dived into the water of the pond. Like Nārada he emerged as a girl, and was thus enwrapped in the fabric of another life."

This is a medieval, literary version of the myth. The story is still told in India, as a kind of nursery tale, and is familiar to many from childhood. In the nineteenth century, the Bengal saint, Ramakrishna, employed the popular form of the tale as a parable in his teaching.* The hero in this case was again Nārada, the model devotee. Through prolonged austerities and devotional practices, he had won the grace of Vishnu. The god had appeared before the saint in his hermitage and granted him the fulfilment of a wish. "Show me the magic power of your Māyā," Nārada had prayed, and the god had replied, "I will. Come with me"; but again with that ambiguous smile on his beautifully curved lips.

From the pleasant shadow of the sheltering hermit grove, Vishnu conducted Nārada across a bare stretch of land which blazed like metal under the merciless glow of a scorching sun. The two were soon very thirsty. At some distance, in the glaring light, they perceived the thatched roofs of a tiny hamlet. Vishnu asked: "Will you go over there and fetch me some water?"

"Certainly, O Lord," the saint replied, and he made off to the distant group of huts. The god relaxed under the shadow of a cliff, to await his return.

When Nārada reached the hamlet, he knocked at the first door. A beautiful maiden opened to him and the holy man experienced something of which he had never up to that time dreamed: the enchantment of her eyes. They resembled those of his divine Lord and friend. He stood and gazed. He simply forgot what he had come for. The girl, gentle and candid, bade him welcome. Her voice was a golden noose about his neck. As though moving in a vision, he entered the door.

The occupants of the house were full of respect for him, yet not the least bit shy. He was honorably received, as a holy man, yet somehow not as a stranger; rather, as an old and venerable acquaintance who had been a long time away. Nārada remained with them impressed by their cheerful and noble bearing, and feeling entirely at home. Nobody asked him what he had come

---

* *The Sayings of Sri Ramakrishna* (Mylapore, Madras, 1938), Book IV, Chapter 22.

for; he seemed to have belonged to the family from time immemorial. And after a certain period, he asked the father for permission to marry the girl, which was no more than everyone in the house had been expecting. He became a member of the family and shared with them the age-old burdens and simple delights of a peasant household.

Twelve years passed; he had three children. When his father-in-law died he became head of the household, inheriting the estate and managing it, tending the cattle and cultivating the fields. The twelfth year, the rainy season was extraordinarily violent: the streams swelled, torrents poured down the hills, and the little village was inundated by a sudden flood. In the night, the straw huts and cattle were carried away and everybody fled.

With one hand supporting his wife, with the other leading two of his children, and bearing the smallest on his shoulder, Nārada set forth hastily. Forging ahead through the pitch darkness and lashed by the rain, he waded through slippery mud, staggered through whirling waters. The burden was more than he could manage with the current heavily dragging at his legs. Once, when he stumbled, the child slipped from his shoulder and disappeared in the roaring night. With a desperate cry, Nārada let go the older children to catch at the smallest, but was too late. Meanwhile the flood swiftly carried off the other two, and even before he could realize the disaster, ripped from his side his wife, swept his own feet from under him and flung him headlong in the torrent like a log. Unconscious, Nārada was stranded eventually on a little cliff. When he returned to consciousness, he opened his eyes upon a vast sheet of muddy water. He could only weep.

"Child!" He heard a familiar voice, which nearly stopped his heart. "Where is the water you went to fetch for me? I have been waiting more than half an hour."

Nārada turned around. Instead of water he beheld the brilliant desert in the midday sun. He found the god standing at his shoulder. The cruel curves of the fascinating mouth, still smiling, parted with the gentle question: "Do you comprehend now the secret of my Māyā?"

From the period of the early Vedas down to the Hinduism of the present, water has been regarded in India as a tangible manifestation of the divine essence. "In the beginning, everything was like a sea without a light," declares an ancient hymn;* and to this day, one of the most common and simple objects of worship in the daily ritual is a jar or pitcher filled with water, representing the presence of the divinity and serving in the place of a sacred image. The water is regarded, for the period of the worship, as a residence or seat (*pīṭha*) of the god.

In our two stories of Nārada the significant trait was the transformation worked by the waters. This was to be read as an operation of Māyā; for the waters are understood as a primary materialization of Vishnu's Māyā-energy. They are the life-maintaining element that circulates through nature in the forms of rain, sap, milk, and blood. They are substance endowed with the power of fluidal change. Therefore, in the symbolism of the myths, to dive into water means to delve into the mystery of Māyā, to quest after the ultimate secret of life. When Nārada, the human disciple, asked to be taught this secret, the god did not disclose the answer by any verbal instruction or formula. Instead, he simply pointed to water, as to the element of initiation.

Boundless and imperishable, the cosmic waters are at once the immaculate source of all things and the dreadful grave. Through a power of self-transformation, the energy of the abyss puts forth, or assumes, individualized forms endowed with temporary life and limited ego-consciousness. For a time it nourishes and sustains these with a vivifying sap. Then it dissolves them again, without mercy or distinction, back into the anonymous

---

* *Rig Veda*, X. 129.3. See also *Ib.*, X. 121. 8., *Śatapatha Brāhmaṇa*, XI. 1. 6. 1., etc.

energy out of which they arose. That is the work, that is the character, of Māyā, the all-consuming, universal womb.

This ambivalence of the dreadful-yet-benign is a dominant trait in all Hindu symbolism and mythology. It is essential to the Hindu concept of divinity. Not alone the Supreme Godhead and Its Māyā, but every godling in the teeming pantheons of the mighty tradition, is a paradox: potent both to further and to destroy; to entangle with benefactions and to redeem with a stroke that slays.

3.

The Waters of Non-Existence

THE symbolism of Māyā is developed further in a magnificent myth describing the irrational adventures of a mighty sage, Mārkandeya, during the interval of non-manifestation between the dissolution and re-creation of the universe. Mārkandeya, by a miraculous and curious accident, beholds Vishnu in a series of archetypal transformations: first, under the elemental guise of the cosmic ocean; then as a giant reclining on the waters; again, as a divine child, alone at play beneath the cosmic tree; and finally as a majestic wild gander, the sound of whose breathing is the magic melody of the creation and dissolution of the world.*

The myth begins with a review of the deterioration of the cosmic order, during the slow but irreversible passage of the four yugas. Holy Dharma vanishes, quarter by quarter, from the life of the world, until chaos supervenes. Men are filled, at last, with only lust and evil. There is no one, any more, in whom enlightening goodness (sattva) prevails: no real wise man, no saint, no one uttering truth and standing by his sacred word. The seem-

---

* *Matsya Purāṇa,* CLXVII. 13-25.

ingly holy brahmin is no better than the fool. Old people, destitute of the true wisdom of old age, try to behave like the young, and the young lack the candor of youth. The social classes have lost their distinguishing, dignifying virtues; teachers, princes, tradespeople, and servants sprawl alike in a general vulgarity. The will to rise to supreme heights has failed; the bonds of sympathy and love have dissolved; narrow egotism rules. Indistinguishable ninnies conglomerate to form a kind of sticky, unpalatable dough. When this calamity has befallen the once harmoniously ordered City of Man, the substance of the world-organism has deteriorated beyond salvage, and the universe is ripe for dissolution.

The cycle has completed itself. One day of Brahmā has elapsed. Vishnu, the Supreme Being, from whom the world first emanated in purity and order, now feels growing within himself the urge to draw the outworn cosmos back into his divine substance. Thus the creator and maintainer of the universe comes to the point of manifesting his destructive aspect: he will devour the sterile chaos and dissolve all animate beings, from Brahmā on high, the inner ruler and cosmic life-spirit of the universal body, down to the ultimate leaf of grass. The hills and the rivers, the mountains and the oceans, gods and titans, goblins and spirits, animals, celestial beings, and men, all are to be resumed by the Supreme.

In this Indian conception of the process of destruction, the regular course of the Indian year—fierce heat and drought alternating with torrential rains—is magnified to such a degree that instead of sustaining, it demolishes existence. The warmth that normally ripens and the moisture that nourishes, when alternating in beneficent co-operation, now annihilate. Vishnu begins the terrible last work by pouring his infinite energy into the sun. He himself becomes the sun. With its fierce, devouring rays he draws into himself the eyesight of every animate being. The whole world dries up and withers, the earth splits, and through deep fissures a deadly blaze of heat licks at the divine waters of the subterranean abyss; these are caught up and swallowed. And when the life-sap has entirely vanished from both the egg-shaped cosmic body and all the bodies of its creatures, Vishnu becomes the wind, the cosmic life-breath, and pulls out of all creatures the enlivening air. Like desiccated leaves the sear substance of the universe leaps to the cyclone. Friction ignites the whirling tumult of highly inflammable matter; the god has turned into fire. All goes up in a gigantic conflagration, then sinks into smoldering ash. Finally, in the form of a great cloud, Vishnu sheds a torrential rain, sweet and pure as milk, to quench the conflagration of the world. The scorched and suffering body of the earth knows at last its ultimate relief, final extinction, Nirvāna. Under the flood of the God-become-Rain it is taken back into the primal ocean from which it arose at the universal dawn. The fecund water-womb receives again into itself the ashes of all creation. The ultimate elements melt into the undifferentiated fluid out of which they once arose. The moon, the stars, dissolve. The mounting tide becomes a limitless sheet of water. This is the interval of a night of Brahmā.

Vishnu sleeps. Like a spider that has climbed up the thread that once issued from its own organism, drawing it back into itself, the god has consumed again the web of the universe. Alone upon the immortal substance of the ocean, a giant figure, submerged partly, partly afloat, he takes delight in slumber. There is no one to behold him, no one to comprehend him; there is no knowledge of him, except within himself.

This giant, "Lord of Māyā," and the cosmic ocean on which he is recumbent, are dual manifestations of a single essence; for the ocean, as well as the human form, is Vishnu. Furthermore, since in Hindu mythology the symbol for water is the serpent (nāga), Vishnu is represented, normally, as reposing on the coils of a prodigious snake, his favorite symbolic animal, the serpent Ananta, "Endless." So that, not only the gigantic anthropomorphic form and the boundless elemental, but the reptile too is Vishnu. It is on a serpent ocean of his own immortal substance that the Cosmic Man passes the universal night.

Inside the god is the cosmos, like an unborn babe within the mother; and here all is restored to its primal perfection. Though without there exists only darkness, within the divine dreamer an ideal vision thrives of what the universe should be. The world, recovering from decline, confusion, and disaster, runs again the harmonious course.

And now, it is during this spellbound interlude that there occurs—according to the tale—a fantastic event:

A holy man, Mārkandeya by name, is wandering inside the god, over the peaceful earth, as an aimless pilgrim, regarding with pleasure the edifying sight of the ideal vision of the world. This Mārkandeya is a well-known mythical figure, a saint endowed with life unending. He is many thousands of years old, yet of unaging strength and alert mind. Wandering now through the interior of Vishnu's body, he is visiting the holy hermitages, gratified by the pious pursuits of the sages and their pupils. At shrines and holy places he pauses to worship, and his heart is made glad by the piety of the people in the countries through which he roams.

But now an accident occurs. In the course of his aimless, unending promenade, the sturdy old man slips, inadvertently, out through the mouth of the all-containing god. Vishnu is sleeping with lips a little open; breathing with a deep, sonorous, rhythmical sound, in the immense silence of the night of Brahmā. And the astonished saint, falling from the sleeper's giant lip, plunges headlong into the cosmic sea.

At first, because of Vishnu's Māyā, Mārkandeya does not behold the sleeping giant, but only the ocean, utterly dark, stretching far in the all-embracing, starless night. He is seized by despair, and fears for his life. Splashing about in the dark water, he becomes presently pensive, ponders, and begins to doubt. "Is it a dream? Or am I under the spell of an illusion? Forsooth, this circumstance, utterly strange, must be the product of my imagination. For the world as I know it, and as I observed it in its harmonious course, does not deserve such annihilation as it seems now suddenly to have suffered. There is no sun, no moon, no wind; the mountains have all vanished, the earth has disappeared. What manner of universe is this in which I discover myself?"

These searching reflections of the saint are a kind of commentary on the idea of Māyā, the problem "What is real?" as conceived by the Hindu. "Reality" is a function of the individual. It is the result of the specific virtues and limitations of individual consciousness. While the saint had been wandering about the interior of the cosmic giant he had perceived a reality which had seemed to him congenial to his nature, and he had regarded it as solid and substantial. Nevertheless, it had been only a dream or vision within the mind of the sleeping god. Contrariwise, during the night of nights, the reality of the primal substance of the god appears to the human consciousness of the saint as a bewildering mirage. "It is impossible," he ponders, "it cannot be real."

The aim of the doctrines of Hindu philosophy and of the training in yoga practice is to transcend the limits of individualized consciousness. The mythical tales are meant to convey the wisdom of the philosophers and to exhibit in a popular, pictorial form the experiences or results of yoga.* Appealing directly to

---

* Yoga, from the root yuj, "to yoke, join together, harness; to come into union or conjunction with; to concentrate or fix the mind; to bestow anything upon any one; to grant, confer." Yoga is a strict spiritual discipline, practiced in order to gain control over the forces of one's own being, to gain occult powers, to dominate certain specific forces of nature, or finally (and chiefly) to attain union with the Deity or with the Universal Spirit.

The three principal stages of yoga are, 1. fixed attention (dhāranā), 2. contemplation (dhyāna), and 3. absorption (samādhi). [These three stages correspond to the European consideratio, contemplatio, and excessus or raptus.—AKC.] The attention is directed exclusively and long upon a single object. (Any object, con-

39

intuition and imagination, they are accessible to all as an interpretation of existence. They are not explicitly commented upon and elucidated. The dialogues and speeches of the principal figures contain moments of philosophical exposition and interpretation, yet the story itself is never explained. There is no explicit commentary on the meaning of the mythological action. The tale goes straight to the listener through an appeal to his intuition, to his creative imagination. It stirs and feeds the unconscious. By an eloquence rather of incident than of word, the mythology of India serves its function as the popular vehicle of the esoteric wisdom of yoga experience and of orthodox religion.

An immediate effect is assured, because the tales are not the products of individual experiences and reactions. They are produced, treasured, and controlled by the collective working and thinking of the religious community. They thrive on the ever-renewed assent of successive generations. They are refashioned, reshaped, laden with new meaning, through an anonymous creative process and a collective, intuitive acceptance. They are effective primarily on a subconscious level, touching intuition, feeling, and imagination. Their details impress themselves on the memory, soak down, and shape the deeper stratifications of the psyche. When brooded upon, their significant episodes are capable of revealing various shades of meaning, according to the experiences and life-needs of the individual.

---

crete or abstract, mortal or divine, may be selected, according to the character and purpose of the yogī.) Various physical disciplines are prescribed, for example, controlled posture, controlled breathing, diet, continence. The immediate aim is a one-pointed concentration of all the psychic energies and a total identification of consciousness with the object, this identification being Samādhi.

Yoga is described in the Aphorisms of Patañjali (cf. Swami Vivekānanda, *Rāja Yoga*, New York, 1897, 1920), in *The Bhagavad Gītā* (cf. translation by Swami Nikhilānanda, New York, 1944), and in the *Saṭ-cakra-nirūpaṇa* and *Pādukā-pañcaka* (two basic works translated with introduction and commentary by Arthur Avalon (Sir John Woodroffe), *The Serpent Power*, 3rd revised edition, London, 1931). An extensive discussion will be found in W. Y. Evans-Wentz, *Tibetan Yoga and Secret Doctrines* (Oxford University Press, 1935).

The myths and symbols of India resist intellectualization and reduction to fixed significations. Such treatment would only sterilize them of their magic. For they are of a more archaic type than those familiar to us from the literature of the Greeks—the gods and myths of Homer, the heroes of the Athenian tragedies of Aeschylus, Sophocles, and Euripides. The latter have been re-fashioned by poetic master-minds, are largely individual creations, and in this respect resemble our modern attempts to deal with traditional forms. As in the works of Shelley and Swin-burne, or, above all, Wagner, there is always in the post-Homeric productions of the Greeks an attempt to stamp old mythological coins with new meanings, new interpretations of existence based on individual experience. On the other hand, in the myths of India we are brought the intuitive, collective wisdom of an age-less, anonymous, and many-sided civilization.

One should feel diffident therefore when offering to comment on any Hindu myth. There is always the risk that the opening of one vista may be the closing of another. Details familiar to the Hindu listener as part of his experience and tradition, but strange to the Western reader, must be explained; yet the formu-lation of definite interpretations should be as far as possible eschewed. The predicament, therefore, of Mārkandeya we shall respectfully leave to speak for itself.

The saint, forlorn in the vast expanse of the waters and on the very point of despair, at last became aware of the form of the sleeping god; and he was filled with amazement and a beatific joy. Partly submerged, the enormous shape resembled a moun-tain range breaking out of the waters. It glowed with a wonder-ful light from within. The saint swam nearer, to study the pres-ence; and he had just opened his lips to ask who this was, when the giant seized him, summarily swallowed him, and he was again in the familiar landscape of the interior.

Thus abruptly restored to the harmonious world of Vishnu's dream, Mārkandeya was filled with extreme confusion. He could only think of his brief yet unforgettable experience as a kind of vision. Paradoxically, however, he himself, the human being unable to accept any reality that transcended the interpretative powers of his limited consciousness, was now contained within that divine being, as a figure of its universal dream. And yet to Mārkandeya, who had been suddenly blessed with a vision of the Supreme Existence—in and by itself, in its all-containing solitude and quietude—that revelation likewise had been but a dream.

Mārkandeya, back again, resumed his former life. As before, he wandered over the wide earth, a saintly pilgrim. He observed yogīs practicing austerities in the woods. He nodded assent to the kingly donors who performed costly sacrifices, with lavish gifts for the brahmins. He watched brahmins officiating at sacrificial rituals and receiving generous fees for their effective magic. All castes he saw piously devoted to their proper tasks, and the holy sequence of the Four Stages of Life he observed in full effect among men.* Graciously pleased with this ideal state of affairs, he wandered in safety for another hundred years.

But then, inadvertently, once again, he slipped from the sleeper's mouth and tumbled into the pitch-black sea. This time, in

---

* The Four Stages (āśrama) of the Hindu scheme of life are: (1) that of student (brahmacārī), i.e., youth: discipleship under the spiritual guidance of a priest versed in revealed wisdom, religious study as a sacramental initiation into the rituals of life, a stage marked by chastity and obedience; (2) that of householder and head of the family (gṛhastha), i.e., manhood: married life, the begetting of children, the exercise of the inherited profession, the fulfilment of sacramental duties to the gods and ancestors, in submission to the spiritual authority of the brahmins; the supporting of brahmins and holy men by gifts; (3) that of hermit (vānaprastha), i.e., spiritual maturity: renunciation of worldly possessions and family life (with the coming of age of the sons), retirement into the forest, solitary life in the wilderness, introversion into hermit existence, purification of the soul from secular tendencies through ascetic practices and simple living, centering of the mind on devotional exercises, yoga practice, realization of the Eternal in man and the universe; (4) that of homeless mendicant (sannyāsī), i.e., old age: quitting of the hermit hut and the idyll of the forest, homeless mendicancy, asceticism of the beggar saint, who walks along the roads apparently aimlessly, yet actually on the path of liberation from the worldly bondage of rebirth.

the dreadful darkness and water-desert of silence, he beheld a luminous babe, a godlike boy beneath a fig tree, peaceful in slumber. Then again, by an effect of Māyā, Mārkandeya saw the lonely little boy cheerfully at play, undismayed amidst the vast ocean. The saint was filled with curiosity, but his eyes could not stand the dazzling splendor of the child, and so he remained at a comfortable distance, pondering as he kept himself afloat on the pitchy deep. Mārkandeya mused: "Something of this kind I seem to remember having beheld once before—long, long ago." But then his mind became aware of the fathomless depth of the shoreless ocean and was overcome with a freezing fear.

The god, in the guise of the divine child, gently addressed him. "Welcome, Mārkandeya!" The voice had the soft deep tone of the melodious thundering of an auspicious rain cloud. The god reassured him: "Welcome, Mārkandeya! Do not be afraid, my child. Do not fear. Come hither."

The hoary, ageless saint could not recall a time when anyone had presumed either to address him as "child," or to name him simply by his first name without any respectful appellation referring to his saintliness and birth. He was profoundly offended. Though weary, pained with fatigue, and at a very great disadvantage, he burst into a display of temper. "Who presumes to ignore my dignity, my saintly character, and to make light of the treasure of magic power stored in me through my ascetic austerities? Who is this who slights my venerable age, equal to a thousand years—as the gods count years? I am not accustomed to this sort of insulting treatment. Even the highest gods regard me with exceptional respect. Not even Brahmā would dare to approach me in this irreverent manner. Brahmā addresses me courteously: 'O Long-Lived one,' he calls me. Who now courts disaster, flings himself blindly into the abyss of destruction, casts away his life, by naming me simply Mārkandeya? Who merits death?"

When the saint had thus expressed his wrath, the divine child resumed his discourse, unperturbed. "Child, I am thy parent, thy father and elder, the primeval being who bestows all life. Why do you not come to me? I knew your sire well. He practised severe austerities in bygone times in order to beget a son. He gained my grace. Pleased with his perfect saintliness, I granted him a gift, and he requested that you, his son, should be endowed with inexhaustible life-strength and should never grow old. Your father knew the secret core of his existence, and you stem from that core. That is why you are now privileged to behold me, recumbent on the primal, all-containing cosmic waters, and playing here as a child beneath the tree."

Mārkandeya's features brightened with delight. His eyes grew wide, like opening blossoms. In humble surrender, he made as if to bow and he prayed: "Let me know the secret of your Māyā, the secret of your apparition now as child, lying and playing in the infinite sea. Lord of the Universe, by what name are you known? I believe you to be the Great Being of all beings; for who else could exist as you exist?"

Vishnu replied: "I am the Primeval Cosmic Man, Narāyana. He is the waters; he is the first being; he is the source of the universe. I have a thousand heads. I manifest myself as the holiest of holy offerings; I manifest myself as the sacred fire that carries the offerings of men on earth to the gods in heaven. Simultaneously, I manifest myself as the Lord of Waters. Wearing the garb of Indra, the king of gods, I am the foremost of the immortals. I am the cycle of the year, which generates everything and again dissolves it. I am the divine yogī, the cosmic juggler or magician, who works wonderful tricks of delusion. The magical deceptions of the cosmic yogī are the yugas, the ages of the world. This display of the mirage of the phenomenal process of the universe is the work of my creative aspect; but at the same time I am the whirlpool, the destructive vortex, that sucks back whatever has been displayed and puts an end to the procession of the yugas. I put an end to everything that exists. My name is **Death of the Universe.**"

From this self-revelation of Vishnu it appears that Mārkandeya was far more privileged than Nārada. Both saints plunged into the water, the substantial aspect of Vishnu's Māyā, Nārada intentionally, Mārkandeya inadvertently. To each the waters disclosed "the other side," "the totally different aspect," the *totaliter aliter.* But Nārada, who in his fervent devotion and loving surrender (*bhakti*) was apparently on such familiar terms with the god's secret essence, broke into another existence, another entanglement of earthly suffering and joy. The transformation bound him with those very ties which he, in his fervent asceticism, had been striving to ignore and overcome. The waters initiated him into the unconscious side of his own being; introduced him to longings and attitudes still alive within him, which had been screened from his consciousness by the one-pointedness of his endeavor. "You are not what you fancy yourself to be," was the lesson implied in the startling experience that overwhelmed him when he was for but an instant submerged.*

---

* The imagery of the Hindu myth allows for a cautious, intuitive reading in terms of psychology—the psychology of the conscious and unconscious. Among other interpretations this approach is indeed demanded, for Māyā is as much a psychological as a cosmic term.

The individualized, differentiated forms of the universe—earth as well as the higher and lower spheres of the heavens and underworlds—are supported by the formless fluid element of the depth. All have evolved and grown out of the primary fluid and are maintained by its circulation. Likewise, our individual, conscious personality, the psyche of which we are aware, the character-role that we enact socially and in solitary seclusion, is supported, as a mental and emotional microcosm, on the fluid element of the unconscious. The latter represents a potentiality in largest part unknown, distinct from our conscious being, far wider, far stranger than the cultivated personality, yet supporting it as its deep foundation and communing with it, circulating through it, as an enlivening, inspiring, and frequently disturbing fluid.

The water represents the element of the deeper unconscious and contains everything—tendencies, attitudes—which the conscious personality, striving in the case of Nārada for perfect saintliness, has ignored and pushed aside. It represents the indiscriminate, comprehensive potentiality of life and nature present in the individual, though split off from the perceived, realized, consciously enacted character.

Mārkandeya was a holy man of a different character. Contained within the world-dream in the body of the sleeping god, he was only one of many figures, yet was delighted to play his role as the ever-enduring saint-pilgrim, gratified by the ideal state of human affairs. He had no obsessive craving to transcend the Māyā-spell by penetrating the miracle of the mirage.

When Mārkandeya slipped from the god's mouth, he fell out of existence, in so far as existence is comprehensible and bearable. He found himself confronted by what amounted to the Great Nothingness, the vast desert of the shoreless sea. The world familiar to him had vanished. In sudden succession he had experienced two contradictory, incompatible aspects of the one essence, and his human mind failing to co-ordinate the two, Vishnu taught him the identity of opposites, the fundamental unity of everything in God. Stemming from His sole substance, thriving and perishing in God, all melts away again into the only source.

Vishnu teaches the identity of opposites, first by manifesting himself as the babe, unafraid though utterly solitary in the infinite expanse of the abysmal waters and the starless night; again, by addressing the age-old saint as "child," and by calling him by his first name, as an old friend or relative, though apparently the two had never met.

The secret of Māyā is this identity of opposites. Māyā is a simultaneous-and-successive manifestation of energies that are at variance with each other, processes contradicting and annihilating each other: creation *and* destruction, evolution *and* dissolution, the dream-idyll of the inward vision of the god *and* the desolate nought, the terror of the void, the dread infinite. Māyā is the whole cycle of the year, generating everything *and* taking it away. This "and," uniting incompatibles, expresses the fundamental character of the Highest Being who is the Lord and Wielder of Māyā, whose energy is Māyā. Opposites are fundamentally of the one essence, two aspects of the one Vishnu. That is the wisdom which this myth undertakes to disclose to the Hindu devotee.

The deep-booming voice of the child continued, and instruction rolled from his lips in a wonderful, soul-gratifying stream: "I am the holy order (*dharma*), I am the glowing fervor of ascetic endeavor (*tapas*), I am all those appearances and virtues through which the true essence of existence manifests itself. I am the Lord-Creator-and-Generator-of-all-Beings (*prajāpati*), the order of the sacrificial ritual, and I am called the Lord of Sacred Wisdom. As celestial light, I manifest myself, as wind and earth, as the water of the oceans, and as the space extending to the four quarters, lying between the four quarters and stretching above and below. I am the Primeval Being and the Supreme Refuge. From me originates whatever has been, shall be, or is. And whatever you may see, hear, or know in the whole of the universe, know me as Him who therein abides. Cycle after cycle, I produce out of my essence the spheres and creatures of the cosmos. Consider that in your heart. Obey the laws of my eternal order and wander in happiness through the universe within my body. Brahmā lives in my body and all the gods and the holy seers. Know me as Him who manifests, yet whose manifesting magic remains unmanifested and not to be grasped. I am beyond the goals of human life—gratification of the senses, pursuit of prosperity, and pious fulfilment of sacred duties—yet I point out those three goals as the proper aims of earthly existence."

With a swift motion, then, the Primeval Being brought the holy Mārkandeya to his mouth and swallowed him, so that he vanished again into the gigantic body. This time, the heart of the saint was so flooded with beatitude, that instead of wandering further he sought rest in a solitary place. There he remained in lonely quietude and joyfully listened to "The Song of the Immortal Gander": the at first hardly audible, secret, yet universal melody of God's life-breath, flowing in, flowing out. And this is the song that Mārkandeya heard: "Many forms do I assume.

And when the sun and moon have disappeared, I float and swim with slow movements on the boundless expanse of the waters. I am the Gander. I am the Lord. I bring forth the universe from my essence and I abide in the cycle of time that dissolves it."

This melody and song, with its figure of the cosmic gander, is the last of the series of archetypal revelations of the god, made to the pious saint, Mārkandeya. In Hindu mythology the wild goose is associated, generally, with Brahmā. Just as Indra rides on an elephant, Shiva on the bull Nandī, Shiva's son, the war-god Skanda-Kārttikeya, on the peacock, and "The Goddess" (devī) on the lion, so Brahmā soars through the atmosphere on a magnificent gander. These vehicles or mounts (vāhana) are manifestations on the animal plane of the divine individuals themselves. The gander is the animal mask of the creative principle, which is anthropomorphically embodied in Brahmā. As such, it is a symbol of sovereign freedom through stainless spirituality. That is why the Hindu ascetic, the mendicant monk or saint who is supposed to have become freed from the bondage of rebirth, is said to have attained to the rank of "gander" (haṁsa), or "highest gander" (paramahaṁsa). These are epithets commonly applied to the orthodox teacher-saints of present-day Hinduism. Why, we must ask, is the gander such an important symbol?

The wild gander (haṁsa) strikingly exhibits in its mode of life the twofold nature of all beings. It swims on the surface of the water, but is not bound to it. Withdrawing from the watery realm, it wings into the pure and stainless air, where it is as much at home as in the world below. Flying through space it migrates south and north, following the course of the seasons. Thus it is the homeless free wanderer, between the upper celestial and the lower earthly spheres, at ease in both, not bound to either. When the gander wishes, it alights upon the waters of the earth; when it wishes, it withdraws again to the void on high. Hence it symbolizes the divine essence, which, though embodied in, and abiding with, the individual, yet remains forever free from, and unconcerned with, the events of individual life.

On the one hand earth-bound, limited in life-strength, in virtues and in consciousness, but on the other hand a manifestation of the divine essence, which is unlimited, immortal, virtually omniscient and all-powerful, we, like the wild goose, are citizens of the two spheres. We are mortal individuals bearing within ourselves an immortal, supra-individual nucleus. Shrouded by the limiting, individualizing stratifications of the tangible gross frame of our physical nature, and by the subtle sheaths of our animating psyche, is the Self (*ātman*), fundamentally unaffected by the processes and activities of the conditioning layers, isolated and steeped in beatitude. Without knowing it, we are immaterial, divine, exalted, though also changing, subject to experiences, joys and griefs, decay and rebirth.

The macrocosmic gander, the divine Self in the body of the universe, manifests itself through a song. The melody of inhaling and exhaling, which the Indian yogī hears when he controls through exercises (*prāṇāyāma*) the rhythm of his breath, is regarded as a manifestation of the "inner gander." The inhalation is said to make the sound, *haṁ*, the exhalation, *sa*. Thus, by constantly humming its own name, *haṁ-sa, haṁ-sa,* the inner presence reveals itself to the yogī-initiate.

Mārkandeya is listening to this song. He is listening to the breathing of the Highest Being. That is why he sits alone in a solitary place and does not care any more to follow the course of the world, no longer delights to roam around and observe the ideal state of human affairs. He is released from the spell of endless, though delightful, sight-seeing, liberated from the compulsion to migrate through supernal landscapes. The most divine melody imaginable is absorbing his entire attention.

The song of the inner gander has a final secret to disclose. "*Haṁsa, haṁ-sa,*" it sings, but at the same time, "*sa-'ham, sa-'ham.*" *Sa* means "this" and *'ham* means "I"; the lesson is, "This am I." I, the human individual, of limited consciousness, steeped in delusion, spellbound by Māyā, actually and fundamentally am This, or He, namely, the Ātman, the Self, the Highest Being, of unlimited consciousness and existence. I am not to be identified with the perishable individual, who accepts as utterly real and fatal the processes and happenings of the psyche and the body. "I am He who is free and divine." That is the lesson sung to man by every movement of inhalation and exhalation, asserting the divine nature of Him in whom breath abides.

Mārkandeya's doubts as to what is "real" are put at rest by this song. "Many forms do I assume," the god is singing. That is to say, through the creative energy of his Māyā the Divine Being transmutes himself and exfoliates into the hosts of perishable individuals and universes—into the universe, for instance, of which Mārkandeya forms a part. *"And,"* sings the glorious bird, "when the sun and moon have disappeared I float and swim with slow movements on the boundless expanse of the waters."

Thus the opposing views of reality, which so baffled and disturbed the saint when he fell out of the familiar world into the starless night of the fathomless ocean, are for him now reconciled and identified as one. *I am the Lord,* and *I am the Gander."* I am the supreme All-Being, whose playful transmutation is the macrocosm, *and* I am the innermost principle in man—in the microcosm; I am the divine life-principle revealed in the melody of the breath. I am the Lord, the all-containing cosmic giant *and* the Self, the imperishable, divine life-center in man. "I bring forth the universe from my essence *and* I abide in the cycle of time that dissolves it." The operation of Māyā was revealed in Mārkandeya through alternating cosmic visions. Whereas Nārada experienced the enigma through a personal dream-transformation, Mārkandeya beheld the wonder of the play on a scale that was universal.

The myth opened with a description of the dissolution of the eon, it concludes now with an account of the re-beginning:

The Highest Being, in the form of water, gradually gathered and stored within himself a glowing energy. Then, in his boundless strength, he determined to produce again the universe. He who is himself the Universal visualized the form of the universe in its five elements of ether, air, fire, water, and earth. Calm lay over the ocean, fathomless and subtle. Vishnu, having entered the water, gently stirred it. Waves rippled. As they followed each other, there was formed among them a tiny cleft. This cleft was space or ether, invisible, intangible, the most subtle of the five elements; carrier of the invisible, intangible sense-quality of sound. Space resounded, and from the sound arose the second element, air, in the form of a wind.

Wind, spontaneous motor force, had space at its disposal in which to grow. Pervading space, it relentlessly expanded far and wide. Violently rushing, fiercely blowing, it aroused the waters. From the resultant commotion and friction the third element, fire, originated—a mighty divinity whose path is black with smoke and ash. Fire, increasing, devoured a great quantity of the cosmic water. And where the water had disappeared, there remained a mighty void, within which came into existence the upper sphere of heaven. The Universal Being who had permitted the elements to proceed from his essence, now rejoiced to behold the formation of heavenly space. In preparation for the bringing forth of Brahmā he centered his mind.

It is the nature of the Supreme Being to take delight in himself in the cosmic ocean. Presently, out of his cosmic body, he puts forth a single lotus, with a thousand petals of pure gold, stainless, radiant as the sun. And together with this lotus he puts forth the God-Creator of the Universe, Brahmā, who is seated in the center of the golden lotus, which expands and is radiant with the glowing energy of creation.

The rank and role of Brahmā is entrusted to a perfect yogī, in full control over himself and the powers of the universe. Whenever a human being, purified through fervent austerities, and through initiation spiritually reborn into sacred wisdom, achieves supreme enlightenment and becomes the highest of all yogīs, he is recognized in his full dignity by the Supreme Being. When the universe again evolves, the later processes of creation are committed to his charge.

Brahmā is four-faced, and with his faces he controls the quarters and the whole field of the universe.

The lotus of Brahmā is called, by the sages versed in sacred tradition, "the highest form or aspect of the earth." It is marked with the symbols of the element earth. It is the goddess Earth, or Moisture. Out of this Earth arise the holy, towering mountains, saturated with the life-sap of the lotus: the Himalaya, the mountain Sumeru, Mount Kailāsa, the Vindhya mountain. Sumeru, or Meru, is the central peak of the world, the main pin of the universe, the vertical axis. Kailāsa is the residence of the god Kubera, king of the genii (yakṣas); also a favorite resort of Shiva. The Vindhya mountain, which separates the North-Indian plain from the highlands of the Dekkan, is the summit over which the sun rises to begin its daily transit of the firmament. All these peaks are the abodes of hosts of gods, celestial and superhuman beings, and accomplished saints, who bestow on the pious the fulfilment of their wishes. Furthermore, the water that flows down from these mountains is as salutary as the elixir of immortal life. It runs into rivers that are the holy goals of pilgrimage. And the filaments of the lotus are the innumerable mountains of the world, filled with precious metals. The outer petals contain the inaccessible continents of foreign peoples. On the underside of the petals dwell the demons and the serpents. But in the center of the pericarp, amidst the four oceans that extend to the four quarters, is the continent of which a part is India.

Thus came into being again, out of the Māyā-power of the brooding god, the whole vast dream of the universe, to resume the majestic round of the four yugas. Another cycle, to be identical with all that had gone before and with all that ever would come to pass, now moist and radiant with the living substance of its source, expanded wonderfully in the sweet dawn.

4·

Māyā in Indian Art

IN the hills of the west coast of India, at Bhājā near Bombay, is a Buddhist cave-monastery, dating from the second century B.C. To the right of the entrance is a magnificent stone relief showing Indra, the king of gods. (Figure 1.) He is seated on his giant elephant, Airāvata, the celestial ancestor of all earthly elephants, animal-shaped archetype of the rain-bestowing monsoon-cloud. Compared with the earth below, which is seen in the relief as if half from above, the god and his mount are of enormous size. Minute, toy-like figures cover the landscape beneath. In the center is a holy tree, surrounded by a fence. To the left is a court scene: a king seated under an umbrella on a wicker throne, attended by musicians and dancers. The celestial elephant, with uplifted trunk, carries a mighty tree which he has uprooted in his course, symbolizing the irresistible fury of the storm.

This Bhājā relief is executed in a distinctly "visionary style" and resembles rather a plastic painting than the work of a chisel in stone. Subtle yet bold, with a fluent, vigorous stroke, it testifies to a long antecedent tradition, of which the earlier documents have not as yet been found. The figures emerge from the rock and cover its surface in thin, rippling layers, like subtle waves of cloudlike substance; so that, though carved from solid rock, they suggest a kind of mirage. The substance of the stone seems to have assumed the contours of lightly fleeting emanations. Formless, undifferentiated, anonymous rock is in the very process, as it were, of transforming itself into individualized and animate forms. Thus the basic conception of Māyā is reflected in this style. It represents the apparition of living forms out of formless primal substance; it illustrates the phenomenal, mirage-like character of all existence, earthly and divine.

But the view of the universe as Māyā is not the only world-interpretation known to India. In fact this view, this mode of experience, represents a considerable philosophical victory, obtained during the first millennium B.C., over an earlier, strictly concretistic, dualistic system of belief, such as persists to this day in the teachings of the Jaina sect, and which may have flourished generally, in pre-historic times, among the pre-Aryan populations of the Indian sub-continent.

The Jains numbered, in 1931, only 1,252,105 members, for the most part wealthy traders, bankers and merchants, settled in the larger cities—this prosperous lay community supporting an all-important inner circle of extraordinarily austere, advanced ascetics, both monks and nuns. But at one time the Jains were numerous, and their teachings have played an important part in the history of Indian thought. Their last great prophet, Mahāvīra (d. ca. 500 B.C.), was a contemporary of the Buddha (563–483 B.C.), and was himself a follower of the much earlier Jaina prophet, Pārshvanātha (872?–772? B.C.), who is regarded as the twenty-third of the Jaina saviors. The twenty-second, Neminātha, is said to have preceded him by 84,000 years. The first, Rishabhanātha, existed in an earlier epoch of the world, when husbands and wives were born together as twins, had sixty-four ribs apiece, and were two miles tall. For many centuries Jainism flourished side by side with orthodox Hinduism, attaining to a peak of prosperity in the fifth century A.D. But since the Mohammedan invasions and massacres some seven centuries later (especially, since the conquest of the region of Gujarāt by Alā-ud-dēn, "The Bloody," in 1297–8), the sect has steadily declined. Its present almost vestigial state was long foretold by its seers: with the decline of virtue in the world, during the slow, irreversible course

54

of the cycle of the ages, the true religion should steadily dwindle, until, at last, with the fall of the world into utter degradation, it should disappear. The last Jaina monk should be named Duppasahasūri, the last nun Phalgushrī, the last layman Nāgila, the last laywoman Satyashrī.*

Jainism is characterized by a profound and absolute pessimism with respect to the nature of the world. Matter is not finally a transformation of spirit, but a permanently existing substance, concrete and ineradicable, made up of atoms and capable (like clay) of taking many forms. Different from matter, imprisoned within it and working upon it from within, like a yeast, to give it forms, are the souls (*jīva*, "the lives"), which are practically innumerable (the world is literally filled with them), and which, like matter itself, are never to dissolve. The goal of Jaina religious practice is to release these Jīvas from their entanglement with matter (matter is "non-jīva," *ajīva*). In order to accomplish this end, an elaborate and gently graduated system of life-rules and vows is carefully maintained, to conduct the layman by slow degrees to the ultimate state of the advanced ascetic. Man is fettered because he goes on acting and doing, every deed bringing an accumulation of new entanglements; the way to victory, therefore, resides in absolute inaction. When this state has been properly and very gradually attained, every trace of Ajīva will have been put away by the time the moment of death occurs. The Jīva then breaks free into absolute release (*kaivalya*, "perfect isolation"). This condition is not regarded by the Jains as reabsorption into any ultimate Universal Substance; for they know of no such all-subsuming, non-dual state of being. On the contrary, the individual Jīva, the Monad, simply ascends, like a free

---

* The Jaina cycle, it should be noted, differs from that of the Māyā-world of Vishnu. The universe never dissolves, but after a long period of unmitigated horror begins again gradually to improve, until the religion of the Jains reappears again, men increase in stature, the universe grows beautiful, and all presently returns to the perfect state from which the decline begins anew.—Cf. Mrs. Sinclair Stevenson, *The Heart of Jainism* (Oxford University Press, 1915).

balloon, to the zenith of the organism of the universe, there to remain, forever and forever, together with all the other free balloons—each absolutely self-existent and self-contained, immobile, against the ceiling of the world. The space occupied by each of the perfected ones is boundless. The perfected ones are all-aware.*

Although the perfected state, Kaivalya, is far beyond and above the worldly spheres presided over by the gods, the Jains admit to their popular household devotions (for the aid and consolation of lay-people in their daily affairs, until the higher reaches of spiritual clarification shall have been attained) certain of the divinities of the Hindu pantheon. But these are understood to partake of a distinctly inferior mode of being. Like the world over which they preside, they are heavy with the stuff of temporal existence. And this weightiness, this durable materiality, is reflected in their representation in the works of Jaina art.

Figure 2 shows a Jaina image of Indra, the heavenly rājā, king of the gods. This is a work dating from about A.D. 850; it stands in a Jaina sanctuary at Elūrā, a monolithic temple cut into the living rock of a cliff. Jaina art of all periods is characterized by a puppet-like stiffness, barrenness, and rigidity. Sometimes it draws a certain vigor and vitality from its close kinship to popular art: its images often resemble the fetish figures of the primitive levels of the population. Like the doctrine and life-experience that it renders and interprets, it is archaic, fundamentalist, inflexible—unsophisticated by any alleviating insight. Nothing

---

* The universe is represented by the mythological symbolism of the Jains as a giant in human form, the Cosmic Giant, which may be represented either as a male or as a female. In the lower part of its body, from the waist to the soles of the feet, are the under-worlds, the purgatories and dwelling-places of the demons. The world of man is at the level of the waist. In the great chest, neck, and head are the heavens. Moksha (*mokṣa*, "freedom, release") the place of the Pure Jīvas, is at the crown. The relationship of Moksha to the cycles of history and rebirth is repre-presented diagrammatically like this: ꖜ

56

ever dissolves into undifferentiated, transcendent, subtle essence. Nothing finally ceases to be. The everlasting contrariety of primal matter and the living, straining souls is never resolved.

Indra, king of the gods, with a dignified, almost threatening heaviness, sits on his mount, the elephant. He is flanked by two attendants and overshadowed by a tree, a "wish-fulfilling tree" (*kalpa-vṛikṣa*): the inhabitants of Indra's paradise gather from the branches of this arboreal symbol of life the fruits of their desires—jewels, precious garments, and other delightful objects of vanity and pleasure. But the god, the tree, and all that they can give, are loaded with the heaviness of corporeality. In the clear contours and ornaments of this work the vigor and solid resistance of the rock are made to serve the intended effect. The stone of the image retains its solidity. Mineral, animal weight is what we here behold. There is no conversion of the stone into something subtle and fleeting, no hint of cloud-like transciency. Life-force is expressed in terms of massiveness and bulk, with a thoroughly respectable realism and an utterly prosaic devotion. Here are stateliness and the beatitude of vegetable-animal nature, but in the higher mode of an immortal god. This Indra is the stout and sturdy master of the sensuous, living world, out of whose pale the Jaina saint is strenuously exercised to escape. Little wonder if the monk should be forced to the most extraordinary extremes of physical self-castigation, in order to break free.

An epoch-making philosophical and psychological victory over this literal-minded religiosity is represented in the subtle, mirage-effects of the art of Bhājā. Here the entire manifested world is dissolved, and yet permitted to remain—"like a burnt string, which would disappear at the breath of a breeze."

57

CHAPTER THREE

THE GUARDIANS OF LIFE

I.

The Serpent,
Supporter of Vishnu and the Buddha

WHEREAS the myths of emanation and dissolution revolve with a cold and ruthless impersonality that reduces to virtual non-entity the great world of human weal and woe, popular lore abounds with divinities and genii warmly sympathetic to the life-illusion. The sages Nārada and Mārkandeya were vouch-safed magical experiences of the impalpability of Māyā. On the other hand, the millions of mankind dwell and labor within the net of the dream-web. They are beguiled, surrounded, supported, and comforted in their lives by an abundant company of homely guardian-figures, whose function it is to preside over the local and continuous efficacy of that cosmogonic power which in the beginning shaped the world. Genii (*yakṣa*), representing the forces of the soil, and the mineral treasures, precious metals, and jewels of the earth; serpent kings and queens (*nāga, nāginī*), personifying and directing the terrestrial waters of the lakes and ponds, rivers and oceans; the goddesses of the three sacred streams, Gangā (the Ganges), Yamunā (the Jumna), Sarasvatī (the Saraswatī); dryads or tree goddesses (*vṛikṣa-devatā*), pa-tronesses of the world of vegetation; sacred elephants (*nāga*— same term as for "serpent"), who originally had wings and con-sorted with the clouds, and who, even now, on earth, retain the power to attract their rain-bearing, earlier companions: these bestow upon the children of the world all the boons of earthly happiness—abundance of crops and cattle, prosperity, offspring, health, long life.

The terrible heat of the devouring sun is regarded in India as a deadly power. The moon, on the other hand, conferring the refreshing dew, is the abode and source of life. The moon is the controller of the waters; and these, circulating through the universe, sustaining all living creatures, are the counterpart on earth of the liquor of heaven, Amrita,* the drink of the gods. Dew and rain becoming vegetable sap, sap becoming the milk of the cow, and the milk then being converted into blood:— Amrita, water, sap, milk, and blood, represent but differing states of the one elixir. The vessel or cup of this immortal fluid is the moon. The most conspicuous and generally beneficent of its manifestations on earth are the mighty rivers, and particularly the great sacred three: Ganges, Jumna, Saraswatī.

The mythology of India is rich in personifications of the life-giving power of the waters. Chief among these is Vishnu himself, the supreme procreator of the universe. Second to him is the goddess Padmā ("Lotus"), his spouse and queen—called also Lakshmī and Shrī ("Prosperity," "Fortune," "Beauty," "Virtue"). The god and goddess are depicted on Indian shrines in close association with the multitudinous local genii who typify the play of the living waters in the created world.

A beautiful relief in the temple of Deogarh (Figure 3) displays Vishnu recumbent on the coils of Ananta, the cosmic serpent (*Viṣṇu Anantāśāyin*). The work—in the Gupta style of about A.D. 600—is of the same period as the classic Purānic narratives that enumerate and describe the ten avatārs or incarna-

---

* *A*—meaning "non"—and *mṛita* meaning "dead"; this word is etymologically related to the Greek *ambrosia*. [Cf. A. M. Fowler: "A Note on ἄμβροτος," *Classical Philology*, XXXVII, Jan. 1942, and "Expressions for 'Immortality' in the early Indo-European languages, with special reference to the Rig-Veda, Homer, and the Poetic Edda," Dissertation, Harvard.—AKC.]

tions of this supreme divinity. The anthropomorphic figure, the serpent coils that form his bed, and the water on which this serpent floats, are triune manifestations of the single divine, imperishable, cosmic substance, the energy underlying and inhabiting all the forms of life.

In a graceful, relaxed posture the god reclines in slumber, as if absorbed in the dream of the universe inside him. At his feet, in the humble place assigned to the Hindu wife, is Lakshmī-Shrī, the goddess Lotus, his spouse. Her right hand holds his foot, her left hand gently strokes the leg. Such stroking is part of the worship traditionally paid by the Hindu wife to the feet of her lord.

From the navel of the god grows a lotus, which is a duplicate-manifestation of the goddess at his feet. The flower bears on its corolla Brahmā, the four-faced demiurge-creator. Arrayed above are major divinities of the Hindu pantheon. The figure to the right of four-faced Brahmā is Indra, mounted on Airāvata, his elephant. The couple seated on a bull and soaring through space are Shiva and his spouse, "The Goddess." A boyish personage is to be distinguished in the right hand corner, exhibiting several profiles; this is probably the six-faced war god, Skanda Kārttikeya.

Below are aligned five masculine figures and a woman: apparently the five Pāndava princes with their wife, the heroes of the epic of the *Mahābhārata*. These are associated with Vishnu as celebrated recipients of his favor. According to the great story, they lost their kingdom to their cousins, the Kauravas, in a gambling match, and were then supported in the struggle to recover it by the High God himself. Vishnu, in the human form of their companion, Krishna, served them as advisor and charioteer. Before the onset of the final battle, he revealed to their leader, Arjuna, the blessed gospel of the *Bhagavad Gītā*, thus bestowing on him eternal freedom as well as victory on earth.—In the Deogarh relief the central personage is apparently Yudhishthira; the two to his left are Bhīma and Arjuna, and those to his right,

Nakula and Sahadeva, the twins. The common wife of the five, Draupadī, is in the corner.*

Returning now to the problem of the great serpent-bed, we may review the whole subject of the snake symbol in Indian iconography. Vishnu's shoulders and head are surrounded and protected by nine serpent heads with expanded hoods; he couches on the mighty coils. This multiheaded snake is an animal-counterpart of the anthropomorphic sleeper himself. It is named Endless (*ananta*), also The Remainder, The Residue (*śeṣa*). It is a figure representing the residue that remained after the earth, the upper and infernal regions, and all their beings, had been shaped out of the cosmic waters of the abyss. The three created worlds are afloat upon the waters; i.e., they balance on the expanded hoods. Shesha is the king and ancestor of all the snakes that crawl the earth.

The shield of expanded serpent-hoods surrounding the shoulders and head is a characteristic feature of serpent-genii in Indian art. A typical representation was discovered during the excavation of the great Buddhist monastery-university of Nālandā in northeast India. (Figure 4.) This is a work in the mature classic style of the later Gupta period, about the fifth century A.D. The serpent prince, or nāga, in human form is represented sitting in a devotional attitude, in meditative posture, with a rosary slung around the palm of his right hand. From the back spreads the characteristic halo: an uneven number of expanded cobra-hoods, forming a part of the body and shielding the head.

---

* These heroes are regarded as themselves incarnations. Yudhishthira is a human manifestation of Dharma, the Sacred Order of Life. Bhīma represents the Wind God, Vāyu; he is characterized by the huge iron club with which he smashed (by a foul) the thighs of the leading hero of the opponents, whom he had engaged in single combat. Arjuna is a human counterpart of Indra. Nakula and Sahadeva incarnate the twin "Horseman Gods," the Ashvin (Hindu parallels to the Greek Dioscuri). Draupadī, finally, is a duplicate of Indrānī, the queen of the gods and spouse of Indra. Her polyandrous marriage to the five brothers is an extraordinary and exceptional case in the Brahmin tradition.

Occasionally the sinuous body of the snake is represented as running down the back. Or again, at the hips, the human figure may become serpentine, after the manner of a mermaid. In a gigantic relief depicting the myth of the Descent to Earth of the Ganges (which we shall discuss at the conclusion of the present chapter) two such figures, a male and a female, are to be seen. (Figures 27-8.)

Nāgas are genii superior to man. They inhabit subaquatic paradises, dwelling at the bottoms of rivers, lakes, and seas, in resplendent palaces studded with gems and pearls. They are keepers of the life-energy that is stored in the earthly waters of springs, wells, and ponds. They are the guardians, also, of the riches of the deep sea—corals, shells, and pearls. They are supposed to carry a precious jewel in their heads. Serpent princesses, celebrated for their cleverness and charm, figure among the ancestresses of many a South Indian dynasty: a nāginī or nāga in the family tree gives one a background.

An important function of the nāgas is that of "door guardian" (dvāra-pāla). As such they frequently appear at the portals of Hindu and Buddhist shrines. In this role their proper attitude is one of pious devotion (bhakti), fervent and loving concentration on the inward vision of the god or the Buddha whose precincts they attend. It is extremely interesting and important to observe that the Buddhist and Hindu representations of such popular divinities do not differ from each other, either essentially or in detail; for Buddhist and Hindu art—as also Buddhist and Hindu doctrine *—were in India basically one. Prince Gautama Siddhārtha, the "historical Buddha," who taught in the sixth and fifth centuries b.c., was a reformer, a monastic reformer, remaining within, and taking for granted, the context of Indian civilization. He never denied the Hindu pantheon or

---

* Cf. Ananda K. Coomaraswamy, *Hinduism and Buddhism* (The Philosophical Library, New York, no date).

broke with the traditional Hindu ideal of release through enlightenment (*mokṣa, nirvāṇa*). His specific deed was not that of
refuting but of re-formulating, on the basis of a profound personal experience, the ageless Indian teaching of redemption from
the toils of Māyā. The new order of mendicant monks that he
established for the practice of his special code of disciplines was,
in India, one order among a multitude. "I have seen the ancient
Way," he is reported to have said, "the Old Road that was taken
by the formerly All-Awakened, and that is the path I follow." *

Like every considerable Indian saint, Gautama was venerated
even during his lifetime as a human vehicle of Absolute Truth.
After his passing, his memory became clothed with the standard
accouterments of myth. And when the Buddhist sect expanded,
developing from the estate of an essentially monastic to that of
a largely secular community,† the great founder became less and
less exclusively an example to be followed (for how can a layman
follow an ascetic and at the same time do justice to family duties?),
more and more a symbol to be venerated—symbol of the re-
demptive power of enlightenment which is latent in every deluded being. During the golden centuries that followed the period
of the Buddha and endured until the fiery arrival in India of
the zealots of Mohammed, Buddhism and Hinduism developed
side by side, submitting to common influences, exchanging argu-
ments and insights. In later Buddhist art we find the Blessed
One throned supreme—as representing the highest personification of the Absolute—amidst the old, old demonic and divine
presences of the fertile land, the heavens, and the hells.

The earliest stone monuments in India date from the Maurya
period (320–185 B.C.), particularly from the epoch-making reign
of the emperor Ashoka (272–232 B.C.). Ashoka was a convert to

---

* *Saṁyutta Nikāya*, II. 106. Quoted by Coomaraswamy, *op. cit.*, pp. 45-6.
† A development to be duplicated, half a millennium later, in the history of
Christianity.

the Buddhist belief and an immensely powerful patron. Not only did his domain embrace the whole of northern India, expanding to include Afghanistan, Kashmir, and the Dekkan, but he sent out missionaries to the south as far as Ceylon, and westward even into Syria and Egypt. He established throughout his empire countless monasteries, and is reputed to have constructed up to eighty thousand dāgabas or stūpas (Buddhist reliquary shrines). It is among the ruins of his era that the pictorial tradition of Indian myth and symbol first breaks for us, like a torrent, into the light of day.

It is apparent, however, from the sophistication, the degree of perfection, and the variety of the work that abruptly appears in the period of Ashoka and then rapidly increases, that already in the earlier centuries (though invisible to us, because committed to the perishable materials of ivory and wood) the torrent of Indian religious art must have been flowing strong. The craftsmen who wrought the elaborately decorated gates of the "Great Stūpa" at Sāñchī (Figure 63), and the now shattered shrines of Bhārhut, Bodhgayā, and Amarāvatī, in the main translated into stone and skillfully adapted to the special requirements and special legends of the new sect the ancient motifs of their traditional craft. The mirage-like Indra discussed in the last chapter embellishes the entrance to a Buddhist monastery of the second century b.c. Nāgas, vriksha-devatās, yakshas and yakshinīs (serpent kings, tree goddesses, earth genii and their queens) positively teem in the abundant monuments to Buddhist belief. And their position with respect to the central shrine or image of the Enlightened One is hardly distinguishable from that which they exhibit when appearing in conjunction with the orthodox Hindu personifications of the Absolute, Vishnu and Shiva. Figure 5, for example, shows a nāga who stands at the foot of the long flight of steps leading up to the Ruanweli Dāgaba in Ceylon. This graceful prince exhibits in both hands symbols of the fertility of vegetation, for which he, as a guardian and semi-

65

divine serpent-embodiment of the life-sustaining, terrestrial waters, is personally responsible. In his left hand is a tree, in his right a water-jar, the vessel of abundance, out of which is growing a luscious plant. This attitude of the serpent prince as doorkeeper and devotee goes back to the earliest period of Buddhist art.

Between the Buddha and the nāga in India there is no such antagonism as we are used to in the savior *versus* serpent symbolism of the West. According to the Buddhist view, all the genii of nature rejoice, together with the highest gods, upon the appearance of the incarnate redeemer, and the serpent, as the principal personification of the waters of terrestrial life, is no exception. Eager to serve the universal teacher, they watch solicitously his progress toward final enlightenment; for he has come to redeem all beings alike, the creatures of earth, of the heavens, and of the hells.

There is a special Buddha-type that stresses this supreme harmony between the savior who has overcome the bondage of nature and the serpent who represents that very bondage; the type figures conspicuously in the Buddhist art of Cambodia and Siam. (Figure 7.) Like the image of Vishnu on Ananta (Figure 3), this buddha represents a special modification of a traditional Hindu nāga formula. (Figure 5.) The type does not appear among the art works of India proper, yet the legend that explains it forms a part of the earliest Indian Buddhist tradition and is accorded a prominent place in the orthodox canon preserved by the venerable Buddhist community of Ceylon. It is based on an event that is supposed to have occurred shortly after Gautama's attainment of enlightenment.*

When the Blessed One, in the last watch of the Night of Knowledge, had fathomed the mystery of dependent origination, the ten thousand worlds thundered with his attainment of omni-

---

* *Mahā-vagga*, i. 1-3.

science. Then he sat cross-legged for seven days at the foot of the Bo-tree (the Bodhi tree, the "Tree of Enlightenment"), on the banks of the river Nairañjanā, absorbed in the bliss of his illumination. And he revolved in his mind his new understanding of the bondage of all individualized existence; the fateful power of the inborn ignorance that casts its spell over all living beings; the irrational thirst for life with which everything consequently is pervaded; the endless round of birth, suffering, decay, death, and rebirth. Then after the lapse of those seven days, he arose and proceeded a little way to a great banyan-tree, "The Tree of the Goatherd," at the foot of which he resumed his cross-legged posture; and there for seven more days he again sat absorbed in the bliss of his illumination. After the lapse of that period, he again arose, and, leaving the banyan, went to a third great tree. Again he sat and experienced for seven days his state of exalted calm. This third tree—the tree of our legend—was named "The Tree of the Serpent King, Muchalinda."

Now Muchalinda, a prodigious cobra, dwelt in a hole amongst the roots. He perceived, as soon as the Buddha had passed into the state of bliss, that a great storm cloud had begun to gather, out of season. Thereupon he issued quietly from the black abode and with the coils of his body enveloped seven times the blessed body of the Enlightened One; with the expanse of his giant snake-hood he sheltered as an umbrella the blessed head. Seven days it rained, the wind blew cold, the Buddha remained in meditation. But on the seventh, the unseasonable storm dispersed; Muchalinda unloosed his coils, transformed himself into a gentle youth, and with joined hands to his forehead bowed in worship of the savior of the world.

In this legend and in the images of the Muchalinda-Buddha a perfect reconciliation of antagonistic principles is represented. The serpent, symbolizing the life force that motivates birth and rebirth, and the savior, conqueror of that blind will for life, severer of the bonds of birth, pointer of the path to the imperishable Transcendent, here together in harmonious union open to the eye a vista beyond all the dualities of thought. Some of these Muchalinda-Buddhas of the Mon-Khmers (Siam and Cambodia, ninth to thirteenth centuries A.D.) rank among the very finest masterworks of Buddhist art. With the dreamy, graceful voluptuousness of a subtle, unearthly, sensual charm they blend a perfect spirituality and serene aloofness. The bliss of inner absorption in the experience of enlightenment, triumph over the bondage of life, supreme peace, Nirvāna-Release, pervade the substance of the image and emit a radiance, tender, compassionate, and sweet.

It is said by some that when the Buddha began teaching his doctrine, he soon realized that men were not prepared to accept it in its fullness. They shrank from the extreme implications of his vision of the universal Void (śūnyatā). Therefore, he committed the deeper interpretation of reality to an audience of nāgas, who were to hold it in trust until mankind should be made ready to understand. Then to his human disciples he offered, as a kind of preliminary training and approach to the paradoxical truth, the comparatively rational and realistic doctrine of the so-called Hīnayāna division of Buddhism. Not until some seven centuries had passed was the great sage Nāgārjuna, "Arjuna of the Nāgas," initiated by the serpent kings into the truth that all is void (śūnya). And so it was he who brought to man the full-fledged Buddhist teachings of the Mahāyāna.*

---

* For a discussion of Hīnayāna and Mahāyāna Buddhism, see Ananda Coomaraswamy, *Buddha and the Gospel of Buddhism* (New York, 1916).

2.

Divinities and Their Vehicles

WHEREVER we encounter a fairly continuous series of Buddhist monuments dating from the final centuries B.C.—such as have survived the inclemencies of the Indian climate and the vicissitudes of history—representations of serpent genii occur in association with a variety of other divine patrons of fertility, prosperity, and earthly health. These personify under various aspects the life energy—beneficent but blind—which the message of the Buddha broke and dissolved. In attitudes of devout concentration, deep faith, and rapture, they watch now at the shrine of him who pointed the difficult path that leads beyond them: the embodiments of the powers of earthbound life stand in worship of the master of asceticism and release.

Conspicuous among these figures are the voluptuous tree goddesses or dryads, generally represented in a characteristic posture: with one arm entwining the trunk of a tree and the other bending a branch down, the goddess gives the trunk, near the root, a gentle kick. (Figure 19.) This curious formula derives from a ritual of fecundation. According to an ageless belief, nature requires to be stimulated by man; the procreative forces have to be aroused, by magic means, from semi-dormancy. In particular, there is in India a certain tree (aśoka) which is supposed not to put forth blossoms unless touched and kicked by a girl or young woman. Girls and young women are regarded as human embodiments of the maternal energy of nature. They are diminutive doubles of the Great Mother of all life, vessels of fertility, life in full sap, potential sources of new offspring. By touching and kicking the tree they transfer into it their potency, and enable it to bring forth blossom and fruit. Hence, the goddess who represents the life-energy and fertility of the tree is herself most aptly visualized in this magic posture of fertilization.

The tree goddess of Figure 19 is represented standing above an elephant. Such a relationship of anthropomorphic to animal figure is a common trait of Indian iconography. The animal symbol, placed beneath, is interpreted as carrying the human figure and is called the "vehicle" (*vāhana*). It is a duplicate-representation of the energy and character of the god. Shiva, similarly, is depicted on the bull; "The Goddess," his spouse-consort, on the lion. Their son, the elephant-headed god Ganesha, "The Lord and Leader of the Hosts of Shiva," called also "The Lord and Master of Obstacles" (*vighneśvara*), sits above a rat. (Figure 53.) Ganesha forges ahead through obstacles as an elephant through the jungle, but the rat, too, is an overcomer of obstacles, and, as such, an appropriate, even though physically incongruous, mount for the gigantic pot-bellied divinity of the elephant head. The elephant passes through the wilderness, treading shrubs, bending and uprooting trees, fording rivers and lakes easily; the rat can gain access to the bolted granary. The two represent the power of this god to vanquish every obstacle of the Way.

Kubera, overlord of all the genii (*yakṣas*), frequently is represented as standing on a crouching man. His common epithet is "He whose mount or vehicle is a man" (*nara-vāhana*). Kubera and his following are genii of fertility, riches, and prosperity, principally associated with the earth, the mountains, and the treasures of the precious stones and metals underground. They are tutelary divinities of the Indian household, deriving from the pre-Aryan, aboriginal tradition, and playing a considerable role in Hindu and early Buddhist folklore. The man-vehicle beneath his feet distinguishes Kubera from all other superhuman kings and princes, just as the cobra hoods mark for us the superhuman nāga. Primarily the vehicle is a determinant, to let us know precisely who the figure is that is represented in the given work of art.

The device did not originate in India, but was imported, at an early period, from Mesopotamia. Figure 10 shows an Assyrian divinity, Assur, standing or floating above a composite beast with the head of a dragon, the front paws of a lion, eagle-talons on the hind feet, and the tail of a scorpion. The god is surrounded by the symbols of various celestial beings, as well as the sun and moon, the Pleiades, and the planet Venus. In this work the composite monster occupies the place of the vāhana in Indian art and serves the identical function. It represents and embodies, on an inferior plane, the energies of the anthropomorphic god and serves as a vehicle. In the art works of Mesopotamia the device can be traced back to at least 1500 B.C. In the earliest monuments of India (those of the Indus Valley Civilization of the fourth and third millenniums B.C.) * it does not occur.

The origin of the determinative "vehicle" is to be sought in the technique of picture or rebus writing of the ancient Near East. According to a common convention of the hieroglyphic, pictographic scripts—as preserved in the Egyptian and Mesopotamian inscriptions, and as underlying the Hebrew and Phoenician alphabets—characters that originally represented objects were employed to express phonetic values. Then, in order to preclude ambiguity, another symbol, the "determinant," was added, which specified the reference of the original sign. Similarly, in these images of divinities the simple kingly or womanly form of the anthropomorphic figure is somewhat ambiguous; its reference becomes specified by the determinant, or parallel symbol, added underneath.

As we shall see, this device of the animal vehicle is by no means the only instance of Mesopotamian influence on Indian symbolism. There must have flourished, at an early period, a seagoing traffic between the mouths of the Tigris and Euphrates rivers and the western coast of India. The original centers of Mesopotamian civilization were located close to the deltas of the rivers, at the head of the Persian Gulf. It was a matter of only

---

* Cf. pp. 93-6, *infra*.

a few days to India. And we have evidence of influences running in both directions. An early Indian alphabet, the Brāhmī script, was adapted from a Semitic writing style of about 800 B.C.; and there is a Buddhist tale describing an expedition of Indian merchants to Babylon. Babylon is called in the story "Baveru." The men from India are described as having excited the astonishment of the inhabitants of the western city by exhibiting a peacock.

3.

The Serpent and the Bird

AMONG the motifs deriving from early Mesopotamian art and continuing in the traditions of India to the present day is the pattern of the entwined serpent-pair. This ancient device commonly appears on votive slabs erected to serpent genii. Such stone tables, called nāgalkals, variously decorated with serpent forms, are votive gifts from women desiring offspring. They are set up in temple courtyards, at the entrances of villages and towns, near ponds, or under holy trees. (Figure 8.) The ponds are supposed to be peopled by nāgas.

When the sculptor has finished such a stone, it is placed for some six months in a pond, to become imbued with the life force of the watery element. Also, and for the same reason, it is treated with a ritual and with magic formulae (*mantra*). Then the stone is set up, preferably under a pipal or a nimba tree. These two trees often stand together, and are regarded as married couples. The snakes are supposed to inhabit the terrestrial moisture among the roots.

The nāgakals of Figure 8 are from the state of Mysore, South India. The reliefs decorating them are of several kinds. Some exhibit a snake queen of the mermaid type, with serpent tail and human body, and with a halo of expanded cobra hoods; she folds her arms across her breast supporting in them two serpent children who rise above her shoulders. Others exhibit one snake with a number of heads and expanded hoods. Others again show the Mesopotamian serpent pair, heads facing each other, entwined in amorous embrace.

In Mesopotamia this device appears in a very early design traced on the sacrificial goblet of King Gudea of Lagash. (Figure 11.) In this work of the Sumerian period, ca. 2600 B.C., we find the familiar pair of serpents, entwined, and facing each other. The motif must have been diffused into India at an extremely remote era, before the arrival of the Aryans. Together with certain other non-Vedic, pre-Aryan, aboriginal traits, it is preserved to this day in the conservative local traditions, particularly of Central and South Indian folklore. Interestingly enough, in the living Indian traditions as well as in this golden goblet of the archaic Sumerian past, the classical antagonist of the fabulous serpent is the fabulous bird.

The goblet of King Gudea displays a warlike pair of winged, birdlike monsters, standing erect on eagle claws and with the forepaws of a lion. Such bird-beings represent the firmament—the upper, celestial, ethereal realm—just as the serpents represent the life-bestowing, fertilizing element of the terrestrial waters. They stand in eternal opposition to the serpent powers, and, accordingly, constitute with them an archetypal pair of symbolical antagonists, the champions respectively of heaven and of earth.

The eagle belongs to Father Heaven, Father Zeus in the mythology of the Greeks. Serpents, on the other hand, attend the goddess Hera, Zeus' consort, Mother Earth. Many are the mythological episodes delineating the opposition of the two. For example, when Herakles, the child of a clandestine affair between Zeus and the mortal woman Alkmene, was still an infant in the cradle, jealous Hera dispatched her snake attendants to kill him; the little son of Father Heaven, however, was able to slay them. Again, according to Homer's *Iliad*, an eagle appeared to the assembled Greek heroes, one day during the siege of Troy. The bird was observed slowly soaring in the sky, and bearing in its talons a bleeding snake. Kalchas, the priest-soothsayer, interpreted the apparition as an auspicious omen, denoting the triumph of the Greeks over the Trojans. The heavenly bird ravaging the serpent symbolized to him the victory of the patriarchal, masculine, heavenly order of the Greeks over the female principle of Asia and Troy. The latter was typified in the luxurious Asiatic goddess, Aphrodite, and particularly in her immoral deed which had been the cause of the Trojan War: she had persuaded Helen, the wife of Menelaos, to break the ties of her marriage under the patriarchal, masculine order, and to lie with Paris, a mate of her own selection.

The twofold symbol of eagle and serpent is possessed of a vitality that outlasts the ages. In the West it reappears in modern literature in Nietzsche's *Thus Spake Zarathustra*, where the eagle and serpent are the two animal companions of the philosopher's "Solitary Sage." "The proudest and the shrewdest among animals," he calls them. As embodiments of the principal virtues of the first Superman, they symbolize the re-united powers which are to open the way to the New Age.

Probably the symbolism is very much older than the chalice of the ancient Sumerian king, Gudea. Nevertheless, Mesopotamian Sumer may well have been the cradle out of which the formula made its way, on the one hand westward to Greece and modern Europe, on the other hand eastward into ancient India, and then, somewhat later, into remoter Indonesia. The two snakes were regarded in Mesopotamia as symbolical of the god of healing, Ningishzida; hence, in Greece they became attached to the god of medicine, Asklepios. Today they are our symbol of the medical profession.

Like a river winding its way, the serpent creeps along the

ground; it dwells in the earth and starts forth like a fountain from its hole. It is an embodiment of the water of life issuing from the deep body of Mother Earth. Earth is the primordial mother of life; she feeds all creatures out of her substance, and again devours all; she is the common grave. She clasps to her bosom the life she has brought forth, denying to it the unbound freedom of celestial space. In contrast, the infinity of heaven denotes the free sway of the unbound spirit, freely roaming as a bird, disentangled from the fetters of earth. The eagle represents this higher, spiritual principle, released from the bondage of matter and soaring into the translucent ether, mounting to its kin, the stars, and even to the supreme divine being above them. On the other hand, the serpent is life-force in the sphere of life-matter. The snake is supposed to be of tenacious vitality; it rejuvenates itself by sloughing off its skin.

Whereas in Western tradition the *spiritual* antagonism of bird and serpent is commonly understood and stressed, the opposition, as symbolized in India, is strictly that of the *natural* elements: sun force against the liquid energy of the earthly waters. Ablaze with the heat of the glowing sun, drying up the moisture of the land, the "fair-feathered" (*suparṇa*), golden-winged, griffon-like master of the sky violently attacks, ruthlessly and eternally, the embodier and guardian of the vivifying liquid of the all-nourishing earth. The bird is addressed as "He who kills nāgas or serpents" (*nāgāntaka, bhujagāntaka*), "He who devours serpents" (*pannagāśana, nāgāśana*). His proper name is Garuda, from the root *gṛi*, "to swallow." As the relentless annihilator of serpents, he is possessed of a mystic power against the effects of poison; hence is popular in folklore and daily worship. At Puri, in the Indian province of Orissa, persons suffering from snakebite are taken to the main hall of the Great Temple, where they embrace a Garuda pillar filled with the magic of the celestial bird. Garuda is represented, generally, with wings, human arms, vulture legs, and a curved, beaklike nose. Two amusing examples are represented on the endpiece of a balustrade from Siam (Figure 9): in a triumphant attitude above a pair of giant snakes with lifted heads, the sturdy little garudas clutch their conquered victims in their claws.*

Garuda is the vehicle, or vāhana, of the Supreme God, Vishnu. He bears him on his shoulders, the god carrying meanwhile in uplifted hand the sharp-rimmed battle-discus, "Fair to See" (sudarśana), the fiery sun disk of a thousand spokes, the wheel (cakra) which he hurls against his opponents. In Cambodian architecture not Vishnu alone but his whole temple is supported by Garuda. The bird is multiplied and arrayed in caryatid-rows bearing the structure. The temple is regarded as an earthly copy of Vaikuntha, the god's celestial abode.

Thus Vishnu is linked (like Nietzsche's Zarathustra) with both of the eternal antagonists. Shesha, the serpent Endless, representative of the cosmic waters, who is the source of all water whatsoever, is his animal representative; but then so too is Garuda, the conquering principle, the snake's opponent. This is a paradox with reason; for Vishnu is the Absolute, the all-containing Divine Essence. He comprises all dichotomies. The Absolute becomes differentiated in polarized manifestations, and through these the vital tensions of the world-process are brought into existence and maintained.

---

* In the Hellenistic Buddhist art of Gandhāra (Northwest India, first century B.C. to fourth A.D.) the Greco-Roman formula of the eagle, Zeus, bearing away the youth Ganymede is employed to represent the Indian theme of the sun-bird, Garuda, abducting and devouring a young nāginī. [Both Ganymede (later replaced by an ecstatic feminine figure), and the nāginī are symbols of the Psyche caught up by and assimilated to the Spirit, cf. Coomaraswamy, "The Rape of a Nāgī," Boston Museum of Fine Arts Bulletin Nos. 35, 36, 1937.—AKC.]

Vishnu as Conqueror of the Serpent

HAVING already considered Vishnu as the anthropomorphic counterpart of the cosmic snake, we must now review an important series of mythological episodes in which he appears in the role of the conqueror of the serpent force.

A rather isolated myth, not connected with the major cycles of the avatārs of Vishnu, is that of The Deliverance of the Elephant.* A sculptural representation of the event is shown in a relief in the Dasha-Avatār Temple of Deogarh. (Figure 13.) A magnificent elephant, in quest of its fare of lotus stalks and roots, has ventured too far into the watery element, and the serpents of the deep have seized and fettered it. The great animal, struggling in vain, has at last implored the help of the High God. Vishnu has just appeared, seated on Garuda. No deed of Vishnu is required; his presence is enough. The mighty serpent king pays obeisance, together with his queen. The serpents bow with folded hands before the Lord Ruler of the Universe and surrender to him their victim. The elephant's feet are still ensnared by the powerful coils. In this monument of the classic Gupta period (fourth to sixth centuries A.D.) the bird Garuda has something the appearance of an angel. Vishnu is crowned with a diadem, and has four arms.

A more amply developed myth is that of the third incarnation or avatār: Vishnu's apparition in the form of a boar.† In this case, the story of the conquest of the serpent force is integrated with the great cycle of universal evolution. The event is supposed to have occurred at the dawn of the present kalpa, and is termed The Creation by the Boar.

The earth has just come into being, and the world-stage is set

---

* *Bhāgavata Purāṇa*, VIII. 2-3.   † *Viṣṇu Purāṇa*, I. 4.

for the wonderful drama of evolution. On the solid surface warm-blooded creatures will appear, and out of these, then, the history of mankind will unfold. Like a lotus on the quiet surface of a lake, or like human consciousness on the darkness of the unconscious, so the earth now reposes, fresh and fair, on the waters of the cosmic abyss.

But the course of evolution is subject to setbacks. According to the Indian view, it is punctuated by recurrent crises which require the intervention of the Highest God. There exists an ever threatening counter-current, antagonistic to the trend of evolution, which periodically halts, engulfs, and takes back what has already been given form. This force is represented in classical Hindu mythology under the guise of the giant serpent power of the world abyss. Thus it happened at the very dawn of the present day of Time, that the Earth, newly blossomed, was suddenly ravished from the surface of the cosmic sea to the lowest deep.

It was at this juncture that Vishnu assumed the form of a gigantic boar. The boar is a warm-blooded animal belonging to the earthly sphere, yet reveling in swamps, and familiar with the watery element. Vishnu in this form plunged into the cosmic sea. Overcoming the great serpent king and treading him down—the enemy, with folded hands, imploring at last his mercy—the High God incarnate in the animal shape gathered into his arms the lovely body of the still very youthful Mother Earth, and while she supported herself by clinging to his tusk, brought her up again to the surface of the sea.

Vishnu, as the embodied absolute, is intrinsically not at variance with the serpent principle of the water; nevertheless, in symbolic episodes such as this, the god has to interfere with the serpent's action. The serpent must be checked, because it endangers the further evolution of the universe: it represents, indeed, the all-containing substance of Vishnu, but on a primitive level of differentiation. Operating beyond its bounds at a later stage in the cosmic cycle, it threatens to throw the world back to the shapeless, unconscious condition of the beginnings. There was no universe at that time, only night and the interminable sleep of the infinite sea. Vishnu counteracts that retrogressive tendency of his own substance by taking form and playing the role of the World Creator and Maintainer—in the present instance, in the warm-blooded, animal form of a boar.

The event is magnificently depicted in a relief of Udayagiri, Gwalior, dated A.D. 440. (Figure 12.) The celestial beings here watching the exploit of the heroic boar are aligned in regular rows, after the manner of ancient Mesopotamian patterns—like hieroglyphs or cuneiform symbols. This is an astonishing circumstance, as yet unexplained. In fact, no one has hitherto even expressed surprise at the isolated apparition, amidst the totally different forms of the classic Hindu style, of this rigid, ornamental composition, obviously and very strongly influenced by the hieroglyphics of the ancient Near East.

A third instance of Vishnu as opponent and conqueror of the serpent principle is recounted in connection with the life story of his most popular incarnation, Krishna. The tale is told in the Vishnu Purāṇa,* and since it is fraught with highly significant myth-motifs, is well worth reviewing at considerable length.

The account opens with a review of the circumstances of Krishna's coming into the world.† As usual, the titans or demons having won a victory over the gods, a savior-incarnation was to be born, to restore the balance of the powers. This particular example of the recurrent crisis is regarded as having occurred at the close of the yuga just preceding our own, i.e., at the close of the Dvāpara Yuga that terminated 3102 B.C.‡ A race of demons had sprung into existence over the whole surface of the earth, and having unseated the gods, had established a reign of terror, injustice, and disorder. The life-processes of the cosmos itself were endangered. The goddess Earth, crushed by the terrible

---

* *Viṣṇu Purāṇa*, V. 7.   † *Ib.*, V. 1-4.   ‡ Cf. pp. 14-15, *supra.*

burden, finally could bear the anquish no longer. She ascended to the summit of Mount Meru, the central mountain and axis of the universe, and there gained entrance, as a petitioner, to the Assembly of the Gods.

Before Brahmā and the celestials the goddess Earth prostrated herself. "The God of Fire is the paternal protector of gold," she said, "and the Sun God the protector of cows. My paternal protector is Vishnu. He is venerated by the entire world.

"My Lords, over the realm of mortal beings a demon-host is swarming. Day and night cities howl, the land blazes. Villainous personages too numerous to name, demons celebrated throughout the yugas for their wickedness, have been born again, into the families of powerful kings, and they are working their intolerable deeds without restraint. Even Kālanemi, the infamous devil slain of old by Vishnu, has returned. He is now Kamsa, the son of King Ugrasena. My body is so burdened by iniquities, that I can no longer sustain them. They are shattering my sinews. O ye Mighty Ones, save me; see to it, or I shall sink, overcome, to the bottom of the Abyss."

Brahmā heard. The gods urged him to relieve the goddess. Brahmā spoke:

"O ye Celestials! Myself, Shiva, and You—all beings—are no more than a portion of Vishnu. We know that the manifestations of Vishnu's boundless substance are moved by an ever-changing tide. Violence and weakness alternate with order and strength; there is a continuous waxing and waning of his grace. Let us proceed, therefore, to the shores of the Milky Ocean—which is the abode of Vishnu—and there humbly communicate to him, the Highest Being, this complaint and petition of the Earth. For, as we have so often seen, Vishnu is ever willing to send a minute particle of his essence down into the world—the world being but a manifestation of his pleasure; and thus he has repeatedly re-established the orderly course of the Day."

Brahmā, together with the Earth and all the gods, resorted

therefore to Vishnu. Bowing before him whose emblem is Garuda, the sun-bird, Brahmā composed his mind in meditation and gave praise to the Highest Being.

"Adoration to Vishnu with his myriads of forms and of arms, his manifold faces and feet! Adoration to the Infinite One, who is simultaneously the manifestation, the preservation, and the dissolution of the universe! Thou art subtle beyond all discovery of the senses. Thou art prodigious in thine essence. Thou art of everything the root. Thou bringest forth spirit—that primal substance from which arose and arises speech and the senses. O Thou Highest of All, have mercy! Here, seeking in thee her refuge, comes the Earth. Thou end without end, beginning without beginning, final refuge of all beings, the goddess begs of thee redemption from her burden. Demons, earthborn, are shattering her rocky sinews. Indra, myself, and all the gods, beseech of thee thy counsel: tell us, O Lord and Essence of our Immortality, tell us what we must do."

Vishnu plucked two hairs from his head, a fair one and a dark, and then addressed himself to the assemblage on the shore:

"These two hairs of my head shall descend to the Earth and take away her burden. All the gods, too, shall go down to her, each in a portion of his essence, and rescue the Earth by conquest of the demons. There is a certain princess, Devakī, the wife of Vasudeva, and she is like unto a goddess among men. This dark hair of mine is to become the eighth fruit of her womb. I shall descend into her and be born of her, and shall kill again the demon Kālanemi, in his present incarnation, Kamsa."

Vishnu vanished, and the gods, falling to their knees, paid homage to the Invisible. Then all descended from the summit of Mount Meru.

The hairs became presently a brother-pair of hero saviors. The dark hair became Krishna; the fair one was born as Krishna's older and lighter half-brother, Balarāma—whose mother was another wife of Vasudeva, named Rohinī. Kamsa attempted to slay the two but they were rescued by miraculous devices. Among a tribe of cowherds they passed their childhood in hiding from the enemy. Here, among the children of the good and simple folk, tending the flocks and playing in the woods and fields, they passed a series of idyllic years which have become a favorite theme of Hindu myth and contemplation. The cycle of boyhood deeds associated with this period is one of the most charming passages among the mythologies of the world. The little savior, time after time, playfully baffled and amazed the cowherds with marvelous deeds out of all proportion to his childlike guise, yet never disclosed to them his divinity. At last, misinterpreting the phenomena as ominous of earthquake or other imminent evil, the whole community moved for safety—herds and carts and all—to the mighty forest of Vrindāvana, on the bank of the sacred Yamunā, just across from Kamsa's capital city, Mathurā.* There they constructed a crescent-shaped camp of carts and fences, set their flocks to graze, their children to play, and resumed their ageless way. Krishna, their divine charge, regarded with pleasure the new surroundings, benignly blessed the forest and bestowed welfare on the cows. Immediately, though the merciless heat of the summer was at its height, the meadows—as though it were the rainy season—brought forth fresh grass.

It behooves a superhuman savior, when he has been born of an earthly mother, to conform to the environment he has chosen to inhabit. To all appearances, he is as much enmeshed in Māyā as everybody else. But then, of a sudden, a superhuman deed or gesture betrays his supernatural essence. So it was with Krishna in the Vrinda forest. In this way it happened, that, even as a boy, he met and overcame a certain serpent king, Kāliya by name, who inhabited the waters of the river near his home.

Krishna and his brother, Rāma, played among the cowpens

---

* Modern Brindaban, on the Jumna, opposite Muttra. This is a great center of Vishnu-Krishna worship.

and tended the calves; and they played in the wilderness, making wreaths of grass and leaves, and weaving garlands of wild flowers. They made drums of leaves, and Krishna blew the flute. Laughing and frolicking, they romped among the great trees, sometimes alone, sometimes together, sometimes with a host of other boys.

It was when wandering alone, on a little exploring expedition, that Krishna came to a place along the river where the water was whirling, white with foam. This was the region of the underwater den of the great serpent king, Kāliya, whose poisonous, fiery breath, spreading about, had burned all of the trees overhanging the stream. Even birds flying above the horrible abode were scorched and fell to their death.

Krishna, the adventuring seven-year-old, came to this dangerous place and curiously peered into the depths. "Here dwells the wicked Kāliya," he brooded, "whose weapon is venom. Already, I have subdued him.* If released by me, he will vanish into the vast ocean. Because of this Kāliya the whole of the Yamunā, from here to the sea, has become impure. Neither men nor cattle may quench their thirst in these waters. Therefore, I shall vanquish this king of serpents and release the inhabitants of the country from their continual dread. It was to make them happy and free, and to chastise the wicked who dwell in the paths of evil, that I descended into the world. All right—I shall climb up yonder broad-branched tree overhanging the water, and jump."

The boy girded his loins, made his way up the tree, and jumped with a great leap into the depths. His impact shook the Abyss. The flaming water splashed high into the trees along the bank, setting them afire. The firmament seemed ablaze. Then with his palms Krishna smote the water, and the snake king, challenged by the unwonted noise, came forth, eyes red with wrath, hoods puffing with fiery poison. Kāliya was surrounded

* A reference to the coming battle.

by swarms of red serpent warriors. Serpent queens and serpent maidens attended him by the hundred. The writhing bodies, adorned with glittering necklaces of pearl, sparkled as they rose in undulating coils, lifting their innumerable heads. The serpents sprayed Krishna with their poison. They bit him with mouths running with venom, and they fettered his limbs with their coils.

A little group of the cowherds, watching in horror near by, saw Krishna sink, inert and unconscious, entangled by the swarm of serpents. Overwhelmed, they hurried home. "Krishna, in a fit of madness," they cried, "has jumped into the den of Kāliya. The serpent king is devouring him. Hurry! Help!"

The cowherds rushed for the river, followed by their wives and children. "Alas, alas, where have you gone?" the women cried as they stumbled among the trees.

Balarāma led the way. He pointed out to the people Krishna lying powerless at the bottom, fettered by the coils. Nanda and Yashodā, the boys' foster parents, stood aghast when they beheld the face of their child. The other women, looking on, wept and stammered without hope. "In the abyss of Kāliya we all will join you," they cried; "for we cannot return to the cowpens without you, our beautiful boy! What is day without the sun, or night without the moon; what are cows without milk, and what will our homes be without Krishna?"

Balarāma saw his foster-mother, Yashodā, in a swoon, and the heartbroken Nanda staring into the stream. Then, because of his secret knowledge of Krishna's divine nature, Balarāma addressed him, gazing down at him with a piercing eye: "Divine Lord of the Gods, why do you exhibit this human frailty? Are you not aware of your divine essence? You are the navel of the universe, the support of the gods, the creator, destroyer, and guardian of the worlds. The universe is your body. These who have been your relatives since our descent to man, the cowherds and their wives, are overwhelmed with despair. Have mercy on them! You have played the babe and the boy; you have enacted the human weakness. Display now your infinite power; arise and conquer the mighty fiend!"

The words rang in Krishna's ears. They reminded him of his true essence. Over his face there moved a smile, and his eyes gradually opened. His arms stirred; his hands began to beat the coils that entwined him. With a burst, he released his limbs from the serpent coils, and, springing free, placed his foot on the serpent king. He lifted his knee, and began to dance on the mighty head. Whenever the monster attempted to rear its neck, the divine boy trod it down; again and again this happened, until finally the snake grew weak and fainted. Krishna continued his dance until the great king spat blood, and lay stiff as a stick.

The queens then in awe, beholding their lord with battered and bloodied head, implored Krishna in the following words: "Divine Master of the Gods, Supreme Ruler of the Universe, we recognize you now! Who is worthy to praise your world-transcending greatness? Be merciful, and spare the life of this our king!" (Figure 14.)

The exhausted Kāliya recovered somewhat at this prayer, and with faltering voice implored the victor: "I have only acted according to my nature. As you created me with strength and endowed me with my poison, so have I behaved. Had I comported myself otherwise, I should have violated the laws laid down by you for every creature according to its kind; I should have challenged the order of the universe and been liable therefore to punishment. But now, even in striking me, you have blessed me with the highest boon, the touch of your hand. My force is broken, my poison spent; I implore you to spare my life to me and declare what I must do."

Krishna, in his mercy, replied: "You shall not henceforth reside in the waters of the Yamunā, but in the vastness of the ocean. Depart! Moreover, I declare to you that Garuda, the sun-bird of gold, arch enemy of all serpents and my vehicle through the reaches of space, forever shall spare you, whom I have touched."

The serpent king bowed, and with his kinsfolk withdrew to the ocean. The cowherds embraced Krishna, as one who had been miraculously restored to life. Shedding tears upon his head, they rejoiced in his deed, which had restored to the waters of the river their beneficent quality. Extolled by the cowherds, praised by the women and girls who surrounded him in flattering dalliance, Krishna, the boy hero, incarnation of the All Highest, returned to the camp circle and the cows.

This very popular and often repeated tale is freighted with many charges of meaning, and can be interpreted from a number of points of view. In terms of religious history, it means that a local nature divinity, a demon dwelling in the river Yamunā, the spirit of the water, a wrathful power very difficult to propitiate, was conquered and dislodged. A primitive serpent-cult was superseded by the worship of an anthropomorphic divine savior. Through the intermediary, Krishna, the special cult of a local demon became merged into the widespread, general cult of Vishnu, the Supreme Being, and thus was linked into a context of superior symbolic import, representing concepts and intuitions of a general validity.

In Greek mythology and religious history a similar circumstance is registered in Apollo's conquest of the earthbound serpent lord of Delphi. This python would send up revelations through a fissure in the rock; a priestess, the Pythea, inhaling the potent fumes, would be inspired to give voice to cryptic utterances: the prophecies of the Oracle of Delphi. But then the great god, Apollo, challenged and overcame the dragon-demon; slew it and took its seat. Thereafter, Delphi was the sanctuary of the anthropomorphic Olympian, a god related to solar power and standing for enlightenment, wisdom, moderation and proportion. A higher, celestial principle had replaced the terrestrial presence—and yet, had not completely erased it. The priestess remained in her ancient role; the beneficent power of the earth still spoke to man; the Delphic Oracle continued in operation. Only now, the patron and owner of the sanctuary was no longer a primitive earth demon but an Olympian: Apollo, as the Pythic god.

Likewise, Kāliya was dislodged by Krishna. In this case, the demon was not killed; he had only to resign his power and withdraw to the remote sea, so that the idyllic life of man, as represented by the camp-circle of the cowherds, should not be injured by the blaze of his poison. Krishna played the role rather of moderator than of annihilator. He liberated mankind from a threat and a peril, favoring life against the slaying breath of the serpent, and yet recognized the rights of the destructive power; for the venomous serpent was as much a manifestation of the Supreme Being as were the pious cowherds. It was a manifestation of one of the darker aspects of God's essence, and had appeared out of the all-producing, primary, divine substance. There could be no elimination, once and for all, of this presence which to man seemed wholly negative. Krishna effected only a kind of boundary settlement, a balanced judgment as between demons and men. For the good of the human kingdom, Kāliya was assigned to a remoter sphere, but he was allowed to remain unchanged both in nature and in power. Had he been transformed, redeemed, or altogether eliminated, the counter-play between human and demonic, productive and destructive energies would have been disrupted—and such an eventuality was far from the intent of the Highest Being.

Vishnu's role as the maintainer of the world involves this function of mediator, or moderator, between the antagonistic energies that are active in the life-process of the universe. He restrains the overbearing impact of the destructive, disruptive powers. This he does by descending into the universe in one or another of his avatārs, curbing and subduing the terrible forces that threaten general ruin, and finally restoring a working equilibrium of opposites. Yet, as the Supreme Being, the all-containing Substance, he cannot be fundamentally at variance with the demons of the realm of water. Indeed, one of his principal manifestations is Shesha, the cosmic snake. We must not be surprised, therefore, to find that Krishna, Vishnu's human avatār and the conqueror of Kāliya, may be represented with the typical attributes of the serpent genii.

Figure 6 shows Krishna in conjunction with the nāga-symbol. This is a bronze figure from Bengal; an example of the Pāla style of the first half of the ninth century A.D. The divinity has four arms, and holds the discus (*cakra, sudarśana*) and the iron club (*kaumodakī*). Vishnu's two queens are at either hand: Shrī-Lakshmī, the goddess of earthly welfare, and her opponent, Sarasvatī, patroness of speech, song, and wisdom.* They are rivals, as the two wives of one male must be. It is said that whenever one of them bestows her boons on a man the other remains away: the wise are not wealthy and the wealthy are not wise. But at Vishnu's feet the two are subdued to antagonistic co-operation. Here the charm of the youthful god-incarnate is blended with the grandeur of the cosmic being. The human aspect discloses the Krishna for whom the hearts of all women and maidens were moved with love—first, during the years of his boyhood idyll among the cowherds, later on, at the courts of the princely clans. The nāga-symbol, on the other hand, forming the background, represents that divine nature which the hero-savior concealed from those whom he gladdened by his human presence and amazed by his deeds. This is the sign of his real character, the

---

* Sarasvatī (the river Saraswatī) is related also to Brahmā, who is wisdom and revelation incarnate; though, preferably, Brahmā's consort is Sāvitrī, the anthropomorphic embodiment of a certain holy prayer from the Rig Veda that confers initiation. This prayer invokes Divine Energy, bidding it enter into and take possession of the soul.

spirit that breathed through his human mask. For the human avatār is a blending of opposites. Such a blending also, are we ourselves, though unaware of our twofold nature: we are at once the illimited, unconditioned, divine Self, and the shrouding attributes of personality-experience and ego-consciousness.

In the case of Krishna's half-brother, Balarāma, the nāga character is strongly emphasized. He is a human embodiment, a partial incarnation, of Shesha himself, and this character is exhibited particularly in the story of his end. He is described as sitting beneath a tree on the shore of the ocean, lost in thought; whereupon a large snake crawls out of his mouth, leaving the human body of the hero-savior inanimate. This is his Shesha-nature, his secret life-essence, going back to the watery deep. As it winds its way in gigantic undulations, serpents sing its praises. The ocean itself arises in the form of a mighty serpent king to salute the great guest, its own higher Self, the serpent of the universal waters. The serpent essence of the divine hero goes back into the formlessness of the Abyss—returning into itself after having accomplished the momentary role of companion and supporter to a human avatār.

In the mythologies of the West analogous themes are to be found, but here the antagonism is not resolved. The semi-divine hero, Herakles, son of Father Heaven, Zeus, and thus a part of the celestial energies, is a relentless enemy of the snakes of the earth. As an infant, he strangles the serpents that the old earth-goddess, Hera, sends into his cradle. Later on, he conquers the Hydra, a destructive monster almost unconquerable—blind life-force, growing seven heads for every one severed from its body. Christ, too, crushes the serpent's head, though he falls victim to its sting.

In the West, the hero-saviors descending from heaven to inaugurate a new age on earth are regarded as embodiments of a spiritual and moral principle superior to the blind, animal life-force of the serpent power. In India, on the other hand, the serpent and the savior are two basic manifestations of the one, all-containing, divine substance. And this substance cannot be at variance with either of its polarized, mutually antagonistic aspects. Within it the two are reconciled and subsumed.

5.

The Lotus

WHEN the divine life substance is about to put forth the universe, the cosmic waters grow a thousand-petaled lotus of pure gold, radiant as the sun. This is the door or gate, the opening or mouth, of the womb of the universe. It is the first product of the creative principle, gold in token of its incorruptible nature. It opens to give birth first to the demiurge-creator, Brahmā. From its pericarp then issue the hosts of the created world. According to the Hindu conception, the waters are female; they are the maternal, procreative aspect of the Absolute, and the cosmic lotus is their generative organ. The cosmic lotus is called "The highest form or aspect of Earth," also "The Goddess Moisture," "The Goddess Earth." It is personified as the Mother Goddess through whom the Absolute moves into creation.

This goddess does not figure in the earlier, classic tradition of the Vedas.* Like the lotus plant itself, she is a product of the vegetation of India proper, and was therefore foreign to the Aryan invaders who poured in from northern homelands. Among the thousand and sixty-eight hymns of the Rig Veda—the earliest literary monument of the exclusively Aryan, brahminical tradition—there is not one addressed to the Lotus Goddess or even so

---

* [Not, that is to say, specifically as a goddess. But Vasishtha, i.e., Agni, is born of the lotus, earthly counterpart of Urvashī, whence Agni's constant epithet, "lotus-born" (cf. Rig Veda VI. 16. 13 and VII. 33. 11); and this lotus is the later goddess Padmā.—AKC.]

much as mentioning her. Nor does she appear among the divinities of the Vedic pantheon.

The first literary work containing evidence of her existence is a relatively late hymn, one of the so-called Khilas or "Supplements," appended to the ancient corpus of the Rig Veda.* Here, in twenty-nine stanzas, she is celebrated and described. Most significantly, all the traits that are to characterize her in the still later, "classical" period of Hindu mythology and art, already are announced in this earliest hymn. Not improbably, she existed among the people long before the priests of the invaders deigned to grant her recognition. Ageless as the basic culture-forms of India itself, she comes down, as it were, from everlasting to everlasting, without essential change.

In this apocryphal hymn appended to the Rig Veda the Lotus Goddess is already called by her two classic names, Shrī and Lakshmī, and is associated in every possible way with the lotus symbol. She is praised as "lotus-born" (*padmasaṁbhavā*), "standing on a lotus" (*padmeṣṭhitā*) "lotus-colored" (*padmavarṇa*), "lotus-thighed" (*padma-ūrū*), "lotus-eyed" (*padmākṣī*), "abounding in lotuses" (*padminī, puṣkarṇinī*), "decked with lotus garlands" (*padmamālinī*). As the tutelary deity of the rice-growing agriculture of native India, she is called, "The One Possessing Dung" (*karīṣiṇī*). Her two sons are Mud (*kardama*) and Moisture (*ciklīta*), personifications of the ingredients of a rich soil. She is "honey-like" (*mādhavī*), and is said to grant "gold, cows, horses, and slaves." She wears "garlands of silver and gold." She bestows health, long life, prosperity, offspring, and fame. Fame personified is another of her sons.† She is "made of gold" (*hiraṇ-*

---

* Khila, no. 8. Cf. I. Scheftelowitz, "Zeitschrift der Deutsch-Morgenländischen Gesellschaft," Bd. 75 (1921), pp. 37ff., where the hymn is translated and analyzed.
† The Hindu kings, besides being married to their chief queen and other wife-consorts, are said to be married to Shrī-Lakshmī, who is their kingly fortune and good luck incarnate. When this "Kingly Fortune" (*rāja-lakshmī*) forsakes them, under the ordinance of Fate, the king is doomed to lose his realm.

yamayī), "of golden hue" (*hiraṇyavarṇā*), imperishable, beautiful, and valuable, as gold. She is called *harivallabhā* and *viṣ-ṇupatnī*, "The Beloved Spouse of Vishnu."

As other divinities are represented in human form above their animal symbols, so this goddess Padmā, or Lotus, stands above or is seated upon a lotus. She is associated with this flower as invariably as is Vishnu with the Milky Ocean. The goddess "to whom the lotus is dear" (*padmapriyā*) is among the principal figures sculptured on the richly decorated gates and railings of the earliest Buddhist stupas—those of Sāñchī and Bhārhut (second and first centuries B.C.). In Figure 15, from Bhārhut, she is shown in one of her classic poses. Out of a jar filled with water, the vessel of abundance, five lotus blossoms stem, two supporting a flanking pair of elephants. From uplifted trunks the animals gently pour water over the broad-hipped patroness of fertility—Gajā-Lakshmī, "Lakshmī of the Elephants"—who smiles, and with the right hand uplifts her fully rounded breasts in a gesture of maternal benevolence.

The hymn attached to the Rig Veda addresses her: *prajānām bhavasi mātā*, "Thou art the mother of created beings"; and as the Mother she is called, *kṣamā*, "Earth." She is thus a special aspect or local development of the Mother Earth of old: the great mother goddess of the Chalcolithic period, who was worshiped over a wide area of the world, and of whom innumerable images have been found throughout the ancient Near East, in the lands of the Mediterranean, the Black Sea, and in the Danube valley. She is a sister, or double, of the well known goddesses of early Sumero-Semitic Mesopotamia; and thus she furnishes a clew to pre-Aryan linkages between India and the sources of our Western tradition of myth and symbol.

An archaic image of the goddess Lotus appears on a terracotta plaque from Basārh, dating from about the third century B.C. (Figure 16.) She stands on a lotus pedestal, with two lotus blossoms and two buds at her sides. She wears armlets on her upper arms and rich, pearl-fringed bracelets—Hindu ornaments such as are familiar from other monuments of the era. But the elephants, her characteristic animal-companions, are missing; instead, she has wings—a rare and astonishing feature for India.

Wings, common in Western tradition, do not figure among the attributes of Indian gods or superhuman beings, except in the case of Garuda, the birdlike carrier of Vishnu. In general, the celestial beings of India either float through space without visible support or are carried by their vehicles. On the other hand, in ancient Mesopotamian art winged divinities or genii were the rule. This Indian figure betrays connection with that tradition. That is the sphere from which are derived the wings of our divinities of the West, the Greek victory-goddesses as well as the Christian angels.

We have already noted and briefly discussed the commercial intercourse between India and the Land of the Two Rivers, which must have flourished in archaic times.* A dramatic spot of light was thrown on the problem, during the second decade of the present century, when a series of excavations along the Indus River suddenly disclosed a hitherto unsuspected chapter of ancient Indian history. Up to that time, the Tigris-Euphrates and the Nile had represented to us the dawn of civilization. Now, abruptly, the Indus flashes its claim. Highly developed ancient cities were discovered, giving abundant evidence of an advanced civilization that apparently reached its climax about 2500 B.C. It extended over an area very much larger than either Egypt or Sumer. Of the three principal sites investigated, Mohenjo-Daro, Harappa, and Chanhu-Daro, the first two were explored by the India Archaeological Survey under Sir John Marshall, the third by the American archaeologist, Dr. Ernest Mackay. Their magnificent finds opened a new epoch in Oriental archaeology, ad-

---

* Cf. pp. 71-2, *supra*.

ding to the history of civilization an early chapter fascinating for the problems it poses and the fresh clews it supplies.*

The early date of the Indus Valley Civilization is attested by the distribution of certain characteristic and unmistakable seals, bearing animal figures and pictographic legends, that have not yet been deciphered. (Figures 21-3.) These appear in great abundance among the ruins, and are undoubtedly the productions of India; yet isolated specimens have been found at Susa, the capital of ancient Elam, and at several sites in Mesopotamia, in stratifications that can be dated as of the period prior to King Sargon I (ca. 2500 B.C.). In the ancient Mesopotamian site of Eshnunna (Tell Asmar, fifty miles northeast of Bagdad), in a stratum dating from the so-called Early Dynastic Period (ca. 3000-2550 B.C.), was found a seal cylinder with a frieze of such elephants and rhinoceroses as occur nowhere but on the seals of Harappa and Mohenjo-Daro.† Correspondences in pottery decoration and design, beads apparently from Egypt unearthed among the Indian remains, and a number of other very suggestive fragments of evidence, bespeak a commerce of some kind—its proportions as yet impossible to estimate—during the remotest centuries of the third millennium B.C.

Wells, drains, waterchutes—a solid, elaborate, intricately ramified system of sanitation of almost modern character—are among the most striking features of the remains of the city of Mohenjo-Daro. A high degree of luxury is indicated by this elaborate system of drainage. The great majority of the buildings, constructed of well-baked bricks, appear to have been ordinary dwelling houses or shops. They are divided into good-sized rooms. Each house is furnished with its own wells and bathrooms, and pro-

---

* Sir John Marshall, *Mohenjo-Daro and the Indus Civilisation* (London, 1931), three monumental volumes. Ernest Mackay, *The Indus Civilisation* (London, 1935), a very much briefer account.

† H. Frankfort, *Tell Asmar, Khafaje, and Khorsabad* (Oriental Institute Communications, No. 4, Chicago, 1932).

vided with covered drains that in turn are connected with larger sewers in the side streets. The domestic and civic architecture at Mohenjo-Daro is much more highly developed than that of either Egypt or Mesopotamia of the same period.

Now it is very interesting to observe that among the substructures and outlines of the innumerable houses excavated at Mohenjo-Daro none has been found of proportions great enough to suggest the site of a temple or public sanctuary. In the Mesopotamian excavations, on the other hand, temple sites are exceedingly prominent. Nevertheless, in the center of the city of Mohenjo-Daro were discovered the substructures of an imposing edifice that contained a large bathing pool. The tank is sunk eight feet below the floor level, is thirty-nine feet in length and twenty-three in breadth; the outer wall is more than eight feet thick; a row of chambers is ranged along the east side. Probably this establishment was not meant for purely secular purposes: it very strongly suggests the innumerable holy bathing-places of the popular religion of later India, such as are to be found today along the sacred rivers and in the center of the temple compounds. These are the resorts of pilgrimage, for the washing away of sins, evils and sufferings of every kind. Apparently here we have evidence of a continuous tradition from the bathing place of Mohenjo-Daro to the river sanctuaries of the present day.

Other evidences of continuity over the long millenniums include the forms of ox-carts and of tools, as well as the art of the domestication of the elephant. The Mohenjo-Daro seals supply the earliest known representations of the elephant. They exhibit the animal both in domestic and in fabulous roles—which corresponds to the situation in later classic Indian tradition. The elephant is depicted standing before a feed-trough, so that it must already have played a role in the human household.

Conspicuous among the Indus Valley religious symbols is the phallus—to this day the most common object of worship in the sanctuaries of Hinduism, where it represents the generative male-energy of the universe, and is symbolic of the great god Shiva. (Figure 25.)* Furthermore, the complement to the male symbol, in Mohenjo-Daro as well as in modern India, is our goddess with the lotus in her hair. (Figure 24.) She exhibits her breasts with the familiar maternal gesture; they are the source of the abundant milk that gives life to the universe and its beings.

And so now it appears that though the earliest literary evidence of the existence of the goddess Lotus-Shrī-Lakshmī is a late and apocryphal hymn attached to the Aryan corpus of the Rig Veda, this mother of the world was actually supreme in India long before the arrival of the conquerors from the north. The occlusion of the Indus Civilization together with its goddess queen must have resulted from the arrival of the strictly patriarchal warrior-herdsmen, and the installation of their patriarchal gods. The Mother was removed from her lotus and Brahmā seated in her stead, she herself relegated—as in the shrine of Vishnu Anānta-shayin (Figure 3)—to the servile position of the brahmin wife. Nevertheless, in the hearts of the native population, her supremacy was maintained, and with the gradual merging, through the centuries, of the Vedic and pre-Vedic traditions, gradually she returned to her position of honor. She is visible everywhere in the monuments of early Buddhist art, and in the works of the classic period she stands triumphant on every side. Today she is the greatest power in the Orient.

The ubiquitous lotus is a sign of her presence even where her human features do not appear. And not uncommonly the masculine divinities even copy her traditional poses. A characteristic attitude of the goddess, that known as "lotus in hand" (*padma-hastā, padmapāṇī*), is taken over in the iconography of Mahāyāna Buddhism by the universal savior Padmapāni ("Lotus in Hand"), the greatest among the Bodhisattvas, or immortal helpers of the Buddhas. A lovely, small, copper figure of this benign personifi-

---

* Compare Figures 29-30, and see also pp. 126-30, *infra*.

cation exhibits the refined and graceful style of the classical art of Nepal, ninth or tenth century A.D. (Figure 18.) The right hand is held downward in the "gesture of granting gifts" (*varadā-mudrā*), while the left holds up the lotus symbol. The stalk, passing through the fingers, has been broken and is missing up to the elbow. But the beauty is not destroyed. In the sweet melody of the contours and proportions, and in the subtle musicality of the posture, the virtues of the Bodhisattva are appropriately expressed. Here are embodied his infinite mercy and loving compassion, his unearthly spirituality and angelic charm.

In Indian Buddhist tradition, Padmapāni, or Avalokiteshvara, is of an ambivalent or polyvalent character. He is, like Vishnu, the master of Māyā, and is possessed of the divine power of assuming forms at will. According to the needs of the situation, he may appear as man or woman, or as animal; he may appear as a fabulous winged horse named "Cloud" (*valāhaka*), or as an insect. His manner of manifestation depends upon the particular group of living beings he may wish to assist on the path of salvation through enlightenment. Padmapāni is the Hindu prototype of the Chinese Buddhist goddess Kwan-yin and the Japanese Kwannon; in this Far Eastern version of the Bodhisattva the female character prevails—as if the figure were returning to its archetypal nature.

Not only the "lotus in hand," but also the lotus pedestal, becomes detached from the goddess Lotus and consigned to other powers. The pictographic device, adapted from the vegetable realm and "written" beneath Shrī-Lakshmī's anthropomorphic image after the manner of the determinator in hieroglyphic script, migrates, during the course of the millenniums, from the one goddess who was originally its only reference to other divine or supernatural figures of the Hindu and Buddhist pantheons. Perhaps the most surprising of the new assignments is that to Prajñā-Pāramitā, the highest feminine personification in Mahā-yāna Buddhism.

The wisdom (*prajñā*) * that leads to Nirvāna is the highest virtue (*pāramitā*): it is the very essence of the Buddhas, the wholly enlightened ones, and the Buddha-in-the-making, the Bodhisattva, must bring it to perfection. In a magnificent image from thirteenth century Java we see this supernal quality in its anthropomorphic symbolization. (Figure 20.) The ancient pattern of the goddess Lotus—with lotus beneath her and in her right hand—has undergone a radical transformation of meaning. Under the influence of mature Buddhist and late Hindu conceptions, the maternal goddess of earthly goods and happiness, of fertility and earthbound life, the wife-consort and embodied energy of the cosmic sleeper—Vishnu, dreamer of the world—has become here the highest representative of world-transcending wakefulness, the most spiritual feminine symbol in all the iconographies of the East.

Prajñā-Pāramitā is "The Culmination of the Virtue (*pāramitā*) of Enlightening Transcendental Wisdom (*prajñā*)." † Or, according to another etymological explanation sanctioned by the sacred commentaries, she is "Enlightening Wisdom (*prajñā*) now gone to and abiding upon (*itā*) the Other Shore (*pāra*)." That Other Shore, or Farther Bank, is the realm of ultimate truth and transcendental reality in contradistinction to This Shore— the bank on which we are standing, moving, and talking, fettered by desire, subject to suffering, steeped in ignorance—the realm of unenlightened beings. Thus our goddess Lotus, the ageless Mother Earth, the Magna Mater of Antiquity, procreative energy and fortune on the physical plane, now transfigured under the aspect of Prajñā-Pāramitā, has become the queen of the spiritual kingdom attained through enlightenment (*bodhi*), representing the extinction (*nirvāṇa*) of both individualized consciousness and

---

* Pronounced *pra-gyaa* (*g* as in "give").

† *Prajñā* is etymologically related to the Greek *prognó-sis* [implying a knowledge of things not derived from the things themselves: knowledge a priori, as distinguished from *saṁjñā*, empirical knowledge by observation.—AKC.]

the cosmic manifold of biological, human, and godly being. Prajñā-Pāramitā is the very essence of the Buddhas and of such "great Bodhisattvas" (*mahābodhisattva*) as Padmapāni-Avalokiteshvara, who, out of compassion for the world, postpone their own extinction in order to rescue countless beings from the round of rebirth. On the one hand, she represents the termination of delight in earthly or even celestial existences, the extinction of every craving for individual duration; on the other hand (but this amounts to the same realization differently described) she is the adamantine, indestructible, secret nature of all and everything, itself devoid of all limiting, differentiating characteristics.

Now, according to the Buddhism of the medieval, Tantric period—where Buddhist and Hindu conceptions were mingled in a magnificent harmonization—the great Bodhisattvas and historical Buddhas (the historical Prince Gautama being now regarded as but one Buddha-manifestation among many) who descend as saviors to walk the earth and who go down even into the purgatories to rescue the suffering inmates, or who preside over paradises and everywhere spread the gospel of release-through-enlightenment, teaching and working miracles in a timeless career of saviorship, are but radiations of One Transcendental Enduring Essence, which is called "The Buddha of the Beginnings" (*ādi-buddha*), or again, "The Lord of the Universe" (*lokeśa*). In the Buddhist pantheon this Primeval Buddha occupies much the same position as the Highest Being in Hinduism. He is the sole source of all temporal appearances—the only real reality. The Buddhas and Bodhisattvas go forth from him into the phenomenal mirage of the universe, just as the avatārs go forth from Vishnu. And just as Lakshmī is the consort of the Hindu God, so is Prajñā-Pāramitā the female aspect of the Universal Buddha. As the active energy (*śakti*) of the supreme wisdom that guides and enlightens, she is not only the consort of the Ādi-Buddha but the animating virtue of *all* redeemers. The Buddhas and Bodhisattvas are but projections, reflections in the mirror-spheres of phenomenal existence, of her operation. She is the meaning, the very truth, of the Buddhist Law.*

A manuscript appears on the lotus beside the image of Prajñā-Pāramitā. Brahmā, the four-headed spiritual demiurge, is often represented with manuscripts of the Holy Vedas in his hands; the so-called "Prajñā-Pāramitā Texts" are the corresponding literary manifestation of the transcendent wisdom of the Buddha. In the present image these have supplanted Brahmā himself. Thus the ancient calyx of spontaneous procreative energy has been made to carry the symbol of the wisdom that transcends it, the wisdom that leads beyond the spell of Māyā. The lotus of the world supports the symbol of the enlightenment that dispels the darkness of the naïve ignorance inherent in all living beings. The lotus symbol, which originally gave birth to beings and existences in unending succession, now carries the powerful wisdom of Nirvāna: the Word that puts an end to all individualized existence, whether in heaven or on earth.

To sum up: As the goddess Lotus is characterized by the vegetable symbol beneath her and carries at her left the lotus flower, so Prajñā-Pāramitā is invariably characterized by the lotus seat and the lotus at her left supporting the manuscript. As Lakshmī is Vishnu's consort, representing his creative energy, so Prajñā-Pāramitā is the female consort of the transcendent Universal Buddha and represents his nature, the nature of eternal, blissful quietude in enlightenment—limitation and individualization being extinguished. Lakshmī is the universal mother of life in her benevolent life-bestowing, life-increasing aspect; similarly Prajñā-Pāramitā sends forth the rays of enlightening wisdom that give release from the relentless deadly round of rebirth—she sends

---

* The texts devoted to Prajñā-Pāramitā go back to the first and second centuries A.D. The Buddhist philosophy of transcendental idealism, the teaching of Nāgārjuna and others, is based on the conception of Prajñā-Pāramitā; so also the present-day Buddhism of Tibet, China, and Japan.

forth transcendental life and reality, for she is its embodiment and source.

The Javanese statue, like most images of Indian extraction, is less than life size; yet in a wondrous way it reconciles charm with monumentality. The background, a shield in slightly ogived form, has a rim of gentle flames, radiating the spiritual energy of enlightenment. The oval head is majestically elongated by the huge, rich diadem. The pure oval halo expresses something of the supreme Void of the transcendental essence. The countenance is perfectly symmetrical and a model of womanly beauty. The fingers touch each other in the gesture that indicates meditation on the cycle of causation, the cycle of life, suffering, and death. Prajñā-Pāramitā is the Buddhist version of Sophia, the mother and source of enlightening knowledge.

It is interesting to note that this representation of a most lofty abstraction is at the same time, presumably, a portrait-effigy. Among the Hindu and Buddhist rulers and princes of Java and Cambodia the custom prevailed of erecting "consecration figures" after death or during the lifetime. In "consecration figures" the princely person is portrayed in the attitude, and wearing the dress, ornaments, and symbols, of a divine being, a Hindu divinity or a Buddha. In order to express the assumption of the human person after death into the divine supramundane essence, or in order to indicate that the living prince is an emanation, incarnation, reflex, or avatār of the highest essence, he is identified with the superhuman being. The idea is that the prince, and, fundamentally, all beings, all of us, are brought forth from the divine creative essence, are virtually parts of the Highest Being. This is a concept insisted upon in later Hinduism and Buddhism. It is but a logical consequence of earlier basic concepts. It is implied in the monistic idea developed in the philosophy of the Upanishads and illustrated through the pictorial script of classic Hindu mythology—the idea, namely, of man's Inner Self (*ātman*) as identical with the only Universal Self (*brahman*).

This figure of Prajñā-Pāramitā is a "consecration portrait" celebrating the divinization of a certain Javanese queen. Probably she is Queen Dedes of the dynasty of Singasari. In 1220 the ruling king was overthrown by an adventurer, Ken Arok, who married Queen Dedes and ascended the throne under the title, Rajasa Anurva-bhumi. He extended his conquests until his death in 1227. This figure represents, then, an enormous democratization of the lotus pedestal and the lotus-in-the-hand. Formerly the exclusive attributes of the great Mother Earth, fertile Nature, now they are available to every prince and queen.

The lotus here finally expresses the idea that we are all virtually Buddhas, emanations or reflexes of the transcendent imperishable sphere. The unenlightened behold only Māyā, the differentiated realm of delusory forms and notions, but by the enlightened ones all is experienced as the Void beyond differentiation. The inborn, transcendent character of man is insisted upon by this assignment of the lotus seat to human rulers. The secret of man's intrinsically divine existence is boldly revealed, in order to encourage each to hold with his mind to that truth so difficult to realize, the ultimate truth concerning himself.

6.

The Elephant

THE elephant as a "determinant" placed beneath the anthropomorphic symbols of divine powers is a common feature in the early Buddhist reliefs at Bhārhut. Most of the divinities are not labeled and cannot be identified; others bear the names of certain yakshas and yakshinīs—male and female earth genii, patrons of fertility and wealth. The association of a pair of elephants with the figure of the goddess Lotus is also a feature of the Buddhist art of the second and first centuries B.C. (Bhārhut and Sañchī;

cf. Figure 15.) From there it can be traced through the whole extensive course of Hindu and Buddhist iconography, down to the late Hindu temples of the South. In Hindu miniatures and present-day popular drawings it is a constantly recurring motif. Furthermore, on the very early seals of Mohenjo-Daro—among the earliest art works not only of India but of human civilization —the elephant is depicted, sometimes standing before a manger; but no clew is offered to the symbolic meaning of the animal. We well may ask: What is the function and connotation of this majestic form?

Little help is offered by the religious monuments, but much can be learned from a study of the traditional medical encyclopedias devoted to the domestication and care of the elephant. The owning of elephants, it appears, was a prerogative of kings. Elephants were hunted and captured in the wilderness and then kept on forest reservations, or in garrisons, for the purposes of warfare—they served as a corps of heavy and highly mobile cavalry, a sort of armored division on legs; or the elephants were assigned to the royal stables, to serve as mounts of state and for purposes of magic.*

The standard encyclopedia on the subject is the *Hastyāyurveda*, "The Sacred Wisdom (*veda*) of the Longevity (*āyus*) of the Elephants (*hasti*)." It is a compendium of over 7600 verse-couplets, in addition to chapters in prose. There is also a briefer treatise, "The Playful Treatise on the Elephants" (*mātaṅgalīlā*), which contains a number of remarkable mythical details.

We learn, for example, from the latter work,† that when

---

* [In the Vedas the elephant is a symbol of royal splendor, and Indra is "as it were an elephant"; the symbolism survives in Ganesha, and the Buddha is more than once still called an elephant.—AKC.]

† *Mātaṅgalīlā*, I. Edited by T. Ganapati Shāstri, Trivandrum, Sanskrit Series, No. X, 1910 (German translation by H. Zimmer, *Spiel um den Elefanten*, Munich and Berlin, 1929). An edition of the *Hastyāyurveda* by Shivadattasharman appears in the Ānandāshrama Sanskrit Series, No. 26, Poona, 1894.

Garuda, the Fair Feathered One (*suparṇa*), the golden-winged sun-bird, came into existence at the beginning of time, the elephants also were born. The moment the celestial bird broke from its egg, Brahmā, the demiurge-creator, took the two half eggshells in his hands and sang over them seven holy melodies (*sāman*). Through the virtue of these incantations Airāvata came forth, the divine elephant that was to become the mount of Indra.

The name Airāvata sounds like a metronymic appellation—as though, according to some as yet undiscovered tradition, this elephant were the son of a female called Irāvatī. Irrawaddy, we know, is the name of the principal river and life-artery of Burma; also, it is the alternate name of a great river in the Punjab, the Rāvī. *Irā*, furthermore, means water, any drinkable fluid, milk, refreshment, the liquid contained in the cosmic Milky Ocean. *Irāvatī* then would be "She who is possessed of fluid" (*irā*). This "She" would be the river itself; for rivers and waters are feminine, maternal, fostering divinities, and water is a female element.

Pursuing the genealogy one step further: *Irā* ("Fluid") is one of the daughters of an archaic demiurge or creator-god named Daksha, "The Dexterous One," a figure parallel to, and in function partly identical with, Brahmā, the Lord Creator of Beings (*prajā-pati*). Irā, in another context, is known as the queen-consort of still another old creator-god and father of creatures, Kashyapa, the Old Tortoise Man, and as such she is the mother of all vegetable life.

Airāvata is thus related in many ways, through his mother, to the life-fluid of the cosmos. This relationship is evinced further by the fact that the name Airāvata is used to designate both the rainbow—which is regarded as Indra's weapon—and a certain type of lightning: the two most conspicuous luminous manifestations of thunderstorm and rain.

Airāvata was the first divine elephant to proceed from the eggshell in the right hand of Brahmā; he was followed by seven more males. From the shell in Brahmā's left then appeared eight female elephants. The sixteen constituted eight couples, and became the ancestors of all elephants, both in heaven and on earth. They became also the Dig-Gajas, or "elephants (*gaja*) of the directions of space (*dik*)." * They support the universe at the four quarters and four points between.

Elephants are the caryatids of the universe. As such they very properly appear in the rock-cut Shiva-temple at Elūrā, "The Temple of the Lord of Mount Kailāsa." (Figure 26.) This is one of the great classic monuments of Hindu religious architecture. It dates from the eighth century A.D. Nowhere has more adequate and dignified expression been given to the majesty and grandeur of the elephant—this sole surviving representative of the ancient species of the giant mastodon, more ancient than the rhinoceros, hippopotamus, and other pachyderms. In these figures there is an intimate feeling for the character of the elephant, at once realistic and monumental, testifying to the long and close companionship of the Hindu with this mighty beast.

Another and totally different account of the origin of Airāvata and his consort, Abhramū, appears in the celebrated myth of the Churning of the Milky Ocean.† After the gods and titans had labored at their task for a thousand years, a curious assortment of personifications and symbols began to arise out of the milk of the universe. Among the earlier figures were the goddess Lotus, and Airāvata, the milk-white elephant. Finally appeared the physician of the gods bearing the Amrita, the elixir of immortality, in a milk-white bowl.

A special value is attached to the so-called "white elephants"— albinos showing light or rosy spots—because they suggest the origin of their ancestor from the Universal Milk. They are endowed to a heightened degree with the peculiar magic virtue of

---

* In Sanskrit, final *k* becomes *g* before an initial sonant; therefore, *dik-gaja* becomes *dig-gaja*.

† *Mahābhārata*, I. 17ff. Also *Viṣṇu Purāṇa*, I. 9, *Matsya Purāṇa*, CCXLIX, 13-38, etc., etc. Cf. pp. 17-18, *supra*.

the elephant, the virtue, that is to say, of producing clouds. Abhramu, the name of Airāvata's consort, denotes this special power: *mu* means "to fashion, to fabricate, to bind or knit"; *abhra* means "cloud." *Abhramū* is "Producing Clouds," "She Who Knits or Binds the Clouds"—specifically, the beneficent monsoon-clouds that quicken vegetation after the scorching period of summer heat. When these fail to appear, there will be drought, no crops, and a general famine.

In the wonderful age of the mythological beginnings, the off-spring of the original eight elephants had wings. Like clouds, they freely roamed about the sky. But a group of them lost the wings through heedlessness, and the majestic race, ever since, has been forced to remain on the ground. The story is told of how a flight of elephants had the misfortune to incur the sudden wrath of a saint-ascetic—a type that must be approached with only the ut-most respect and then treated very cautiously, for ascetics are of a most susceptible and irascible nature. Inadvertently, these blithe, winged elephants one day alighted on the branch of a giant tree north of the Himālayas. An ascetic named Dīrghatapas, "Long Austerity," had his seat beneath it and was at that moment teaching—when the heavy arm of the tree, unable to support the load, broke and fell upon the pupils' heads. A number were killed, but the elephants, not worrying in the least, nimbly caught themselves in flight and settled on another bough. The angry saint cursed them roundly. Henceforth they and their whole race were deprived of their wings, and remained on the ground sub-servient to man. And what was more: together with their faculty of roaming through the air, they forfeited also the divine power—which is characteristic of the clouds and of all divinities—of as-suming various forms at will.*

It is said that horses, too, originally had wings. Indra sheared them off with his thunderbolt, to make the free-ranging animals

---

* *Mātaṅgalīlā,* I.

docile, so that they might draw the chariots both of the celestials and of the king-warriors of earth.* Furthermore, even the towering mountain ranges—whose snow-capped summits intermingle with the clouds and so closely resemble them that sometimes it is very difficult to say whether the form be cloud or mountain—were winged in the beginning; indeed, they were a variety of cloud. Indra deprived them of the power of flight in order to steady with their weight the shaky surface of the land.†

As Airāvata belongs to Indra, so elephants belong to kings. In stately processions they are the king's symbolical mount; in warfare they are the watchtower and citadel from which he controls the strategy of battle. But their most important function is to attract their celestial relatives, the clouds, the heavenly elephants. Hence Hindu kings keep elephants for the welfare of their subjects; and to give a white elephant away would make the ruler very unpopular among his people.

But precisely such a deed, inspired by compassion for the sufferings of a neighboring kingdom, is ascribed to the Buddha in his next to last existence. At that time, as a Bodhisattva, or Buddha-in-the-making, he was born as the prince Vishvantara.‡ Practicing the highest virtues of self-detachment, self-sacrifice, generosity and compassion, he gave away the white elephant of his father's realm to a neighboring country suffering from drought and famine. His subjects thereupon felt betrayed and forsaken, and forced him into exile. This is à very popular tale, and occurs among the "Stories of the Former Existences of the Buddha" (*Jātaka*). § It is frequently depicted in Buddhist paintings and

---

* *Aśva-cikitsita*, I. 8. (Cf. Jayadatta Suri, *The Aśva-vaidyaka*, Calcutta 1887; appendix.)
† *Rāmāyaṇa*, V. 1.
‡ "All (*viśvam*) saving (*tara*)." The Pāli form of the name is Vessantara.
§ See, *The Jataka, or Stories of the Buddha's Former Births*, translated from the Pali by various hands under the editorship of E. B. Cowell, Vols. I-VI (Cambridge, 1895-1907). The above is story #547, the last of the series.

reliefs, the earliest representations appearing on the gates of the Great Stūpa of Sāñchī, first century B.C.

In a yearly ritual devoted to rainfall, the fertility of crops, the fecundity of cattle and man, and the general welfare of the kingdom, the white elephant, so constantly associated with the goddess Lotus, plays a significant and conspicuous role. Such a festival is described in the *Hastyāyurveda*.* The elephant is painted white with sandal paste, and then led in solemn procession through the capital. Its attendants are men wearing women's dresses and making merry with clownish, salacious remarks and witticisms. Through this ritualistic female disguise they do honor to the cosmic female principle, the maternal, procreative, feeding energy of nature, and by the ritualistic utterance of licentious language stimulate the dormant sexual energy of the living power. (The occurrence together of these two devices can be traced over the entire world.) The elephant is finally worshiped by the high officials of the realm, both civil and military. The text remarks: "If they did not pay worship to the elephant, the king and the kingdom, the army and the elephants, would be doomed to perish, because a divinity would have been disregarded. Contrariwise, if due worship is paid to the elephant, they will thrive and prosper together with their wives and sons, the country, the army, and the elephants. Crops will sprout in due time; Indra, the rain god, will send rain in due time; there will be no plague, no drought. They will live a hundred years (a full lifetime) with many sons and many cattle and will have a sturdy progeny. Whoever wishes to have sons will have sons, and longings after riches and other goods will also be fulfilled. The earth will abound in treasures of precious metals and jewels."

Thus the worship of the white elephant, as a divinity not to be disregarded, bestows on man all those earthly blessings which the goddess Lotus, Shrī-Lakshmī, Fortune and Prosperity, the

* IV. 22.

108

Mother Earth, fertile and abundant with water and riches, has in store. The symbolic character and significance of the animal is clearly announced in the two appellations that are used to designate it when it is being honored as a divinity; it is called Shrī-gaja, "The Elephant of Shrī," and Megha, "Cloud." The elephant, that is to say, is a rain cloud walking on the earth. By its magic presence it conjures the winged fellow clouds of the atmosphere to approach. When the earthly elephant cloud is duly worshiped, its celestial relatives feel gratified and are moved to show forth their gratitude by favoring the country with abundant rain.

Another name for the Elephant of Shrī is "Son of Airāvata." Son, in the language of myths and symbols, means "double," "alter ego," "living copy of the father," "the father's essence in another individualization."

7.

The Sacred Rivers

EXCEEDINGLY potent among the powers of world-abundance are the rivers, and particularly the three majestic watercourses of the Ganges, Jumna, and Saraswatī. Allahābād (called by the Hindus Prayāg), where the light yellow stream of the Ganges meets and mingles with the dark blue of the Jumna, has been for millenniums an important resort of pilgrims. The rivers are female divinities, food and life bestowing mothers, and as such are prominent among the popular divinities represented in the art works of the classic period. They stand—like the serpent princes and other nature genii—at the entrances to temples in the humble role of door guardians, or appear in niches within the sacred precincts. Accompanied by aquatic birds and wild geese, standing on tortoises, sea monsters, or lotuses, in attitudes of fervent devotion (*bhakti*), sweet repose, or benign protection, the images are sometimes hardly distinguishable from those of the goddess Shrī-Lakshmī.

A splendid specimen of late mediaeval Bengalese art, in the twelfth century style of the Sena dynasty, represents the goddess Gangā in a posture of graceful solemnity and benign repose. (Figure 17.) The material is black steatite, the principal stone for sculpture in Bengal. Gangā is known as "the mother who both bestows prosperity (sukha-dā), and secures salvation (mokṣa-dā)"; she represents joy (in this life) and hope (for the life to come). She washes away the sins of him whose ashes or corpse are committed to her waters, and secures for him rebirth among the gods in a realm of celestial bliss. As the main life-artery of the great province of Bengal, the source of health and wealth for the people, the Ganges is divine grace flowing in tangible form to the very doorsteps of men. She spreads fertility over the rice-growing country, and pours purity into the heart of the devotee who bathes, in his daily morning ritual, in her fruitful stream.

Shiva himself sings a hymn in her praise in one of the Purānas.* "She is the source of redemption. . . . Heaps of sin, accumulated by a sinner during millions of births, are destroyed by the mere contact of a wind charged with her vapor. . . . As fire consumes fuel, so this stream consumes the sins of the wicked. Sages mount the staired terrace of the Ganges; on it they transcend the high heaven of Brahmā himself: free from danger, riding celestial chariots, they go to Shiva's abode. Sinners who expire near the water of the Ganges are released from all their sins: they become Shiva's attendants and dwell at his side. They become identical with him in shape; they never die—not even on the day of the total dissolution of the universe. And if the dead body of a person somehow fall into the water of the Ganges, that person abides with Vishnu for as many years as there are pores in the skin of his body. If a man on an auspicious day begin to bathe in

---

* *Brahmavaivarta Purāṇa*, Kṛiṣṇa-janma Khaṇḍa, 34, 13ff.

110

the Ganges, he dwells cheerfully in Vishnu's heavenly world, Vaikuntha, for the number of years equal to the number of his footsteps."

Gaṅgā is a prototype of all the rivers of India. Her magic power of salvation is shared—only to a lesser degree—by all the bodies of water in the land. In the beautiful black image from Bengal she is represented as an embodiment of both celestial and earthly vitality and sweetness. She is a personification of health and abundance, dignity and prowess. A rich diadem frames her forehead; a necklace descends to her breasts; the rich ornaments and chains of her girdle and loincloth designate her wealth-bestowing virtue. She stands upon a sea-monster (*makara*), which serves her as a vehicle. The gentle ripples of the giant stream, as though its surface were animated by a light breeze, play over her firm and slender body. Much like a Bengal bride or happy young housewife, she is intended to procreate new life and to rule in the house. In the image of this river goddess is embodied the idyllic, earthbound aspect of prosperous Hindu peasant life—its devout union with the divine forces that pervade the living organism of the universe; its recognition of the gentle play of divinity in the simple wonders of the surrounding world.

Physical contact with the body of the goddess Gaṅgā has the magic effect of transforming automatically the nature of the devotee. As if by an alchemical process of purification and transmutation, the base metal of his earthly nature becomes sublimated; he becomes an embodiment of the divine essence of the highest eternal realm. In the hymn just quoted, that realm is conceived under the image of Shiva's supernal mansion, again as Shiva's divine form. It is to be regarded not as something remote from the world of man, but as the core of every least existence, the source of every moment of life. The Ganges itself is regarded as flowing directly from that realm—and thus the heart is conducted back along its blessed course to the place of the Beginning and the End. The Ganges commonly is said to proceed

111

from Vishnu's big toe: she flows from the giant body of Nārāyana, the anthropomorphic personification of the divine life-substance of the Milky Ocean.

The most extensive work of relief-sculpture extant in Indian art—one of the largest, most beautiful and dramatic reliefs of all time—is the representation of a great and celebrated myth describing the descent of the Ganges from heaven to earth. (Figure 27.) A huge wall of rock, rising vertically in the fierce sunshine of southern India, has been converted into a prodigious masterpiece, teeming with hosts of gods, titans, genii, serpent princes, human beings, and animals, all converging towards a great cleft in the middle of the composition. The tableau, measuring twenty-seven meters in length by nine in height and covered with more than a hundred figures, stands amidst a number of other astonishing sculptural works, on the shore of the Indian ocean, at Māmallapuram, near Madras. These are the remains of a gigantic artistic and religious enterprise, undertaken by the Pallava kings of South India in the seventh century A.D. The intention was to transform a striking group of natural cliffs and boulders into a cluster of little temples and great shrines, all cut from the living rock.

The Descent of the Ganges is rendered in a realistic style. Furthermore, on the upper surface of the ledge immediately above the central perpendicular cleft, we find today a number of prepared channels: there was originally a cistern up there, about twenty-three feet square, with plastered walls; rock-cut steps lead up from the ground. Apparently, on certain festival occasions, the cistern was filled and the water allowed to flow down the cleft in the form of a cascade, simulating the descent of a mountain torrent—Gaṅgā falling from heaven to the Himālayas, and streaming, then, down to earth.

The myth is recounted in the *Rāmāyaṇa.** It is a tale extolling

---

* *Rāmāyaṇa*, I. 38-44; also *Mahābhārata*, Vanaparvan 108-109; again *Bhāgavata Purāṇa*, IX. 9.

the miraculous power of certain superhuman saints. The first of these is Agastya, patron saint of southern India, who is supposed to have played an important role in the colonization of that part of the country. He is represented as a great philosopher, kind-hearted, and unsurpassed in the science of archery. In Vedic tradition he is reputed to have been born from the seed of the two great gods, Mitra and Varuna. When the Vindhya Mountains, at one time, in an excess of pride, so enlarged themselves that they fairly eclipsed the sun and even blocked its path, this mighty ascetic, by the magic power of his will, humbled them, forced them to prostrate themselves before him, and thus saved the world.

He is famous especially for the marvels accomplished by his digestive juices. There was, for example, a certain demon in the shape of a ram, who, believing himself to be absolutely undigestible, had developed a cruel trick: disguising himself as a palatable dish of meat, this malicious being would permit himself to be served by his brother to the prospective victim. And when he thus gained entrance into the stomach of his enemy, the brother who had served the dish would cry: "Come out, Brother!" Whereupon the demon would burst forth and the victim explode. However, when he tried his stratagem on Agastya he was fooled; for the saint—who somehow is related to solar energy and its fierce devouring power in the south of India—digested the tasty meal in less than no time. When the other called, "Come out, Brother!" nothing was left to escape but a little wind.

Now Agastya one day put the devouring tropical solar heat of his gastric energy to a major test: he swallowed the entire ocean. His intentions were good and the deed a brave one, but incidentally it had the effect of depriving the earth and all beings of the necessary life-maintaining water. That was what made it necessary for the Gaṅgā, the celestial river, a kind of Milky Way, to descend from the sky. The story goes, that there had been a group of demons annoying certain brahmin hermits by constantly disturbing their sacred ascetic routines. They would be chased into the ocean, but by night would emerge, as fresh as ever, and harass the holy men. The latter, in desperation, appealed to the celebrated saint. Agastya solved the problem at a stroke by simply swallowing the sea. But now the earth was left without its water, and all its creatures were brought to the point of perishing. When a person tries to be particularly helpful, he sometimes causes more trouble than he removes. So it was, at any rate, in the case of Agastya with his boundless digestive fire.

It fell to the share of another superhuman saint to put an end to the terrible drought. This hero, the pious king, Bhagīratha, was the scion of a long lineage of kings descending from Manu Vaivasvata,* and he was sorely in need of water to appease and gratify the ashes and souls of a host of his deceased forefathers who had perished in another, earlier, mythical catastrophe. He decided to force his will upon the celestial powers and compel them to release the heavenly Ganges itself, to send it down to succor the earth. Committing the administration of his realm to his ministers, he proceeded to a celebrated center of pilgrimage sacred to Shiva, a place called Gokarna, "Cow's Ear," in the south. Here, for a thousand years, he devoted himself to fierce penances. With unflinching determination he accumulated superhuman energy through self-inflicted bodily sufferings. Standing with arms uplifted (*ūrdhavabāhu*) he practiced the "penance of the five fires" (*pañcatapas*).† Eventually Brahmā, pleased and attracted by this ascetic fervor, manifested himself, declared himself satisfied with Bhagīratha's perfect asceticism, and promised to grant a wish. Whereupon the kingly saint asked the god to let Gangā descend to the earth.

---

* The Solar Dynasty, reigning in Oudh (Ayodhyā), whose most famous issue was Rāma, hero of the *Rāmāyana*.
† The ascetic sits beneath the merciless sun, with four great fires blazing around him, one in each of the four directions.

Brahmā was agreeable, but declared that it would be necessary to gain the grace of Shiva. For if the mighty river of heaven, with her gigantic weight of water, should fall directly onto the ground, the tremendous torrent might cleave the earth and shatter it. Someone would have to break the fall by receiving the full weight of the cataract on his head, and there was no one but Shiva capable of such a deed. Brahmā advised Bhagīratha to continue his austerities until the High God should be touched, and moved from his supernal seat.

Shiva is the Divine Yogī, the model and arch-ascetic of the gods. He sits in splendid isolation on a solitary summit of the Himālayas, unconcerned with the worries of the world, steeped in pure and perfect meditation, absorbed in the crystal-clear, supreme Void of his own divine essence. It would be a hero-task to assail him, to induce him to co-operate in this timely matter. Bhagīratha fully understood the nature of his problem, betook himself to the Himālayas, and there spent another penitential year, fasting, existing on dry leaves, finally on merely water and air, standing on one foot erect, both arms uplifted, will-power concentrated on the god. Shiva responded eventually to the magic of the saint, appeared before him, and acquiesced. The head of the mighty deity received the full impact of the torrential fall. The matted hair piled high on the head ensnarled and delayed the cascading current, which then in meandering through the labyrinth lost its force. The waters descended gently to the Himālayas, and, at last, flowing majestically down to the Indian plains, bestowed on the earth and all its creatures the life-giving boon.

What is glorified by this myth is the omnipotence of ascetic will-power. Through the endurance of self-inflicted sufferings the yogī accumulates an immense treasure of psychic and physical energy. In him the universal life force becomes concentrated to such a focus of blazing incandescence that it melts the resistance of the cosmic divine powers, as personified in the divinities. This store of concentrated energy is called *tapas*, bodily heat.* *Tapas*, heat brought to this tension, is like a high-power electric charge threatening to discharge itself. When it flashes, it cuts through and melts every resistance.

The production of such heat-energy, the storing of it and the using of it for magical purposes, is the aim of the most ancient form of yoga practice.† In the myths of the Vedas such energy is employed by the gods themselves to many ends. It is employed, especially, for the purposes of creation. The god-creator heats himself and thereby produces the universe: by internal incandescence, by giving forth an emanation in the form of perspiration, or by hatching the cosmic egg.

Utter impassivity under self-inflicted mortification elevates the human being above the exigencies and limitations of human nature. It equates him with the superior energy of the cosmic powers. It displays him endowed with that supreme indifference to weal and woe which is inherent in the forces of nature and which is mythologically personified in the impassive semblances of the gods. This semi-divine, self-detached, powerful attitude compels the divine cosmic powers to fulfill superhuman desires, such desires as invalidate the normal course of the order of nature.

---

* The word *tapas* is remotely related to the English, "tepid."

[*Tapas* is fervor, ardor, glowing; never "penance" in the sense of expiation; the sun is "he who glows (*tapati*) yonder." Tapas does not necessarily involve physical austerities, but may refer to mental or vocational activities. It is clear from *Jaiminīya Upaniṣad Brāhmaṇa* III. 32.4 that the heat developed is that of the "Inner Self" (*antarātman*), a burning fire, like Philo's immanent νοῦς, ἔνθερμον καὶ πεπυρωμένον πνεῦμα (*Fug.* 133); the heat is that of our inward Sun. The final effect, analogous to the refinement of gold in a furnace, may be to consume the body, as in the case of the first Satī (Shiva's wife), of whose spontaneous incineration the practice of "suttee" is a mimesis; and in that of the ascension of Dabba, whose body was consumed as he rose, Udāna 93.—AKC.]

† The art of producing and storing heat (cf. *tapas, tibet, tumo*), as practiced today by Tibetan Buddhist yogīs, is described by Alexandra David-Neel, *Mystiques et magiciens du Thibet* (Plon, Paris, 1929).

[The production of physical heat has also been experienced by some European mystics, but it seems to have been only in the Orient that the effect has been controlled.—AKC.]

In the giant Pallava relief the Descent of the Ganges is represented according to a convention which art-historians currently call "continuous narrative." Not only the decisive moment of the story is represented, the dramatic climax or the conclusion of a series of events, but several different moments of time, consecutive phases of the sequence, are depicted in one setting, side by side. The climactic episode sets the stage and dominates the picture, but within its field side-exhibits are inserted. These review the most important stages of the action that led up to the dramatic, central moment. It is on the latter that attention is first and finally brought to focus.

The centralizing episode of the Ganges relief is the descent of the celestial stream. This is depicted in the central cleft of the great rock wall. From the cistern above (which we now have to imagine) water rushes down. A giant serpent king, covered by the torrent, is moving upward, his powerful serpent body undulating with slow movements; shielded by his halo of snake heads and hoods, he greets the water, rejoicing with rapt devotion. (Figure 27.) He is followed by a snake queen in a similar attitude of bhakti, devout rapture and pious bliss. Beneath her, again, is a giant animal-shaped serpent-genius lifting its body. Meanwhile, from all sides flock together gods, celestial beings, demons and genii, men and animals, to observe the miracle that is to rescue life on earth.

But to the left of the cleft, on the lower level, we have a scene that precedes in time the final event. Here we see a sanctuary with a saint squatting before it. (Figure 28.) The saint is Bhagīratha, in yoga posture, lean from fasting, absorbed in concentration, seeking to gain the favor of Brahmā. It is a most impressive representation of ascetic fervor, executed in a bold and graceful style, at once strong and subtle, sparing in detail, convincing and effective. Bhagīratha is squatting before the sanctuary of Gokarna, which is here shown as a little temple in typical Pallava style. Above a horizontal structure with blind, ornamented windows,

117

towers a dome-shaped roof. Out of the horseshoe-shaped window-frames faces are peering. These are the angel faces (*gandharva-mukha*) of the inhabitants of the heavenly palaces of the gods. The word for temple, *devakula, de-ul,* means "the house of a god": a temple is an earthly copy, or symbol, of a god's celestial abode.

Bhagīratha is bent inward. He is conjuring the apparition of the divinity. Two other ascetics are squatting in yoga posture on the other side of the temple-door. (Their heads have been destroyed.) They are the pupils or attendants of Bhagīratha, following him in his ascetic training. The decisive moment of the exercises has been reached. Attracted and bound by the saint's unflinching concentration, the divinity has just made his appearance from the dark interior of the shrine.

This important scene of the conjuring up of Brahmā at Gokarna in the south of India is placed near the lower margin of the relief. Near the top, and to the left of the central cleft, is represented the conjuring of Shiva on the Himālaya height. (This is visible in Figure 27.) The bearded saint is again Bhagīratha. Body emaciated by fasting, he stands in one of the typical postures of tapas-yoga, poised on a single leg in pillar-like rigidity both arms uplifted (*ūrdhvabāhu*), the fingers firmly interlocked. And again, he has just attained the goal of his fervent endeavor: Shiva stands manifest before him, four-armed, of giant stature, left lower hand extended in a boon-bestowing gesture (*varadā-mudrā*), and accompanied by the dwarfish, potbellied spirits of his attendant host (*gaṇa*). The god's head is surmounted by an enormous tiara of matted hair. The emblems in his hands are not clearly discernible: the huge, staff-like weapon may be either his trident (*triśūla*) or his spear.

To the right of the saint are two large aquatic birds, wild geese, winging to the watercourse. Below are a god and goddess floating through space and greeting joyfully the miracle before their eyes. A horned deer, too, is hurrying toward the water.

118

The remaining portion of the left half of the relief is filled, from top to bottom, with joyous swarms of beings and animals of all kinds. Lions and deer press through the forest. Titans and demons of athletic stature strut along. On an upper level of the Himālaya mountain range, a lion and lioness, recumbent, watch the miracle. Celestial couples walk nimbly through the air to greet the downpour of the water. Monkeys hustle through the wilderness.

In a bold and superbly animated style, at once broad and delicate in its effects, the various forms of life—divine, titanic, human, animal—are perfectly differentiated and characterized. Overlooking minute traits and details, this work of art aims to convey the attitudes, the typical motions or postures of repose, of the beings concerned. It insists on the basic kinship of all creatures. All issue from the one life-reservoir and are sustained on their various planes, whether heavenly or earthbound, by the one life-energy. Here is an art inspired by the monistic view of life that appears everywhere in Hindu philosophy and myth. Everything is alive. The entire universe is alive; only the degrees of life vary. Everything proceeds from the divine life-substance-and-energy as a temporary transmutation. All is a part of the universal display of God's Māyā.

A group of human beings are depicted on the lowermost level of the left side, close to the descending torrent of the celestial river. They are a company of young brahmins who have come to the riverbank. The middle one carries on his shoulder a pitcher full of water. Another, having just bathed in the sacred stream that washes away all stains of sin, is wringing out and drying the long tresses of his hair.

On the opposite bank is a family of elephants, a giant bull accompanied by the smaller female, and a cluster of elephant babes taking shelter between the legs of their parents. Above the forehead of the great elephant, on a crag, perch a pair of monkeys, impassive and concentrated, studying the flow of the water. Above these are to be seen a couple of fabulous beings, half human, half bird, with bird legs and wings, called *kinnaras* or *kimpurushas,* meaning "what kind (*kim*) of human being (*nara, purusha*)." The kinnaras are heavenly musicians. Such creatures are supposed to inhabit a semi-celestial region high in the Himālayas where earthly saints who have attained perfection (*siddha*) consort with superhuman beings. Still higher, approaching in swift flight, are more kinnaras with their female companions, and hurrying groups of gods.

In this wonderful relief, as in the Indra-relief of Bhājā, executed some centuries earlier,* the rock transforms itself into a telling procession of animated figures, drifting by, fleetingly passing, like a flock of luminous clouds. The anonymous, undifferentiated substance manifests every kind of being. The figures produced and animated by the divine essence, the mirage-personages of the cosmic dream of the god, are radiant with a blind delight in life, the enchantment or the spell of Māyā. The heavenly couples of gods and goddesses are borne along lightly. They do not share the bulk and weight of earthly creatures. They are made of subtle mind-stuff (*sūkṣma*), such stuff as composes the figures of our dreams and phantasies, or the divine apparitions that come before the concentrated inner vision of the yogī and devotee. They are angelic figures full of sensual spirituality, of a subtle, unearthly voluptuousness. Shining forth from them is their delight in the glorious impalpability of their bodies. Their corporeal incorporeality is a sublime form of Māyā. The melodious, musical character of bodily charm is rendered through a delicate articulation and joyous vitality of their limbs and contours. Distinctive bodily features are as far as possible ignored; the male and female figures resemble each other as closely as sex-difference permits; they are like twin brothers and sisters, conceived in the one spirit of subtle charm and unearthly bliss.

On the highest level, near the upper rim, are represented gods

* Cf. pp. 53-4, *supra*, and Figure 1.

and more gods, approaching the miracle, greeting and worshiping it with uplifted hands: the sun god, recognizable by his solar disk, another with a mighty diadem, accompanied by his queen consort, his embodied energy or specific virtue (*śakti*). No particularizing details or attributes appear which would allow of definite labeling. This is a style that disdains to load the picture with distracting minor traits. What it renders is the dominant note of wonder and delight that fully suffuses all the beings sharing in the life-renovating experience.

The keynote of fervent devotion and pious rapture is established by the giant, mossy, serpent king in the central cleft. From him goes out an atmosphere of religious enthusiasm that suffuses the whole picture and animates its multitude of figures. The idealistic style—suppressing all minor particulars—achieves a sublime simplicity and conveys a mood of dignity, gravity, and austerity of devotion, a restful serenity abounding in latent power. The nāga-king and his queen consort, their hands clasped in the gesture of adoration, lead in the expression of this feeling voiced by the entire monument—the feeling that brought it into being and which should fill the spectator-pilgrims gathered before it: wonder at the flow of God's abundance into the world of his delight.

CHAPTER FOUR

THE COSMIC DELIGHT OF SHIVA

1.

The "Fundamental Form" and the "Playful Manifestations"

THE noun *brahman* is neuter:* The Absolute is beyond the differentiating qualifications of sex, beyond all limiting, individualizing characteristics whatsoever. It is the all-containing transcendent source of every possible virtue and form. Out of Brahman, the Absolute, proceed the energies of Nature, to produce our world of individuated forms, the swarming world of our empirical experience, which is characterized by limitations, polarities, antagonisms and co-operation.

In compliance with the propensities of man's imagination and

---

* Brahman (neuter) and Brahmā (masculine) are not to be confused with each other. The former refers to the transcendent and immanent Absolute; the latter is an anthropomorphic personification of the Creator-Demiurge. Brahman is properly a metaphysical term, Brahmā mythological.

[It must be understood that in Sanskrit grammatical gender is not always a sign of physical sex. Gender infers function, sex infers form; so that an individual may be masculine from one point of view and feminine from another. For example, Prajāpati (the Progenitor, m.) can be referred to as "pregnant," Mitra "inseminates Varuna," Brahman (n.) can be regarded as the "womb" of life; and as in Christianity "this man" and "this woman" are equally "feminine to God." Absolutely, Brahman, although grammatically n., is the principle of all such differentiation; just as in Genesis the "image of God" is reflected in a creation "male *and* female." In general, masculine gender implies activity and procession, female gender passivity and recession, the neuter a static or absolute condition. Essence and nature áre respectively m. and f., logically distinct, but "one in God," who is "neither" this nor that, and therefore "It" rather than "He" or "She" specifically.—AKC.]

emotion, the Absolute, for purposes of worship, is commonly personified. It is represented to the mind as a supreme, anthropomorphic divinity, "The Lord," the all-pervading ruler of the life-processes of the world. This "Lord" is he who brings to pass the Māyā-miracle of evolution, maintenance and dissolution.

We have already seen Vishnu in this role; we have now to study the symbolism of Shiva. Among the divinities of the Hindu pantheon, only those not too closely associated with special functions, activities, or departments of nature, can serve as embodiments of the personified Absolute. Agni, the Fire God, specifically an aspect of the element Fire,* is much too particularized to represent the Source of all five of the elements. Likewise Vāyu, the Wind God, is specialized as the representative of the element Air in motion, hence is incapable of representing the Universal. Indra is the lord, primarily, of clouds, thunderstorm, and rain. Even the figure of Brahmā is unsatisfactory, in spite of the fact that he is a member of the highest Hindu triad of Brahmā the Creator, Vishnu the Preserver, Shiva the Destroyer. For in Hindu mythology Brahmā personifies exclusively the positive aspect of the life-process of the universe, and is never represented as destroying what he has produced. He symbolizes, in a one-sided way, merely the creative phase, pure spirituality. In his myths he does not exhibit, through a multitude of mutually antagonistic attitudes and activities, such an ambivalent, self-contradictory, enigmatic character as would render him fit to represent in personalized form the paradoxical, all-comprehending nature of the Absolute. Vishnu and Shiva, on the other hand, as well as the Goddess Mother of the World, are strongly visualized as both terrible and benign, creative and destructive, hideous and comely. All three are thus eminently qualified to represent the Ultimate Plenum.

Shiva and Vishnu appear in modern Hinduism as gods of equal

---

* The noun *agni* is related etymologically to igneous, ignite, ignition.

stature: respectively, the destroying and maintaining masks or attitudes of the Supreme.* Vishnu in his myths "becomes" Shiva, assumes the appearance of Shiva, when he brings to pass the periodic dissolution of all things. Brahmā, on the other hand, is described as merely an agent of the Maintainer's creative function, the first-born Being, seated on the lotus that stems from Vishnu's navel—an anthropomorphic manifestation of Vishnu's demiurgic energy and not by any means a co-equal of the Great God.†

When Shiva, rather than Vishnu, holds the center of the stage, the role of the personalized Brahman is colored with death and destruction. For, whereas Vishnu evokes a sense of the fairer qualities of life—and thus best typifies the character of the creator-maintainer—Shiva's stern asceticism casts a blight over the fields of rebirth. His presence negates and transcends the kaleidoscope of sufferings and joys. Nevertheless, he bestows wisdom and peace, and is not only terrible but profoundly benign. Just as Vishnu is a destroyer, so is Shiva a creator and maintainer; his

---

* [These masks are actually combined in the concept and iconography of Hari-Hara, i.e., *mixta persona* of Vishnu-Shiva.—AKC.]

† This situation does not pertain in the materials of the Vedic period (ca. 1500-1000 B.C.), where the god Brahmā is unknown and Vishnu and Shiva play only relatively insignificant roles. Shiva was known at that period under the name Rudra, "The Howler." Perhaps Vishnu and Shiva-Rudra were important figures from indigenous, pre-Aryan, non-Vedic pantheons, who were gradually winning recognition in the exclusive tradition of the recently installed conquerors.

[In the Vedic period, nevertheless, Agni-Brihaspati is "the Brahmā," i.e., High Priest of the gods, and so virtually the god Brahmā.—AKC.]

The mythology of Brahmā seems to have developed during the period of the Brahmānas (ca. 1000-700 B.C.), and to have been a product of orthodox Aryan thinking. Brahmā served for a time as a personification of the supreme Brahman, but even during his greatest period the two rivals, Vishnu and Shiva, were rapidly gaining ascendance.

With the triumph of popular Hinduism (as documented in the art works of the classic, medieval, and modern periods, as well as in the Purānic and Tantric texts, the great Epics, and certain passages of the Upanishads) Brahmā is definitely subordinate to Vishnu and Shiva. The modern Hindu is a devotee of either Vishnu or Shiva, or of the Goddess; in serious worship Brahmā now plays no role.

nature at once transcends and includes all the polarities of the living world.

The plenitude of Shiva's mutually antagonistic functions and aspects is made evident by the fact that his worshipers invoke him by a hundred names. He is described also under twenty-five "playful manifestations" (*līlāmūrti*), or according to another tradition, sixteen. Occasionally we find the multitude of expressive aspects reduced to five: (1) The Beneficent Manifestation (*anugrahamūrti*), (2) The Destructive Manifestation (*saṁhāra-mūrti*), (3) The Vagrant Mendicant (*bhikṣāṭanamūrti*), (4) The Lord of Dancers (*nṛttamūrti*), (5) The Great Lord (*maheśa-mūrti*). Among the titles included in the longer lists are The God with the Moon in his Hair (*candraśekhara*), The Supporter of the Ganges (*gaṅgādhara*), The Slayer of the Elephant-Demon (*gajasaṁhāra*), Consort of the Goddess Uma and Father of Skanda, the War God (*somāskanda*), The Lord Who is Half Woman (*ardhanārīśvara*), Lord of the Peak (*śikhareśvara*), Lord of Physicians (*vaidyanātha*), The Destroyer of Time (*kālasaṁhāra*), Lord of Cattle (*paśupati*), The Beneficent (*śaṅkara*), The Propitious (*śiva*), The Howler (*rudra*).

But the basic and most common object of worship in Shiva shrines is the phallus or lingam. This form of the god can be traced back to the worship of primitive stone symbols as early as the neolithic period. Already at Mohenjo-Daro * the lingam occurs, side by side with other important symbols similar to those employed in later Hindu iconography. (Figure 25.) The lingam denotes the male creative energy of Shiva, and in contradistinction to all other representations of the god is called "the fixed, or immovable" (*dhruva*), "the fundamental form" (*mūlavigraha*). Compared with it the other representations are regarded as secondary.

The anthropomorphic images are known as "movable" (*cala*),

---

* Cf. pp. 95-6, *supra*.

"festival, or ceremonial, figures" (*utsavamūrti*), "images for festival enjoyment" (*bhogamūrti*). They are to be carried in processions on occasions of celebration, or placed in the halls and galleries of the temple for the edification of the worshiper. Standing in files along the corridors that surround or lead up to the main shrine, they display the various aspects or manifestations of the god, and compose an instructive picture gallery for the pilgrim devotee.

The great subterranean rock-cut cave-temple of Elephanta, near Bombay, one of the most impressive and beautiful monuments of Hindu religious art, is adorned with many anthropomorphic representations of Shiva, as well as with scenes from his rich mythology. The central sanctuary of this extensive temple is a simple, monumental, square shrine, with four entrances on the four sides, each guarded by a pair of divine door keepers. (Figure 29.) Within is the austere symbol of the lingam, emanating to the four quarters its all-productive energy. This lingam, as the main stone image, forms the center of the innermost cella, the holy of holies or "womb house" (*garbha-griha*). In the innermost recess of the organism of the temple it serenely stands, constituting the life-center of the subterranean cave.

As the symbol of male creative energy, the lingam is frequently combined with the primary symbol of female creative energy, the yoni, the latter forming the base of the image with the former rising from its center. This serves as a representation of the creative union that procreates and sustains the life of the universe. Lingam and yoni, Shiva and his goddess, symbolize the antagonistic yet co-operating forces of the sexes. Their Sacred Marriage (Greek: *hieros-gamos*) is multifariously figured in the various traditions of world mythology. They are the archetypal parents, Father and Mother of the World, themselves the first-born of the pairs of opposites, first bifurcation of the primal, cosmogonic reality, now reunited in productive harmony. Under the form of Father Heaven and Mother Earth they were known to the

Greeks as Zeus and Hera, Uranos and Gaia, to the Chinese as T'ien and Ti, Yang and Yin.

An instructive story is told concerning the origin of the lingam.* It is recounted in explanation of a certain curious phallic image known to the later, South Indian, medieval tradition. (Figure 30.) Shiva in this myth is represented as winning a momentous victory over the other two supreme divinities of the Hindu triad, Brahmā and Vishnu; and this victory, if we may judge from the literary remains, corresponds to an actual, historical development. For in the earlier and classic Purānas † Shiva is no more than a function or mask assumed by Vishnu whenever the moment approaches for the reabsorption of the universe. Only in a later stratification of Purānic myth ‡ do we find Shiva coming to the fore to enact independently and alone all three of the great world roles of creation, preservation, and destruction.

The myth of "The Origin of the Lingam" (lingobhava) § opens with the familiar primeval situation: no universe, only water and the starless night of the lifeless interval between dissolution and creation. In the infinite ocean all the seeds, all the potentialities, of subsequent evolution rest in a dormant state of undifferentiation. Vishnu, the anthropomorphic embodiment of this fluid of life, is floating—as we have seen him before—in and upon the substance of his own essence. In the form of a luminous giant

---

* [The fiery lingam is a form of the Axis Mundi, and can be equated with the shaft of light or lightning (vajra, keraunós) that penetrates and fertilises the yoni, the altar, the Earth, the mother of the Fire,—for "light is the progenitive power": in the older Christian nativities it is represented by the Ray that extends from the Sun above to the interior of the cave in which the Earth-goddess bears her Son.

For another important Purānic version of the origin of the Shiva-lingam and the cult see F. D. K. Bosch and other sources cited in my Yakṣas II, Washington, 1928, pp. 44, 45.—AKC.]

† Viṣṇu Purāṇa, Matsya Purāṇa, Brahmā Purāṇa, and others.

‡ Mārkandeya Purāṇa, Kūrma Purāṇa.

§ Annales du Musée Guimet, Bibliothèque d'études, tome 27; G. Jouveau-Dubreuil, Archéologie du Sud de l'Inde (Geuthner, Paris, 1941), tome II, Iconographie, pp. 24-5.

he is recumbent on the liquid element, radiant with the steady glow of his blessed energy.

But now a new and astonishing event: Vishnu perceives, all of a sudden, another luminous apparition, and it is approaching him with the swiftness of light, shining with the brilliance of a galaxy of suns. It is Brahmā, the fashioner of the universe, the four-headed one, full of yogic wisdom. Smiling, this new arrival inquires of the recumbent giant: "Who are you? How did you originate? What are you doing here? I am the first progenitor of all beings; I am He Who Originated from Himself!"

Vishnu begged to differ. "On the contrary," he protested, "it is I who am the creator and destroyer of the universe. I have created and destroyed it time and again."

The two mighty presences proceeded to contest each other's claims and to quarrel. And while they were arguing in the timeless void, presently they perceived rising out of the ocean a towering lingam crowned with flame. Rapidly it grew into infinite space. The two divinities, ceasing their discussion, regarded it with amazement. They could measure neither its height nor its depth.

Brahmā said: "You plunge; I shall fly upward. Let us try to discover its two ends."

The two gods assumed their well known animal forms, Brahmā the gander, Vishnu the boar. The bird winged into the heavens, the boar dove into the deep. In opposite directions, on and on, they raced but could attain to neither limit; for while the boar descended and Brahmā climbed, the lingam grew and grew.

Presently the side of the prodigious phallus burst open, and in the niche-like aperture the lord of the lingam stood revealed, Shiva, the force supreme of the universe. While Brahmā and Vishnu bowed before him in adoration, he solemnly proclaimed himself to be the origin of them both. Indeed, he announced himself as a Super-Shiva: the triad of Brahmā, Vishnu, and Shiva, Creator, Maintainer, and Destroyer, he at once contained and bodied forth. Though emanating from the lingam, they, nevertheless, abode permanently within it. They were parts of it, constituents, Brahmā the right side, Vishnu the left, but the center was Shiva-Hara, "The Reabsorber, He Who Takes Back or Takes Away."

Thus Shiva appears augmented in the lingam, heightened, enhanced, as the all-comprising, basic element. The role of the destroyer now is only one of his three principal manifestations. Side by side with Brahmā the Creator and Vishnu the Maintainer, Shiva the Destroyer co-exists in Shiva the Supreme.

2.

The Phenomenon of Expanding Form

But let us now consider, for a moment, the monument in which this mythological idea has been represented. (Figure 30.) Some years ago I paid a visit to the Musée Guimet in Paris to see this work of art which the museum had then just acquired. I was already familiar with its myth. And as I stood before it, suddenly there dawned on me an awareness of something which I immediately recognized as characteristic of other Hindu monuments and symbols—a particular phenomenon of style—an aesthetic effect which I have encountered nowhere except in certain of the most remarkable and significant Hindu creations. I should like to call it, "the phenomenon of the growing, or expanding, form."

It is now quite clear to me that this particular monument was not intended to be regarded, deciphered, or understood, as something static, of abiding, concrete dimensions. Rather, it is to be read, in accordance with the suggestion of the tale, as something growing. The column is to be seen extending in length while the Brahmā-gander flies upward and the Vishnu-boar plunges down. This piece of sculpture might be said not merely to commemorate or signify a mythical event, but actually to exhibit the process of its taking place. While Brahmā and Vishnu speed in opposite directions, the substance of the stone correspondingly expands, outmeasuring their movement. The solid rock is apparently animated by an energy of growth. The niche-like split in its side seems actually to be widening, unfolding, to disclose the anthropomorphic apparition within. The solid, static mass of the stone, by a subtle artifice of the craftsman, has been converted into a dynamomorphic, multiple event. In this respect, this piece of sculpture is more like a motion picture than a painting.

The notion that there is nothing static, nothing abiding, but only the flow of a relentless process, with everything originating, growing, decaying, vanishing—this wholly dynamic view of life, of the individual and of the universe, is one of the fundamental conceptions (as we have already seen) of later Hinduism. We discovered it in the tale of the Ant Parade. It is of the essence of the conception of Māyā. We shall study it again in the cosmic Dance of Shiva, where all the features and creatures of the living world are interpreted as momentary flashes from the limbs of the Lord of the Dance. In the phenomenon of the growing or expanding form an effect of this typically Hindu "total dynamism" is imparted to a solid monument; the elusive element of time is woven, with its imperceptible flow, into the pattern and substance of a block of stone.

Once having become aware of the effect, we can rediscover it, again and again; for the Hindu craftsmen have freely employed their subtle artifice. Consider, for example, the celebrated relief from Bādāmī shown in Figure 31. This is a specimen of early Chalukya art, from the sixth century A.D., representing Vishnu in the form of his fifth avatār, as the pigmy who suddenly waxed into the cosmic giant. According to the story, a mighty demon or titan had driven all the lesser divinities from their seats, and in order to wrest the world from the terrible grasp, the essence of all being, Vishnu, maintainer of the universe, descended—as he had so often descended before and would descend so often again—out of his transcendental quietude into the troubled sphere of cosmic event. Born of the good woman Aditi, mother of Indra and Indra's brother divinities, he appeared in the form of a brahmin pigmy, no bigger than a stunted child. And this unimpressive, rather amusing little figure, bearing a parasol such as brahmins are wont to carry, comically craved audience with the demon tyrant, and asked of him a boon. What he wished was only as much space as he might cover with three of his puny strides. But when the titan, entertained, freely granted the trifling favor, lo, the god, mightily waxing, swelling in every limb, with his first stride stepped beyond the sun and moon, with his second reached the limits of the universe, and with his third returned to set his foot on the head of the conquered foe.

In the Bādāmī relief both the pigmy form and that of the giant infinitely expanding are represented side by side, signifying respectively the beginning and the process of the miracle. The victor is depicted as about to step on the head of the foe, either to crush him, or (if he but recognize and pay worship to the Presence) to bless him with the touch of Vishnu's foot. The body of the dilating god crowds with its tiara the upper frame of the composition, as if to burst the bounds of space. The dynamic character of the whole universe, with all its creatures, as conceived by Hindu philosophy, is rendered in this impressive central figure. The work as a whole is to be deciphered and comprehended, not as a static symbol, but as an event; it is a rendition of something actually coming to pass. The quality of time permeates the inert matter of the stone. Flow and growth transform the mineral substance into an organism interminably expanding.

There is a colossal Shiva-image from Parel, near Bombay, in which this peculiar sculptural effect is realized in a particularly striking way. (Figure 32.) The great block of white granite, nearly thirteen and a half feet high, dating from about A.D. 600, was accidentally unearthed during the course of the construction of a road. The details are unfinished. Below, in the center, is the giant figure of the god, firmly standing on both feet (*samapāda-sthānaka*). His right hand, uplifted and carrying a rosary, is held in the gesture of teaching (*vyākhyāna-mudrā*). The object in the lowered left hand was left unfinished, together with many other minor details of the image, and is not clear enough for us to identify. The figure is clad, from the waist to the ankles, in a garment of fine, clinging material, carefully folded and tucked in at the top. The chest and shoulders are bare. The figure is adorned with bracelets and a necklace. The headdress consists of the traditional, piled up, matted hair of the great yogī of the gods.

Emerging upward out of this divinity is a second, its double, holding in the left hand an attribute of Brahmā—the waterpot of the mendicant ascetic (*kamaṇḍalu*)—and making with the right the gesture of meditation (*dhyāna-mudrā*). Then out of this second emerges a third, extending ten arms in a crowning semicircle and holding emblematic implements: a sword, a rosary, and some indistinct object, a noose, a shield, a circular object with a handle, and a waterpot—symbols, on the one hand, of the cosmic hero, the conqueror of demon-powers, and on the other of the archetypal ascetic, the representative of spirituality. All are appropriate to the many-sided Shiva.

But these three central figures, forming a lingam-like pillar, are augmented by others who break from them to right and to left With a violent yet stately impetus these burst like branches in both directions. They probably represent the hosts or *gaṇas* of the god, his followers and attendants, who in countenance, figure, attire, and attributes, resemble the divinity himself. Some carry musical instruments, a tambour, a flute. On the lowermost level of the monument five such figures are crowded, roughly sketched, only one quite finished. These correspond to the five hosts of

Shiva's followers, each host being represented by a single individual. Then to either side of the two upper figures of the central column, as they emerge and grow from each other, the motif of the emanating lateral forms is powerfully restated. Here the multiples of the central god repeat with both hands the gestures (*mudrā*) of the presence of the center and display identical symbols. With their legs in attitudes of flight, they break forth from the axial Shiva-pillar, soaring out from their point of origin. Their faces remain turned back to it, as if to confirm their intrinsic identity with the center.

In this bold and monumental work, accessories, reduced to a minimum, are of an extremely simple style: smooth rings, wristlets, and armlets. Whereas in many Hindu images (born from and meant for inner visualization) the descriptive details and ornamental features so insist upon themselves that they smother the piece in static pedantry, in the present case they are strenuously subdued in favor of a vigorous, effulgent, almost sweeping *élan*. This relief is conceived, and should be read by the eye, as a never-ending process. The giant granite slab seems to be expanding, both vertically and sidewise, with the life-force of the athletic organisms that throb and heave across its surface.

The physical power of the seven principal figures is gathered in their splendid chests. These are fine examples of the typical chest of the lion-like, broad-shouldered, slim-waisted Hindu hero, the Indian Superman (*mahāpuruṣa*); also, the broad chest of the perfect yogī, trained by breathing exercises and capable of storing in infinite quantity the life-element of *prāṇa*, "the Breath."

The piece is a "Shiva Trimūrti," * a rendition of the exfoliation of Shiva into three appearances or aspects (*tri-mūrti*). The Shivaite Purānas declare that this god, the personification of the

---

* [Or rather, Maheśa-mūrti, not strictly a "Trimūrti" (Ekapāda-mūrti), although a Trinity: see T. A. G. Rao, *Elements of Hindu Iconography*, II, pp. 382-385. This means that none of the faces are really representations of Vishnu or Brahmā as such, but of aspects of Shiva himself.—AKC.]

Absolute, becomes manifest first under the aspect of *sattva*, the first of the three *gunas* or qualities of cosmic matter—the quality of serenity and calm. In this phase of manifestation Shiva is Vishnu. In and by itself the divine essence then is resting, unstirred by any creative impulse; all the qualities and energies are counterbalancing each other in a state of harmony without motion. But this static, dormant attitude, this self-contained, all-containing sleep of the Absolute, then becomes converted into movement: the lotus sprouts from the water, Brahmā springs into existence, the universe begins to be evolved. Shiva as Vishnu puts forth as an emanation Brahmā the creator—the central figure in the axial column of the monument. This is the god under the aspect of *rajas*, second of the three *gunas* or qualities—that of activity, fiery energy, and emotion. Here the Highest Being unfolds the phenomenal world out of his own substance. Finally a third aspect develops, that of Kāla-Rudra, all-devouring Time, engulfing everything produced. This is Shiva in his strictly destructive aspect, bringing about the periodical dissolution of the universe. Kāla-Rudra is a personification of the divine substance under the aspect of *tamas*—the quality or principle of darkness, obstruction, anger, dulness, sorrow.

Shiva is called the Great Lord (*maheśvara*) when he is regarded as a personification of the fulness of the Absolute. In this relief it is he who is depicted. The trinity of the central column is one and the same essence in three attitudes; the secondary figures are emanations of this essence into the five elements and the forms of the world.* All the figures of this monument show therefore the same countenance and features; they look alike because they are finally one and the same. Hindu philosophy and enlightened Hindu orthodoxy are fundamentally monistic, monotheistic, in spite of the hosts of gods and super-

---

* According to the Samkhya philosophy, cosmic matter (*prakṛiti*) becomes manifest in the three gunas (*sattva, rajas, tamas*) and these in turn produce the five elements from the intermixtures of which are generated all phenomenal forms.

human beings with which the mythology teems. The multitudes of apparitions are only specializations, specific virtues, attitudes, components, facets. Regarded from the viewpoint of the Divine itself (a position attained in the enlightenment of yoga) the apparently contradictory aspects of existence—creation, duration, dissolution—are one and the same as to origin and meaning and end. They are the changing phenomenal self-expressions of the one divine substance or energy of life, which, though revealed in a threefold way, is finally beyond, and unaffected by, all the changes that it seems to inflict upon itself. The understanding of this unity is the goal of Hindu wisdom. The power not to be confused by the fluent play of Māyā-energy, but to rejoice at the sight of even the most harrowing of its manifestations, constitutes the victory and solace of this view. Hindu wisdom, Hindu religion, accepts the doom and forms of death as the dark-tones of a cosmic symphony, this tremendous music being the utterance, paradoxically, of the supreme quietude and silence of the Absolute. Every moment of experience is suffused with a deep Dionysian joy, deeper far than the pains and disasters that break the surfaces of our lives and worlds. In the Hindu spirit, as in this wonderful, granite masterpiece from Parel, there is an ultimate, marvelous balance between the dynamism of manifestation—process—constant evolution, and the serene, static repose of eternal being. This monument is meant to teach the total union and coincidence of all kinds of opposites in the one, transcendent source. From it they pour and into it they again subside.*

---

* [The representation, in other words, is of the first essence, Sadāshiva, whose intrinsic nature is that of the unity of the "manifested and unmanifested" (*vyaktāvyakta*), i.e., of the two natures of the single essence, prior to the exercise of Lordship (as Īshvara, *kuriós*) and from which nature (as from the "brahmawomb") all things are derived as from a mother (see the *Mahārtha-mañjarī* of Maheśvarānanda, text p. 44). In this "Supreme Identity" all the contraries inhere without opposition, for example *sat* and *asat*, τὸ ὄν and τὸ μὴ ὄν; and this, in (*mokṣa*) is, accordingly, "*from* the pairs of opposites," for example *from* the knowledge of good and evil that man acquired by the Fall.—AKC.]

136

3.

Shiva-Shakti

THERE are many ways of representing the differentiation of the Absolute into antagonistic yet co-operative pairs of opposites. Among the oldest and most usual of these is that based on the duality of the sexes: Father Heaven and Mother Earth, Uranos and Gaia, Zeus and Hera, the Chinese Yang and Yin. This is a convention that has been developed with particular emphasis in the Hindu and later Buddhist traditions, where, though the outward symbolization in images is strikingly erotic, the connotations of all the forms are almost exclusively allegorical. The most elaborate and illuminating readings of this vivid pictorial scripture are those of the so-called Tantras—religious writings representing the Shivaite schools of the latest great period of Hinduism. In the primal couple engendering the spheres of being we are to behold personified the divine essence in its productive aspect, polarized for fruitful self-reflection.*

A splendid example of the God and Goddess in erotic play appears in a Bengalese relief representing Shiva with his consort. (Figure 34.) She sits on his left thigh with her right arm around his shoulder, while his left arm gently holds her by the waist. The two countenances, rigid and mask-like, regard each other with intense emotion. Gazing with a deep and everlasting rapture, they are imbued with the secret knowledge that, though seemingly two, they are fundamentally one. For the sake of the universe and its creatures, the Absolute has apparently unfolded into this duality, and out of them derive all the life polarities, antagonisms, distinctions of powers and elements, that charac-

---

*[Cf. Heinrich Zimmer's "Some Aspects of Time in Indian Art," *Journ. Indian Society of Oriental Art,* I, 1933, esp. p. 48; and my own "Tantric Doctrine of Divine Biunity" in *Annals Bhandarkar Research Institute,* 19, 1938.—AKC.]

terize the phenomenal world. Anklets, wristlets, armlets, rich necklaces, and royal diadems bedeck the magnificent pair. They are seated on the lotus throne, which symbolizes divine creative energy. A minor lotus cushion appears under Shiva's bent left foot, two more such cushions appearing under the two feet of the divine couple that hang toward the ground. Below are reposing their respective animal vehicles (*vāhana*), the lion, counterpart of the Goddess, and Nandī, Shiva's bull.

Shiva has four arms. With one he holds his consort, with two others he exhibits the trident (his weapon as a hero) and the rosary (his emblem as an ascetic), which together symbolize the combination in him of the active principle and the contemplative, the extravert and the introvert. His remaining right hand, before his chest, holds a stalk-like symbol twined with the tendril of a lotus plant and crowned with lotus petals. This evidently is the lingam, emblematic of the divinity's productive essence. Silently he exhibits it to the goddess, while she in her left hand, elevates its complement, a convex, swelled-out symbol marked by a furrow.

On the lowermost level, to the right, appears on a diminutive scale the elephant-headed Ganesha, "Lord (*īśa*) of the Hosts (*gaṇa*)," their son; * the trumpet of this god, the conch, rests near by on a tripod throne. Skanda Kārttikeya, the other son of the divine couple, is depicted opposite, at the left, rattling a drum with the fingers of his left hand and brandishing behind his head a sword. Just above these two are the portraits of the donor and his family, offering flowers with folded hands. The father,

---

*[Ganesha, corresponding to Agni-Brihaspati, "Lord of Hosts" (i.e., of the Maruts, the Breaths, the Powers of the soul) in the Rig Veda, and Skanda represent respectively the Sacerdotium (*brahma*) and Regnum (*kṣatra*), the "hosts" being those of the Commons (*viśa*). Ganesha's elephant's head corresponds to the "elephantine-glory" (*hastī-varcas*) and "force" attributed to the Sun and to Brihaspati in the Atharva Veda. Thus Ganesha is not, as often stated, a concept "of popular origin," but of hieratic origin. Cf. also Alice Getty, *Gaṇeśa*, Oxford, 1926.—AKC.]

on Shiva's side of the composition, is accompanied by his son, and the mother, beside the Goddess, by her two daughters. Thus the human couple are shown to participate in the mystical union of the divine; they, too, are of one flesh.

A pair of celestial attendants stand at either side of the lotus throne—at the level of the chests of the divine couple—holding their fly-whisks downward-turned. Such chowry bearers * generally flank the presences of kingly persons sitting in state, but as a rule the whisks are held uplifted. In the present case, the attendants are so distracted by pious rapture that they are forgetting their appointed office. Indeed, the emotion with which the god and his spouse are gazing at each other affects all of the figures, both human and divine, privileged to behold the spectacle. Not only the donors and chowry bearers, but the hovering swarm of Shiva's hosts, the heavenly musicians, are filled with exalted bliss. The face at the top of the frame surmounting the throne is an ornamental demon-mask which is commonly encountered in Shiva-sanctuaries and above the doors of Shiva-temples. It is an apotropaic device called *Kīrtti-mukha*, "The Face of Glory," a manifestation of the terrible aspect of the god, whose function it is to ward away the impious and to protect the devotee.

In stone and in bronze, again and again, this classic theme of the God and Goddess reappears, variously inflected, in the monuments of Hindu art. The God and Goddess are the first self-revelation of the Absolute, the male being the personification of the passive aspect which we know as Eternity, the female of the activating energy (*śakti*), the dynamism of Time. Though apparently opposites, they are in essence one. The mystery of their identity is stated here in symbol. The God is he whom we

---

* From the Hindustani, *cāurī,* which is derived from the Sanskrit, *cāmarī,* which in turn is developed from *camara,* meaning yak. Fly-whisks are made from the hair of the streaming white tail of this Tibetan beast of burden.

have beheld threefold in the monument of Parel; he who dwells in the "root-figure" of the lingam. The Goddess is the yoni, mother-womb of the ever-cycling eons, of all the universes endlessly extending in space, of every atom in the living cell. She is called "The Universal Power" (*śakti*), "The Fairest of the Three Worlds" (*tri-pura-sundarī*), she has been known in myth as Umā, Durgā, Pārvatī, Kālī, Chāmundā, Gaurī, Haimavatī, Vindhyavāsinī. She has her living counterpart in every woman, as the God in every man.

But these seated couples are static in their presentation of the mystery. A more dynamic symbol—characteristically Indian in its rendition of growing or expanding form—is represented by the profoundly eloquent Shrī Yantra, "Auspicious Yantra," "Yantra above Yantras." (Figure 36.) Though apparently no more than a geometrical device, this intricate linear composition is conceived and designed as a support to meditation—more precisely, to a concentrated visualization and intimate inner experience of the polar play and logic-shattering paradox of eternity and time. But before its meaning can unfold and its effects begin to be experienced in the mind, the beholder must understand the exact relationship of its concise and compendious delineation to the basic principles of Oriental metaphysics. This composition summarizes in a single moment the whole sense of the Hindu world of myth and symbol.

To begin with, then, what is the meaning of the term "yantra"? The suffix -*tra* in Sanskrit is used to form substantives denoting instruments or tools. For example, *khan* means "dig," *khani*, "digging or rooting up"; *khanitra* is "an instrument for digging, a spade, hoe, pickax, shovel, a primitive stick for drawing furrows and for digging holes in which to deposit seed." Similarly, *man* (related etymologically to "mental") means "think or have in mind"; *mantra* therefore is "an instrument for evoking or producing something in our minds," specifically "a holy formula or magic spell for evoking or bringing to mind the vision and inner presence of a god." * Correspondingly, *yantra* is an instrument to make *yam*.

What, however, is the meaning of *yam*? "Curb, subdue, rule, control." The verb *yam* means to gain control over the energy inherent in some element or being. Accordingly, *yantra* denotes, primarily, any kind of machine—machine, that is to say, in a pre-industrial, pre-technical sense: a dam to collect water for irrigation, a catapult to hurl stones against a fort—any mechanism built to yield energy for some definite purpose of man's will. In Hindu devotional tradition, "yantra" is the general term for instruments of worship, namely, idols, pictures, or geometrical diagrams. A yantra may serve as (1) a representation of some personification or aspect of the divine, (2) a model for the worship of a divinity immediately within the heart, after the paraphernalia of outward devotion (idol, perfumes, offerings, audibly uttered formulae) have been discarded by the advanced initiate, (3) a kind of chart or schedule for the gradual evolution of a vision, while identifying the Self with its slowly varying contents, that is to say, with the divinity in all its phases of transformation. In this case the yantra contains dynamic elements.

We may say, then, that a yantra is an instrument designed to curb the psychic forces by concentrating them on a pattern, and in such a way that this pattern becomes reproduced by the worshiper's visualizing power. It is a machine to stimulate inner visualizations, meditations, and experiences. The given pattern may suggest a static vision of the divinity to be worshiped, the superhuman presence to be realized, or it may develop a series

---

* Originally the word *mantra* meant simply a verbal instrument for producing something in our minds. Such an instrument was regarded as possessing power. A word or formula—say, "democracy" or "charity"—represents a mental presence or energy; by it something is produced, crystallized, in the mind. The term *mantra-śakti* is employed to denote this magic power possessed by words when they are brought together in a formula or effective slogan.

of visualizations growing and unfolding from each other as the links or steps of a process.

The latter is the richer, more interesting type, and makes the greater demands upon the initiate. It works in two directions: first, forward as a course of evolution, then backward again as a process of involution, undoing the visions previously unfolded. That is to say, it restates in miniature the stages or aspects of the manifestation of the Absolute in the evolution and involution of the world. Furthermore, the visualizing power of the devotee is required to follow in two ways this twofold process of creation and dissolution: on the one hand, as a temporal and spatial development, but on the other, as something transcending the categories of space and time—a simultaneity of antagonistic aspects in the one and only Essence. Thus, whereas on the one hand the dynamic diagrams suggest a continuous process of expansion from the center of the pattern to the circumference and requiring a passage of time for its course, on the other hand they are to be grasped as an enduring hierarchy, or gradation, of simultaneously manifested degrees of being, with the highest value situated at the center. These degrees symbolize the various transformations, or aspects, of the Absolute on the phenomenal plane of Māyā-Shakti,* and at the same time supply a pictorial analysis of the structure of man's soul and body; for the Highest Essence (*brahman*), which is the core of the world, is identical with the Highest Self (*ātman*), the kernel of man's existence.† The visualizations, meditations, and experiences

---

* For definitions of Māyā and Shakti, cf. pp. 24-6, *supra*.

† *Brahman* is the Life that lives in all things, [Heracleitus' "ever-living Fire," Plato's "ever-progenitive Nature"—AKC]. "It is never born, nor does It ever die, nor, having once been, does It again cease to be. Unborn, eternal, permanent, and primeval, It is not slain when the body is slain." (*Bhagavad Gītā*, 2. 20.) This "It," when experienced introspectively as the root of our individual existence, is termed Ātman (the Self). When intuited as the sustaining Form of external, universal flux, It is Brahman (the Absolute). Brahman-Ātman, the All in all of us, surpasses human reason, cannot be conceived of by the human imagination, and cannot be

generated by the yantra must be regarded, therefore, not only as reflections of the divine essence in its production and destruction of the universe, but at the same time (since the world-processes and the stages of evolution are duplicated in the history and structure of the human organism) as emanations out of the psyche of the devotee. When utilized, in connection with the practice of yoga, the contents of the yantra diagram represent those stages of consciousness that lead inward from the everyday state of naïve "ignorance" (*avidyā*), through the degrees of yoga-experience, to the realization of the Universal Self (*brahman-ātman*).

Typical of the whole class are the elements of the Shrī Yantra (Figure 36): (1) a square outer frame, composed of straight lines broken according to a regular pattern, (2) an inclosed arrangement of concentric circles and stylized lotus petals, (3) a concentric composition of nine interpenetrating triangles. The square framework is called, in the Tantric tradition, "shivered" (*śiśirita*). i.e., trembling, as if with a chill. This curious expression does not refer to its symbolic meaning, but to its shape. What the "shivered" frame represents is a square sanctuary with four doors opening out to the four quarters, a landing before each entrance, and a low flight of steps leading up from the ground to the raised floor of the sanctuary. This sanctuary is the seat (*pīṭha*) of the divinity, and should be thought of as the center of the heart of the devotee. Herein resides his own particular "Chosen Deity" (*iṣṭa-devatā*), who, finally, is to be understood as a symbolization

---

described; yet It can be experienced as the very Life within us (*ātman*), or intuited as the Life of the cosmos (*brahman*).

> "He who knows that It is incomprehensible, comprehends;
> He who conceives of It, comprehends It not.
> It is unknown to the knowing ones,
> Known to the unknowing." (*Kena Upanishad*, 2. 3.)

[Hence only to be known by negations, in *docta ignorantia,* as in Christian theology.—AKC.]

of the divine nucleus of his own existence, his eternal, higher Self.*

The character of the "shivered" line as denoting the four walls of a square sanctuary is particularly obvious when the basic linear pattern is filled in with colors and shapes. This is the common case in Tibet, where a Lamaistic tradition of circular patterns (mandala) amplified into superb paintings has produced an inexhaustible treasury of magnificent forms. This northern Buddhist tradition developed under the influence of doctrines strongly imbued with Hindu—and especially Shiva-Shakti—ideas. For example, in the beautiful temple-ceiling from the holy city of Lhasa that is reproduced in Figure 37, a perfect yantra-diagram appears, but with a Buddha-figure in the position of the Ishta Devatā, and strictly Buddhist amplifications throughout. The personification in the center is the primal, eternal, Ādi-Buddha, or Vairochana. Radiating from him to the four quarters and the four points between are eight doubles or manifestations of his essence, differing in their special colors, gestures, and attributes. These denote the specific constituents going out from the immovable Absolute into the world. Illuminating and holding extended the universe, they are represented as contained within the heart of the cosmic flower. This, in turn, is set within the square sanctuary, and to each of the four quarters stands a meticulously pictured door. Beyond are lesser presences, door guardians, ceremonial umbrellas, and other symbols of the Lamaistic cult. Finally, the outermost rim of the lotus of the created universe is represented as a gigantic corolla of sixty-four varicolored petals.

The significance of the Buddha figure, we must pause a mo-

---

* ["Eternal Self": i.e., self's immortal Self and Leader, the Common Man in this man or woman so-and-so; to whom all worship is ultimately due. "That art thou." "Whoever resorts to any deity as 'other,' thinking 'He is one, and I another,' knoweth not." (Brihadāranyaka Upaniṣad 1. 4. 10.) "Some there are so simple as to think of God as if he dwelt there, and of themselves as here. It is not so; God and I are one." (Meister Eckhart, Pfeiffer, p. 469.)—AKC.]

ment to develop and explain. From the standpoint of the perfect Bodhisattva or Buddha-mind, there is only one essence, to wit, Buddhahood, enlightenment itself, the indescribable state or essence that is realized and attained when all the products and effects of Māyā-ignorance have been transcended. This is the sheer "Such-ness" or "That-ness" beyond differentiating qualifications, definable limitations and characteristics. This is *tatha-tā*, literally, "the state (*-tā*) of being 'so' (*tathā*)." *Tathā* means "yes, so it is, so be it, amen." It is the everyday, wholehearted affirmative. Hence the term *tatha-tā*, "such-ness," represents the utterly positive aspect of Nirvāna-enlightenment, the only really real state or essence, not to be undone or dissolved. All other states of consciousness are built up and dissolved again —the waking-state with its sense experiences, its thinking and its feeling, the dream-state with its subtle apparitions, and even the states of "higher" experience. But the state *tatha-tā* is indestructible; for it is at once the experience and the reality of the Absolute. And it is termed "adamantine" (*vajra*); for it is not to be split, disintegrated, dissolved, or even scratched, either by physical violence or by the power of critical-analytical thought.

The only possible anthropomorphic symbol for *tatha-tā* is the Buddha, he who has attained to the experience of the adamantine. And the most appropriate symbolic object or utensil is the thunderbolt, the weapon of Father Heaven, and in later times of Indra, king of the gods. Accordingly, the thunderbolt (*vajra*, same term as for "adamantine") is the characteristic emblem of a special school of Buddhist doctrine which styles itself Vajrayāna, "The Vehicle of the Irresistible Thunderbolt," "The Way toward the Adamantine Reality of Transcendent Truth." The vajra here commonly figures in every possible phase of iconographic decoration. It appears as a magic wand for the exorcism of evil forces, or as the handle of the bell used to mark time in the recital of sacred texts. (Figure 47.) In the design on the temple-ceiling of Lhasa, eight vajras encircle the central buddha, sixteen the eight emanations, and thirty-two the outer rim of the cosmic lotus. Also, it is the principal attribute of a certain very important, allegorical Buddha-type, known as Vajra-dhara, "He Who Holds, or Wields (*dhara*), the Adamantine Substance, or Weapon (*vajra*)." This figure is regarded as the Supreme Personalization of the Such-ness of Reality; he is called, accordingly, Vajra-sattva, "He Whose Essence, or Being (*sattva*), is the Adamantine Substance." Just as the animal "determinants" of the Hindu gods are in essence identical with the anthropomorphic forms that they support, so also, in the case of this supreme symbol of the Vajrayāna sect, the adamantine bolt is identical with the Buddha who holds it in his hand.

As a symbol of the Absolute, which engenders and sustains the phenomenal world, Vajradhara-Vajrasattva is represented seated on the lotus throne. This lotus having been originally the exclusive sign and "vehicle" of the goddess Padmā—mother, or yoni, of the universe—* it is symbolic of the procreative power (*śakti*) of the immortal, adamantine, eternal Substance. Thus a Buddha on or in the lotus symbolizes the essence of enlightenment as it permeates and sustains the universe of Time.

An alternate symbol of this mystery, based on the Hindu pattern of the God and his Shakti, is commonly encountered in the iconography of Tibet: Vajradhara with a female counterpart in close embrace. (Figure 35.) This is a formula known in Tibetan as "Yab-Yum." The two figures, merging into each other in supreme concentration and absorption, are seated on the lotus throne in a commanding attitude of imperishable calm. Both wear the jeweled attire and the tiaras of crowned Bodhisattvas. Scarcely could the ultimate identity of Eternity and Time, Nirvāna and Samsāra, the two aspects of the revealed Absolute, be represented in a more majestically intimate way.

Returning now to the Shrī Yantra, we may perceive under

---

* Cf. pp. 90-102, *supra.*

the abstract linear design this same primal pair. There are nine triangles in the figure, interpenetrating, five pointing downward, four upward. The downward-pointing triangle is a female symbol corresponding to the yoni; it is called "shakti." * The upward-pointing triangle is the male, the lingam, and is called "the fire" (*vahni*). *Vahni* is synonymous with *tejas*, "fiery energy, solar heat, kingly splendor, the threatening fervor of the ascetic, the bodily heat of the warm-blooded organism, the life-force condensed in the male seed." Thus the vahni-triangles denote the male essence of the god, and the shakti-triangles the female essence of his consort.

The nine signify the primitive revelation of the Absolute as it differentiates into graduated polarities, the creative activity of the cosmic male and female energies on successive stages of evolution. Most important is the fact that the Absolute itself, the Really Real, is not represented. It cannot be represented; for it is beyond form and space. The Absolute is to be visualized by the concentrating devotee as a vanishing point or dot, "the drop" (*bindu*), amidst the interplay of all the triangles. This Bindu is the power-point, the invisible, elusive center from which the entire diagram expands. And now, whereas four of the shakti-triangles link with their represented vahni-counterparts, the fifth, or innermost, remains over, to unite with the invisible Point. This is the Primal Shakti, consort of the transcendental Shiva, creative energy as a female manifestation of the pure, quiescent Brahman, the Great Original.

Like the Shiva-Shakti images, the Shrī Yantra symbolizes Life, both universal life and individual, as an incessant interaction of

---

* Likewise, according to Greek lexicographers, the Greek letter Δ, delta, denotes (though upward-pointing) the female: "Δέλτα, εἴδωλον γυναικεῖον." Furthermore, the European gypsies, in their symbol language, denote the fair sex by triangles, a usage brought by them from their ancient homeland, India. Among the marks that they stealthily leave on fence or doorpost to apprise their fellows of what to expect from the inmates of a house, they write one or more triangles to indicate the number of females within.

147

co-operating opposites. The five female triangles expanding from above and the four male emerging from below, signify the continuous process of creation. Like an uninterrupted series of lightning flashes they delve into each other and mirror the eternal procreative moment—a dynamism nevertheless exhibited in a static pattern of geometrical repose. This is the archetypal Hieros Gamos, or "Mystical Marriage," represented in an abstract diagram—a key to the secret of the phenomenal mirage of the world.

4.

The Great Lord

THIS same polarity of male and female principles has found expression in one of the most magnificent documents of Hindu symbolic art, the great Shiva-Trinity of Elephanta, a masterpiece of the classic period, created in the eighth century A.D. (Figure 33.) It is not the central image of the temple, the principal object of worship being the stone lingam represented in Figure 29.* It is only one of a number of decorative reliefs in the huge, subterranean, rock-cut hall that surrounds the central shrine. Nevertheless, it is a work of art hardly to be matched. What it represents is precisely the mystery of the unfolding of the Absolute into the dualities of phenomenal existence, these being personified and culminated in human experience by the polarity of the female and the male.

The middle head of the threefold image is a representation of the Absolute. Majestic and sublime, it is the divine essence out of which proceed the other two. Over the right shoulder of this presence, perpetually growing out of the central form, is

---

* See discussion, p. 127, *supra*.

the male profile of Shiva, the Great God (*mahādeva*)—virility, will-power, and defiance in its arching contours; haughtiness, valor, and temper flashing about the chin, the forehead, and the root of the nose; manly consciousness exhibited in the twirled mustache. Correspondingly, to the left of the central mask is the profile of the female principle—ineffable attractiveness, the seductive power of nature, blossom and fruit, gentle charm, swelling with the promise of all sweetness. In this alluring mask of womanhood are all the delights of the senses: *das Ewig-Weibliche* (that untranslatable term for which Gérard de Nerval, who first translated *Faust* into French, coined the delightful French equivalent, *le charme éternel*).

But the middle head is self-inclosed in a sublime, dreamy aloofness. By its impassivity it silences the two gestures to right and to left, ignoring completely the display of their antagonistic features. Whereas these two differentiated profiles, perpetually emerging and evolving from the middle personification, are represented in relief, the central head from which they blossom is fully sculptured in the round. As an immovable, massive, central form, magnificent, self-absorbed in lofty and stony silence, it overpowers, dissolves, and fuses into itself the characteristic features of the two lateral physiognomies: power and sweetness, aggressive vigor and expectant receptivity. Great with transcendental quietude, comprehensive, enigmatic, it subsumes them and annhilates in eternal rest the effects of their creative tension. Unaware of their polarity, indifferent to its insubstantial weight, the mighty Middle, this magnificent apparition of the Bindu,* nullifies serenely the primitive, archetypal polarity that is producing forever the Māyā of the world. Apparently, it never feels the joys and agonies of their interaction. Apparently, the processes of the universe and of the living individual, as reflected in human consciousness, this ambiguous presence never knows. At

---

* *Bindu:* "the drop," i.e., the Absolute, cf. p. 147, *supra.*

least, it rests in sovereign indifference, unaffected.—So, likewise, the innermost Self of man, the Ātman, rests unconcerned amidst the sufferings and delights, the organic and psychic processes, of the sheaths that enshroud its adamantine Being.

The central head is the face of Eternity. Insisting on nothing whatsoever, it contains, blended in transcendental harmony, all the powers of the paired existences to either side. Out of its solid silence, time and the life-processes are continuously flowing—or apparently are flowing: from the viewpoint of the Middle, there is nothing flowing. In the august presence of the face of eternity the two expressive relief-profiles become cloud-like. Their drama on the stage of space and time becomes an effect as insubstantial as a play of light and shade. Perpetually asserting themselves to right and to left—yet wholly disregarded by the very essence from which they ceaselessly proceed—they are the producers and directors of the world spectacle, self-multiplying into an infinite number of actors. Their production is visible only to our "nescience" (avidyā); before the awakened eye it disappears. They are and they are not. Like vapor they and their creation come to pass, flow, and vanish away. That is the true nature of Māyā, the phenomenal character of the process of life—whether personal or collective, historical or cosmogonic—as it is experienced by us with our individualized, limited and perishable consciousness, awake or asleep, remembering or forgetting, acting or suffering, laying our hands on things, yet ourselves slipping out of our own grasp.

The two profiles are happening; the universe is happening; the individual is happening. But in what sense are they happening? Do they *really* happen? The central mask is meant to express the truth of the Eternal in which nothing happens, nothing comes to pass, changes, or dissolves again. The divine essence, the solely real, the Absolute in itself, our own innermost Higher Self, abides in itself, steeped in its own sublime Void, omniscient and omnipotent, containing all and everything. This is the portrait of Ātman-Brahman. And here is the paradox of Māyā: the universe and our personalities are as real as—but not more real than—the phenomenal apparitions of these male and female profiles, emerging from the center, but ignored by it. Brahman and Māyā coexist. Māyā is the continuous self-manifestation and self-disguise of Brahman—its self-revelation, yet its multi-colored, concealing veil. Hence the dignity of all perishable things, on all levels. That is why their sum total is worshiped as the Highest Goddess, Mother and Life-Energy of Gods and Creatures, under the formula, Māyā-Shakti-Devī.

5.

The Dance of Shiva

SHIVA, the lord of the lingam, the consort of Shakti-Devī, also is Natarāja, "King of Dancers."

Dancing is an ancient form of magic. The dancer becomes amplified into a being endowed with supra-normal powers. His personality is transformed. Like yoga, the dance induces trance, ecstasy, the experience of the divine, the realization of one's own secret nature, and, finally, mergence into the divine essence. In India consequently the dance has flourished side by side with the terrific austerities of the meditation grove—fasting, breathing exercises, absolute introversion. To work magic, to put enchantments upon others, one has first to put enchantments on oneself. And this is effected as well by the dance as by prayer, fasting and meditation. Shiva, therefore, the arch-yogī of the gods, is necessarily also the master of the dance.

Pantomimic dance is intended to transmute the dancer into whatever demon, god, or earthly existence he impersonates. The war dance, for example, converts the men who execute it into warriors; it arouses their warlike virtues and turns them into fearless heroes. And the hunting-party dance-pantomime, which magically anticipates and assures the successes of the hunting party, makes of the participants unerring huntsmen. To summon from dormancy the nature-powers attendant upon fruitfulness, dancers mimic the gods of vegetation, sexuality, and rain.

The dance is an act of creation. It brings about a new situation and summons into the dancer a new and higher personality. It has a cosmogonic function, in that it arouses dormant energies which then may shape the world. On a universal scale, Shiva is the Cosmic Dancer; in his "Dancing Manifestation" (*nritya-mūrti*) he embodies in himself and simultaneously gives manifestation to Eternal Energy. The forces gathered and projected in his frantic, ever-enduring gyration, are the powers of the evolution, maintenance, and dissolution of the world. Nature and all its creatures are the effects of his eternal dance.

Shiva-Natarāja is represented in a beautiful series of South Indian bronzes dating from the tenth and twelfth centuries A.D. (Figure 38.) The details of these figures are to be read, according to the Hindu tradition, in terms of a complex pictorial allegory. The upper right hand, it will be observed, carries a little drum, shaped like an hour-glass, for the beating of the rhythm. This connotes Sound, the vehicle of speech, the conveyer of revelation, tradition, incantation, magic, and divine truth. Furthermore, Sound is associated in India with Ether, the first of the five elements. Ether is the primary and most subtly pervasive manifestation of the divine Substance. Out of it unfold, in the evolution of the universe, all the other elements, Air, Fire, Water, and Earth. Together, therefore, Sound and Ether signify the first, truth-pregnant moment of creation, the productive energy of the Absolute, in its pristine, cosmogenetic strength.

The opposite hand, the upper left, with a half-moon posture of the fingers (*ardhacandra-mudrā*), bears on its palm a tongue of flame. Fire is the element of the destruction of the world. At the close of the Kali Yuga, Fire will annihilate the body of creation, to be itself then quenched by the ocean of the void. Here, then, in the balance of the hands, is illustrated a counterpoise of creation and destruction in the play of the cosmic dance. As a ruthlessness of opposites, the Transcendental shows through the mask of the enigmatic Master: ceaselessness of production against an insatiate appetite of extermination, Sound against Flame. And the field of the terrible interplay is the Dancing Ground of the Universe, brilliant and horrific with the dance of the god.

The "fear not" gesture (*abhaya-mudrā*), bestowing protection and peace, is displayed by the second right hand, while the remaining left lifted across the chest, points downward to the uplifted left foot. This foot signifies Release and is the refuge and salvation of the devotee. It is to be worshiped for the attainment of union with the Absolute. The hand pointing to it is held in a pose imitative of the outstretched trunk or "hand" of the elephant (*gaja-hasta-mudrā*), reminding us of Ganesha, Shiva's son, the Remover of Obstacles.

The divinity is represented as dancing on the prostrate body of a dwarfish demon. This is Apasmāra Purusha, "The Man or Demon (*puruṣa*) called Forgetfulness, or Heedlessness (*apasmāra*)." * It is symbolical of life's blindness, man's ignorance. Conquest of this demon lies in the attainment of true wisdom. Therein is release from the bondages of the world.

A ring of flames and light (*prabhā-maṇḍala*) issues from and encompasses the god. This is said to signify the vital processes of the universe and its creatures, nature's dance as moved by the dancing god within. Simultaneously it is said to signify the energy of Wisdom, the transcendental light of the knowledge of truth, dancing forth from the personification of the All. Still another allegorical meaning assigned to the halo of flames is that of the

---

* The name in Tamil is *Muyalaka*, also meaning heedlessness or forgetfulness.

holy syllable AUM or OM.* This mystical utterance ("aye," "amen") stemming from the sacred language of Vedic praise and incantation, is understood as an expression and affirmation of the totality of creation. A—is the state of waking consciousness, together with its world of gross experience. U—is the state of dreaming consciousness, together with its experience of the subtle shapes of dream. M—is the state of dreamless sleep, the natural condition of quiescent, undifferentiated consciousness, wherein every experience is dissolved into a blissful non-experience, a mass of potential consciousness. The Silence following the pronunciation of the three, A, U, and M, is the ultimate unmanifest, wherein perfected supra-consciousness totally reflects and merges with the pure, transcendental essence of Divine Reality—Brahman is experienced as Ātman, the Self. AUM, therefore, together with its surrounding silence, is a sound-symbol of the whole of consciousness-existence, and at the same time its willing affirmation.

The origin of the ring of flames is, probably, in the destructive aspect of Shiva-Rudra; but Shiva's destruction is finally identical with Release.

Shiva as the Cosmic Dancer is the embodiment and manifestation of eternal energy in its "five activities" (pañca-kriya): (1) Creation (sṛiṣṭi), the pouring forth or unfolding, (2) Maintenance (sthiti), the duration, (3) Destruction (saṁhāra), the taking back or reabsorption, (4) Concealment (tiro-bhāva), the veiling of True Being behind the masks and garbs of apparitions, aloofness, display of Māyā, and (5) Favor (anugraha) acceptance of the devotee, acknowledgment of the pious endeavor of the yogī, bestowal of peace through a revelatory manifestation. The first three and the last two are matched, as groups of co-operative mutual antagonisms; the god displays them all. And he displays them, not only simultaneously, but in sequence. They are sym-

---

* A and U amalgamate to O.

bolized in the positions of his hands and his feet—the upper three hands being respectively, "creation," "maintenance" and "destruction"; the foot planted in Forgetfulness is "concealment," and the foot uplifted, "favor"; the "elephant hand" indicates the linkage of the three to the two, and promises peace to the soul that experiences the relationship. All five activities are made manifest, simultaneously with the pulse of every moment, and in sequence through the changes of time.

Now, in the Shiva-Trinity of Elephanta we saw that the two expressive profiles, representing the polarity of the creative force, were counterposed to a single, silent, central head, signifying the quiescence of the Absolute. And we deciphered this symbolic relationship as eloquent of the paradox of Eternity and Time: the reposeful ocean and the racing stream are not finally distinct; the indestructible Self and the mortal being are in essence the same. This wonderful lesson can be read also in the figure of Shiva-Naṭarāja, where the incessant, triumphant motion of the swaying limbs is in significant contrast to the balance of the head and immobility of the mask-like countenance. Shiva is Kāla, "The Black One," "Time"; but he is also Mahā Kāla, "Great Time," "Eternity." As Naṭarāja, King of Dancers, his gestures, wild and full of grace, precipitate the cosmic illusion; his flying arms and legs and the swaying of his torso produce —indeed, they are—the continuous creation-destruction of the universe, death exactly balancing birth, annihilation the end of every coming-forth. The choreography is the whirligig of time. History and its ruins, the explosion of suns, are flashes from the tireless swinging sequence of the gestures. In the medieval bronze figurines, not merely a single phase or movement, but the entirety of this cosmic dance is miraculously rendered. The cyclic rhythm, flowing on and on in the unstayable, irreversible round of the Mahāyugas, or Great Eons, is marked by the beating and stamping of the Master's heels. But the face remains, meanwhile, in sovereign calm.

155

Steeped in quietude, the enigmatic mask resides above the whirl of the four resilient arms, cares nothing for the superb legs as they beat out the tempo of the world ages. Aloof, in sovereign silence, the mask of the god's eternal essence remains unaffected by the tremendous display of his own energy, the world and its progress, the flow and the changes of time. This head, this face, this mask, abides in transcendental isolation, as a spectator unconcerned. Its smile, bent inward, filled with the bliss of self-absorption, subtly refutes, with a scarcely hidden irony, the meaningful gestures of the feet and hands. A tension exists between the marvel of the dance and the serene tranquillity of this expressively inexpressive countenance, the tension, that is to say, of Eternity and Time, the paradox—the silent, mutual confutation—of the Absolute and the Phenomenal, the Self-Immortal and the perishable Psyche, Brahman-Ātman and Māyā. For neither one is the entirety it would seem, whereas, on the other hand, the two, invisible and visible, are quintessentially the same. Man with all the fibers of his native personality clings to the duality, in anxiety and delight; nevertheless, actually and finally, there is no duality. Ignorance, passion, egotism, disintegrate the experience of the highest Essence (crystal clear and beyond time and change, free from suffering and bondage) into the universal illusion of a world of individual existences. This world, for all its fluidity, however, *is*—and it never will end.

The bronze, dancing figures of southern India insist on the paradoxical identity of the personality, carried away by experiences and emotions, with the quiet, all-knowing Self. In these figures the contrast of the blissfully dreaming, silent countenance with the passionate agility of the limbs represents, to those ready to understand, the Absolute and its Māyā as a single trans-dual form. We and the Divine are one and the same, precisely as the vitality of these swaying limbs is one and the same with the utter unconcern of the Dancer who flings them into play.

But there is even more to be said about the god of the dance, as represented in the South Indian Bronzes.

Shiva's tresses are long and matted, partly streaming, partly stacked in a kind of pyramid. This is the hair of the model yogī of the gods. Supra-normal life-energy, amounting to the power of magic, resides in such a wilderness of hair untouched by the scissors. Similarly, the celebrated strength of Samson, who with naked hands tore asunder the jaws of a lion and shook down the roof of a pagan temple, resided in his uncut hair.—Furthermore, if we may judge by those magicians, genii, and demons of wondrous spells, who work their incantations on the concert stage, the sorcery of music demands a virtuoso lion-maned. No question either, but that much of womanly charm, the sensual appeal of the Eternal Feminine, *das Ewig-Weibliche, le charm éternel,* is in the fragrance, the flow and luster of beautiful hair. On the other hand, anyone renouncing the generative forces of the vegetable-animal realm, revolting against the procreative principle of life, sex, earth, and nature, to enter upon the spiritual path of absolute asceticism, has first to be shaved. He must simulate the sterility of an old man whose hairs have fallen and who no longer constitutes a link in the chain of generation. He must coldly sacrifice the foliage of the head.

The tonsure of the Christian priest and monk is a sign of this renunciation of the flesh. (Clergymen of denominations in which marriage is not considered incompatible with the saintly office do not wear a tonsure.) Buddhist saint-yogīs and patriarchs, as depicted, for example, in the numerous Chinese portraits of the Lohans,* shave the head entirely. Such heads connote defiance

---

* Chinese, *lohan,* from Sanskrit, *arhant, arahant;* becomes in Japanese, *rakan.* [The root, *arh,* means to be able, qualified, worthy: in the Rig Veda and Brāhmanas *arhana,* qualification, worth, is prerequisite to immortality and the indispensable condition of admission at the Sundoor; in Buddhism, *arhatta,* the state of being an Arhat, all in act, is tantamount to Buddhahood.—AKC.]

157

of the "fascination" * of the generative impulse of the life-cycle of Māyā. These "Worthy Ones," representing the victory of yoga-spirituality, have overcome all seduction by their taking of the monastic vows and following of the ascetic formula. With their voluntary baldness they have broken through to the peace beyond the seasons of growth and change. Almost demonic is the triumphant expression on the face of the Chinese Buddhist patriarch portrayed in Figure 49. It speaks of the power to be won through self-conquest, a vigor calm and challenging, sparkling with the magnetism of supra-normal yoga-capabilities. This is an imaginary portrait of him who has severed all the fetters of the world, him who has transcended the slavery of life's endless, meaningless reproduction of itself, him who has wielded the trenchant sword of discriminating knowledge and cut himself free from all those bonds that tie mankind to the urges and necessities of the plant world and the beast. This "Worthy One" has acquired, through his conquest, a prodigious power. We overhear the sonorous motif of the gods, titans, and Nibelung-dwarfs sounded by Richard Wagner in the *Ring: Nur wer der Minne Macht entsagt. . .* , "only he who renounces the power and spell of love and sex will acquire the Ring that bestows on its possessor the power beyond measure."

The Indian ascetic, be he Buddhist, Jain, or Brahmin, striving for release from the bondage and order of nature, is the counterpart—only spiritualized—of those titanic mythological demons who, by dint of fierce self-mortification, testing and increasing beyond measure their endurance and strength of will, struggle to win for themselves tyrannical powers in the world. The spiritual man is far beyond the temptation to rule the material universe, nevertheless he aspires to, and is carried onward toward, a goal of cosmic mastery. The Buddha was a World Emperor

---

* The Latin *fascinosum* refers originally and literally to the realm of smell, the bewitching odor primarily of sex—for instance, to the fragrance of blossoms opening their chalices and asking to be fertilized.

(*cakravartin*), but on the spiritual, not the political, physical plane. And the prerequisite to mastery, whether spiritual or political, as attested by the conquerors, whether saintly or titanic, is the law of Wagnerian Alberich, the Nibelung. Both the yogīs and the tyrants have learned the teaching of the daughters of the Rhine, those divine maidens who give voice to the primal wisdom of the timeless, cosmic waters—the wisdom of the recumbent Vishnu: *Nur wer der Minne Macht entsagt*. . . .

The lesson of the significance of the shaving of the head may be followed in the story of the "great departure" (*mahā-abhiniṣkramaṇa*) of the Buddha. He had entered upon his last incarnation (the incarnation during which, as the Bodhisattva, he was to attain enlightenment and therewith become the Buddha, the universal savior), and he had been born as the son of a princely house. But his father, wishing to defend the exquisite youth from every risk of disillusionment, so that he might remain with the world and become a mighty king, a "world emperor" (*cakravartin*), saw to it that his eyes should never behold any sign of the sorrowful aspect of existence. When the time was ripe, however, the signs appeared. During the course of four brief excursions out of the pleasure-idyll of his ravishing palace into the real life-world of men, the sensitive and highly intuitive young prince beheld, first an old man, then a person riddled with disease, then a corpse, and finally an ascetic-sage who had renounced the world. Immediately, he grasped and accepted these initiations from the Genius of Life.* Inspired by the glimpse of the ascetic, he straightway departed, that night, out of his father's palace. The genii of the earth held up the hoofs of his horse, so that their clatter should not arouse the sleeping city. His faithful charioteer

---

* The Genius of Life is broadcasting all possible initiations, revelations, and messages, all the time. But then again, this same Genius, under the aspect of Nature, has provided us with the precious gift of a natural blindness and deafness (*avidyā*, nescience, *māyā*), so that we are unable to tune in on station WOB, Wisdom of the Buddha. This problem of tuning in remains for us the major difficulty.

went ahead. The tutelary divinity of the residence flung open the gates of the capital rejoicingly, though in silence. And the rider vaulted the broad boundary-river of the kingdom of his father, on the adventure that would bring redeeming enlightenment to the mortals and the gods.

The first deed of the Buddha-in-the-making, after his departure from within the pale, is depicted in two eleventh century images of the great Ananda Temple of the Burmese city of Pagan. (Figures 44-5.) He severed his long and beautiful hair with his princely blade.* In the earliest canonical Buddhist records, the Pāli Canon, committed to writing in Ceylon during the first century B.C., the event is described in the following stately terms:†

"He thought, 'These locks of mine are not suited to a monk; but there is no one fit to cut the hair of a Future Buddha. Therefore I will cut them off myself with my sword.' And grasping a scimitar with his right hand, he seized his top-knot with his left hand, and cut it off, together with the diadem. His hair thus became two finger-breadths in length, and curling to the right, lay close to his head. As long as he lived it remained of that length, and the beard was proportionate. And never again did he have to cut either hair or beard.

"Then the Future Buddha seized hold of his top-knot and diadem, and threw them into the air, saying,—

" 'If I am to become a Buddha, let them stay in the sky; but if not, let them fall to the ground.'

"The top-knot and the jewelled turban mounted for a distance

---

* [Like many other verbal or visual formulae, the Bodhisattva's tonsure has Brahmanical antecedents; "They cut off the top-knot, for success, thinking 'More swiftly may we attain the world of heaven.' " (*Taittirīya Saṁhitā.* VII. 4. 9.)—AKC.]
† Reprinted by permission of the publishers from Henry Clarke Warren, *Buddhism in Translations* (Harvard Oriental Series, 3) Cambridge, Mass.: Harvard University Press, 1896, p. 66, which in turn is a translation of the Pāli *Introduction to the Jātaka*, i. 64-5.

of a league in the air, and there came to a stop. And Sakka,* the king of the gods, perceiving them with his divine eyes, received them in an appropriate jewelled casket, and established it in the Heaven of the Thirty-Three Gods as the 'Shrine of the Diadem.'

> "His hair he cut, so sweet with many pleasant scents,
> This Chief of Men, and high impelled it towards the sky;
> And there god Vāsava, the god with thousand eyes,
> In golden casket caught it, bowing low his head."

Figure 44 represents the Bodhisattva severing his hair with his own sword. In Figure 45 he holds the top-knot with the jeweled turban in both hands, just before throwing them into the air; and he is concentrating on the conjuration: "If I am to become a Buddha, let them stay in the sky. . . ." Indra, soaring back to his celestial paradise, the heaven of the Thirty-Three Gods, is carrying reverently the jeweled casket. Therein reposes the priceless relic signifying the decisive step towards spiritual enlightenment, the supreme renunciation. The female figure at the right, in an attitude of delight and worship, should be Indra's queen-consort, his shakti or embodied energy, Indrānī-Shachī, queen of the gods.

At the base of the pedestal, beneath the rim of the lotus-seat (*padmāsana*), Channa is depicted, the faithful courtier and charioteer. Channa was sleeping at the threshold of the Bodhisattva's apartments, on duty, when his Lord set forth on the great departure; and he accompanied him, to lead the horse, Kanthaka, by the bridle. Channa's only remaining function now will be to return to the residence and announce to the parents that they have irrevocably lost their son. The prince has renounced his princedom. The Bodhisattva has entered upon the homeless path of the nameless, anonymous ascetic. Gautama's

---

* *Sakka* (Pāli) corresponds to *śakra* (Sanskrit), i.e., the god, Indra. Sakka catching the top-knot is the flying figure in the upper left corner of Figure 45.

quest is to be now the Absolute, beyond the cycle of life and death.

After the Future Buddha had severed his hair and exchanged his royal garments for the orange-yellow robe of the ascetic beggar,* he dismissed his faithful charioteer: "Channa, go tell my father and my mother, from me, that I am well." And Channa did obeisance to the Future Buddha; and keeping his right side towards him, he departed.† But Kanthaka, the horse, who had been standing listening the while, was unable to bear his grief. As he was conducted out of sight, at the thought "I shall never see my master any more," his heart burst and he died. He was reborn in the Heaven of the Thirty-Three Gods, as the god Kanthaka.‡ In a very sensitive way this episode is alluded to in the attitude of the diminutive horse-figure by the pedestal. The utter dejection of the splendid animal, bearing the saddle but never more the rider,§ the bend of its simple, expressive head, and the pleading of the uplifted right foreleg, in protest as it were, supply a delightful specimen of the Indian gesture language, discreet and delicate, expressive, spirited, and full of sympathy for the forms of life.

Figure 46 is from a Buddhist shrine of the second century B.C., a detail from a pillar among the ruins of Bhārhut. It is a representation of Indra's realm at the moment of the inauguration of

---

* Those outside the pale of human society voluntarily adopt the orange-yellow garment that was originally the covering of condemned criminals being led to the place of execution [just as the saffron robes of a religious are put on by the Rajput knight when going forth to certain death in battle against overwhelming odds. Funeral rites are performed for one who becomes an "Abandoner"; the *sannyāsī* is what the Sūfīs call "a dead man walking."—AKC.]

† This is the usual ceremonious way of approaching and taking leave of a venerable person, guru, saint, icon, deity, or object of worship.

‡ Warren, p. 67.

§ [The "horse" is a symbol of the bodily vehicle, and the "rider" is the Spirit: when the latter has come to the end of its incarnations, the saddle is unoccupied, and the vehicle necessarily dies. The Bodhisattva's renunciation, like that of any other *sannyāsī*, is virtually a death.—AKC.]

the sanctuary of the rescued crest of hair. In the upper left-hand quarter is depicted a newly erected, domed tabernacle, bearing an inscription: *devadhammā sabhā bhagavato cūḍā-maha*, "The hall of the Buddha's true law of the gods, the festival (*maha*) of the hair-tuft (*cūḍā*)." Two gods, at either side, are in attitudes of worship; the one at the left, with the uplifted right hand, is throwing the offering of a lotus flower at the foot of the reliquary —in conformity to the non-Vedic Indian injunction: "One should never approach the presence of a divinity (icon, or other object of worship) without the offering of a handful of flowers (*puṣpāñjali*)." Other inhabitants of the celestial mansions are watching the ceremonies, rejoicing and enthusiastic, from the windows and terraces of the heavenly palaces. Below, meanwhile, are the heavenly damsels, the so-called Apsarases, dancers and singers of Indra's princely household, who are contributing their share to the festival by executing a ballet to musical accompaniment. These ever youthful, ever charming damsels form the seraglio of the inhabitants of Indra's paradise. They are the ever desirable, ever willing mistresses of those blessed souls who are reborn into Indra's heavenly world as a reward for virtuous and devout conduct. Apsarases are the perfect dispensers of sensual delight and amorous bliss on a divine scale, and in sheer celestial harmony. They are the embodiments of a strictly supra-earthly quality of sensual love, Divine Love as distinct from, and opposed to, Earthly Love,* which latter is intrinsically fraught with drama and tensions, the misunderstandings, quarrels, and reconciliations of lovers, and a hardly avoidable intimate flavor of dignified, dutiful resignation, such as is intrinsic even to perfect matrimonial adjustment. Apsarases † represent the "Innocence of Nature," "Delight Without Tears," "Sensual Consummation Without Remorse, Without Doubts or Subsequent Misgivings."

---

* As represented, for instance, in the celebrated painting of Titian, "Sacred and Profane Love."
† [Like the Perīs or Hūrīs of the Islamic Paradise.—AKC.]

They are the initiating priestesses of the ever-new ancient mystery of the mutual attractiveness of the sexes, "mystagogues" of those variegated activities that go to the celebration and fathoming of the miraculous depth of this mystery—its colorful monotony, repetitious dullness, and sublime nonsensicality. These very forces of Nature and Life acclaim the supreme sacrifice and conquest of the Future Buddha, though the Buddha's victory is to negate and annihilate their own very power and existence. They hallow his decisive step, his severing of the vegetation of his head, his decision to embark on that adventure of self-conquest which in the end will invalidate, annihilate, simply explode all the heavens and hell-pits together with their inhabitants, both alluring and terrible—revealing them all to be only so many projections, mirages, externalizations, of our own vegetative, animalistic, emotional-intellectual propensities.

In the early records we read that when the Future Buddha severed his hair, "so sweet with many pleasant scents," it became "two finger-breadths in length, and, curling to the right, lay close to the head." The cropped, curly locks remain to this day the canonical hairdress of the Buddha-image. In the classical Buddhist art of eighth century Java this formula was followed faithfully; the many sculptured representations of the eternal supramundane Buddhas that line the upper galleries and terraces of the gigantic mandala-structure of Borobodur bear witness to it. So also in the Mon-Khmer creations of Cambodia, this motif has been both steadfastly and skillfully employed. In the best works it is converted into an impressively simple, ornamental surface, abstract and anonymous. In the case, for example, of a certain mask-like Buddha portrait, which I once saw at an exposition in Paris, it forms a most inspiring frame. (Figure 48.) This is a piece, not much bigger than the palm of the hand, completely corroded by time, soil and rain, brittle and thin as an autumn leaf. It is one of the most knowing and solemn masks of a Buddha —breathtaking in its silence and composure. Seeing through the sufferings of all creatures and perceiving the cause, it is beyond suffering. It makes manifest the redeeming wisdom. The fragility of all transitory beings and things, which itself is the root of suffering, has penetrated and transfigured this indescribable face and nearly destroyed it. Still, it is there—this brittle foil—even enhanced by the added frailty: with the sublime indifference and composure of its features it wipes away the powers of suffering and decay. The relentless processes of time, here executing their sentence of destruction, the doom of that lamentable Samsāra from which the Wisdom of the Buddha brings redemption, have collaborated with the inspiration of an unknown artist to put the finishing touch to this precious document of the human spirit.

Another Buddha head from Cambodia is shown in Figure 50. It is of a portrait-like intimacy. Yet there is about it a sublime, ethereal melodiousness, a subdued musicality, which is effected by its eloquent absence of striking detail. And particularly from the treatment of the skull and hair, this softly ringing silence proceeds. I remember that when I saw for the first time this magnificent symbol of the essence of Buddhism amongst a collection of Cambodian masterpieces assembled in Paris at the Musée Guimet, I was struck by it as by something quite singular. It is said that when the Future Buddha was born, the brahminical soothsayers, reading the physiognomy of the newborn child, foretold for him conquest of the world, and declared that his dominion would be either as Universal Monarch (*cakravartin*) or as Universal Savior (*tathāgata*). This is that fateful physiognomy. This is the mask of him who declined all the kingdoms of the world. And while I was looking at these features with this idea in mind, my thoughts flew from the Musée Guimet on the Place Jena (which is named after Napoleon's decisive victory over Prussia, 1806), across the Seine, to the tomb of Napoleon, the Dome of the Invalides; and before my vision was another mask, the profile of that other Conqueror, the Buddha. In such heads the symbolic and significant mark of asceticism is converted into a symbol of supreme spirituality.

The ascetic hostility to the hair of the human organism is so excessive in the extreme sect of the Jains that they will tolerate no hair whatsoever on the person of an ordained holy-man. Part of their ritual of ordination consists in a thorough weeding out of every single hair growing on the head and body. Here the idea of the tonsure is, so to say, carried to its limit; and correspondingly, the Jaina idea of life-renunciation is drastic beyond bounds. In accordance with their archaic, fundamentalist, and thoroughgoing doctrine, the Jains so schedule their disciplines of bodily mortification, that in old age these ideally culminate in death from an absolute fast. As with the hair so with the last vegetable-requirement of the flesh: the revolt against the principle of life is pressed to the end.

But though the spiritual and even earthly rewards of the ascetic attitude are high, Shiva does not shave or shear his hair, "so sweet with many a pleasant scent." Refusing to take advantage of the symbolical and potent devices of self-curtailment and deprivation, the divine dancer and arch-yogī is forever the unshorn male. The long tresses of his matted hair, usually piled up in a kind of pyramid, loosen during the triumphant, violent frenzy of his untiring dance, and expand, so as to form two wings, to right and to left, a kind of halo—broadcasting, as it were, on their magic waves, the exuberance and sanctity of vegetative life, the charm, the appeal, the solemn command, of the generative forces of procreating Māyā.

Shiva's tresses are commonly represented as filled with little symbolic figures. Those that appear most frequently in his images are the following: (1) a diminutive figure of the goddess Ganges, whom he received on his head when she descended from heaven to earth,* (2) flowers of the datura (from which an intoxicating

---

* Cf. p. 115, *supra*.

drink is prepared), (3) a skull, symbolic of death–the common crown-jewel or forehead-ornament both of Shiva and of the lesser divinities who constitute part of his retinue and realm (the *Memento mori* of the Lord of Destruction), and (4) a crescent moon, called in Sanskrit *śiśu*, "the quickly swelling one, the eagerly growing one," but also, "the newborn babe," which from week to week, clinging to the mother breasts, quickly grows, like the crescent moon.

Shiva is the personification of the Absolute, particularly in its dissolution of the universe. He is the embodiment of Super-Death. He is called Yamāntaka, "The Ender of the Tamer, He who conquers and exterminates Yama the God of Death, the Tamer." Shiva is Mahā-Kāla, Great Time, Eternity, the swallower of time, swallower of all the ages and cycles of ages. He reduces the phenomenal rhythm and whirlpool to nought, dissolving all things, all beings, all divinities, in the crystal pure, motionless ocean of Eternity–from the viewpoint of which nothing whatsoever fundamentally comes to pass. But then again as Shishu, the babe, the crescent moon, Shiva is a sheer delight and the most auspicious thing to see, a promise of life and life-strength, gentle but irresistible. The moon, Shishu, is regarded as the cup of the fluid of life immortal, quickening the vegetable realm and whatsoever grows in the sub-lunar sphere, quickening also the immortals on high, so that they may be fit to perform their beneficent cosmic duties. Shiva as Shishu is this cup, this moon.

Shiva is apparently, thus, two opposite things: archetypal ascetic, and archetypal dancer. On the one hand he is Total Tranquillity–inward calm absorbed in itself, absorbed in the void of the Absolute, where all distinctions merge and dissolve, and all tensions are at rest. But on the other hand he is Total Activity –life's energy, frantic, aimless, and playful. These aspects are the dual manifestations of an absolutely non-dual, ultimate Reality. The two are represented side by side in the sanctuaries of

Shiva: the reality known to the enlightened ones, to the Buddhas, knowers, and yogīs, side by side with that enjoyed by the children of Māyā, who are still under the spell of the world.

It is extremely interesting to observe that among the few remains surviving to us from the Indus Civilization—coming down through a corridor of some six thousand years as echoes of a religiosity antedating the arrival of the Vedic Aryans, an antique religiosity, old as the pyramids of the Nile—the two aspects of the God are already revealed. Figure 42 shows a little faïence plaque from Mohenjo-Daro, on which is engraved a horned deity, seated like a yogī with his heels pressed close together, naked, having three faces, and with phallus erect. The personage wears many bracelets on his arms and a great fan-shaped headdress—perhaps the latter is the piled up, matted hair. He is seated on a little throne or altar, and is surrounded by two antelopes, an elephant, a tiger, a rhinoceros, and a buffalo. (The glyphs along the upper margin cannot be deciphered.) The figure resembles nothing so much as Shiva-Pashupati, "The Lord of Beasts." * Shiva-Natarāja, meanwhile, is powerfully suggested by the significant torso depicted in Figure 41. This is from the Indus Valley city of Harappa. The head is lost; so are the arms; so are the knee, shank, and foot of the left leg. All of these extremities were wrought separately and then fixed to the trunk by means of plugs which have since disintegrated. But the holes into which they were inserted are clearly to be seen. Evidently, it was for the sake of convenience that the figure was not carved from a single block of stone, and this probability supplies a hint as to how the posture of the missing limbs is to be imagined. They cannot have clung closely to the body; perhaps, by virtue of the plugs, they were capable of swinging to and fro. (The children's toys of Mohenjo-Daro and Harappa are equipped with such moving

---

* Cf. discussion by Sir John Marshall, *Mohenjo-Daro and the Indus Civilization* (London, 1931), Vol. I, pp. 52-6.

parts. See, for example, Figure 43.) Particularly significant is the point at which the left shank was affixed to the thigh: it is above the knee. The position suggests that the foot cannot have rested on the ground; it must have hung uplifted, as though in a posture of dance. In fact there is every reason to believe that this archaic torso represents a dancer, not very different in form from those of the much later Nataraja type.* The probability is that we have here a precious symptom of a continuity of tradition over a period of no less than four thousand years. The episode of the invading Aryans, their establishment of their Olympic pantheon of orthodox Vedic divinities, the gradual resurgence of the earlier Indian forms, and their definitive reassumption of power with the triumph of Vishnu, Shiva, and the Goddess over Indra, Brahmā, and their entourage, we must regard as nothing more than a titanic *incident,* which came to pass in the timeless theater of the Indian soul.

The life strength of symbols and symbolic figures is inexhaustible, especially when carried forward by a highly conservative, traditional civilization, such as that of India. Our conventional histories of the development of mankind, the growth of human institutions, and the progress of religion, virtues, and ideals, not infrequently misrepresent the situation totally, by describing as new departures the returns to power of archaic, archetypal forms.†
Very often, as during the greater part of the history of India, evidence for the continuity may be woefully lacking; the materials in which the forms were rendered—wood, largely, and clay

---

* The art of the Indus Civilization did not know the later oriental convention of images with many arms. This device, which was developed in India in medieval times, has immensely enriched the possibilities of iconographic communication.

† ["He who marvels that a formal symbol can remain alive not only for millennia, but that it can spring to life again after an interruption of thousands of years, should remind himself that the power from the spiritual world, which forms one part of the symbol, is eternal . . . It is the spiritual power that knows and wills, and manifests itself when and where its due time comes." (Walter Andrae, *Die ionische Säule, Bauform oder Symbol?* 1933, Schlusswort.)—AKC.]

—were perishable, and have simply disappeared. Oral traditions, furthermore, and the fleeting features of popular festivals, are practically impossible to reconstruct in detail for the centuries and centuries behind us. We have only the living present, and certain accidentally preserved relics—but the latter largely from the upper, official circles of society: how are we to dogmatize for mankind as a whole? Every so often tangible evidence appears—such as that which has suddenly been opened to us with the excavations of Harappa, Mohenjo-Daro and Chanhu-Daro—staggering the imagination with its demonstration of continuities never suspected by the historians. And we are forced to a more humble estimate of all our judgments of the past. We can never be certain but that in one or another of the innumerable undocumented centuries of human history, in one or another of the unexcavated hilltops of the world, there may not lurk some simple fact, which, if disclosed, would refute our least-questioned belief. Evidences of the existence in the third millennium B.C. of forms that were by our scholars thought to have evolved only very much later cannot, and must not, be lightly shrugged away. The vista of *duration* that they open, while it does not precisely refute everything that we are wont to say about progress and change, at least supplies to our accepted view a counter-view—suggesting spiritual continuities persisting through immense reaches of time.

It is, therefore, with a certain sense of the forever lost, that we must study the living traditions of the popular, and perhaps ageless, divinity, Shiva.* Associated with the Dancing Shiva there are to be found, today, many myths and legends. How far we might follow them into the past, could we but relive the buried centuries, we shall never know. Suffice to say, that in all probability, the traditions are immensely old.

---

* Obviously the *Sanskrit* appellation, Shiva, cannot have been applied to this figure in the pre-Aryan past; but the divinity can have been present under another name. "Shiva" means "the Beneficent, the Gracious, the Blessed One."

To begin with, there are two principal and antagonistic kinds of dance, corresponding to the benign and wrathful manifestations of the God. *Tāṇḍava,* the fierce, violent dance, fired by an explosive, sweeping energy, is a delirious outburst, precipitating havoc. On the other hand, *lāsya,* the gentle, lyric dance, is full of sweetness and represents the emotions of tenderness and love. Shiva is the perfect master of the two.

Shiva in his gentle aspect is Pashupati, "The Herdsman, the Owner of Cattle, Lord of the Animals." All beasts (*paśu*) are of his flock, both the wild and the tame. Furthermore, the souls of all men are the "cattle" of this herdsman. Thus the tender symbol of the herdsman watching his flock, which is familiar to us in the figure of Christ, the Good Shepherd, as represented in early Christian art,* is familiar also to the Shiva-devotee. As a member of the shepherd's flock, the worshiper realizes his relationship to the benign aspect of the august god.

In this way, the term *paśu* has come to denote "a follower of Shiva, a Soul." Specifically, *paśu* is a term signifying the uninitiated person, the general and lowermost grade of Shiva devotee. In a spiritual sense, such an uninitiated one is as dumb as a brute and must be goaded by the god. *Paśu,* then, represents the grade opposed to that higher one of spiritual evolution, *vīra,* "The Hero."

As early as the sixth century B.C. the term *vīra* had ceased to be used to denote the valorous knight of the feudal epic, the kingly warrior and hero of the battlefield and of the mythical combats with demons and monsters. The earlier usage is represented by the heroes of the feudal warfare of the *Mahābhārata* and by Rāma of the *Rāmāyaṇa,* conqueror of monsters and demons. But as understood, for example, in the sixth-century name

---

* Paintings, for instance, in the Roman Catacombs, and in the famous mosaic of Ravenna.

Mahāvīra,* *vīra* denotes the ascetic hero, the man perfectly shock-proof, impassive amidst the self-inflicted tortures of ascetic austerity, and amidst temptations and allurements, even threats of death, from without.

Among the followers of Shiva the vīra-grade of the devotee-initiate represents the state of the perfected ascetic, conqueror of the forces of nature, that "victor" who has overcome his cattle-nature and in the perfection of his asceticism is even equal to Shiva himself. The vīra has become the perfect yogī, a true spiritual Superman, a "man-hero," no longer merely the human beast.

The Tāndava-dance, the violent, phrenetic effusion of divine energies, bears traits suggesting some cosmic war-dance, designed to arouse destructive energies and to work havoc on the foe; at the same time, it is the triumphant dance of the victor. There is a myth, instructive in this connection, that represents Shiva as the conqueror of a great demon who had assumed the shape of an elephant. The god, having forced his opponent to dance with him, continued until the victim fell down dead, then flayed him, donned the skin as a kind of mantle, and finally, wrapped in this blood-dripping trophy, executed a horrendous dance of victory. A late but magnificent image representing this warrior-triumph in celebration of the annihilation of the elephant-demon (*gajāsura-samhāra*) is to be seen in the South Indian, seventeenth century, Natarāja Temple of Perūr. (Figure 39.) This is a facile creation in an extremely sophisticated style. The god wears a garland of skulls, and a skull is in his diadem. The two uppermost hands stretch out the skin of the elephant. The next pair of hands bears a pair of weapons, the noose (*pāśa*) and the hook (*aṅkuśa*). The third holds a tusk of the victim and a little hand-drum shaped like an hourglass with which the

---

* Mahāvīra, the restorer of the Jaina doctrine, was a contemporary of the Buddha. [But Mahāvīra, "great Hero," is already Indra's epithet in the Rig Veda, just as by implication (-*jit*) he is a "Conqueror" (*jina*), and these epithets are inherited alike in Jainism and Buddhism.—AKC.]

dancer is beating time. The lowermost pair of hands holds a trident (*triśūla*) and the almsbowl of the vagrant mendicant (*bhikṣāpātra*). In the countenance of the god is a dreamy yet deliberate, sly aloofness, as he enjoys the solemn, slow strides that are holding his delirious energy compressed.

This Shiva dancing in the elephant skin is a "terrific or wrathful apparition" (*ghora-mūrti*) of the god. The divine dancer is encompassed by the skin of his prey, as by a gruesome halo. The ponderous head of the victim, with its large ears, dangles at the bottom; the tiny tail is visible at the top; the four feet hang down at the sides. In the interior, the god extends his eight arms, in his measured, slow, and sophisticated dance. The trident and the other symbolic weapons characteristic of the hero-ruler are carried together with the alms bowl of the ascetic, symbol of the god's supreme aloofness. In his agility he is lizard-like; serpent-like in his slimness and grace.

This pattern represents a perfect, enigmatical blending of polar-opposites. In it we may sense the dionysiac ambiguity, the ominous smile, of the forces of life. Blood-dripping, gruesome, the flayed trophy-skin of the violated victim constitutes a sinister background. In a poem by Kālidāsa * it is told that even the Goddess-Spouse who watched the combat and the subsequent dance of her beloved husband felt alarm at this terrible sight. It sent the shivers up and down her spine. Against the sinister background, however, there flash the divine, youthful limbs, agile, delicate, and graceful, moving with their measured solemnity; and in these is the beautiful innocence of the first athletic powers of young manhood.

Four of the nine "moods" or "flavors" (*rasa*) of the Hindu system of rhetoric—four at least—are blended in this representation. They are the "heroic" (*vīra*), the "wild" (*raudra*), the

---

* *Meghadūta*, "The Cloud Messenger" (translated by Arthur W. Ryder in the Everyman's Library volume, *Shakuntala and Other Writings*).

"charming" (*śṛiṅgāra*), and the "loathsome" (*bībhatsa*); for Shiva contains and enacts all possible aspects of life, and his dance is a marvelous blending of opposites. The dance, like life itself, is a mixture of the terrific and the auspicious, a juxtaposition and unification of destruction, death, and vital triumph, the volcanic bursting-forth of the lavas of life. Here is a blending familiar to the Hindu mind, everywhere documented in Hindu art. It is understood as expressive of the Divine, which in its totality comprises all the goods and evils, beauties and horrors, joys and agonies, of our phenomenal life.

Another seventeenth century South Indian representation of Shiva dancing in the elephant skin appears in "The Great Temple" of Madura. (Figure 40.) Here, however, the attitude has become frozen into a sullen solemnity. The delirious dance of the victorious god has lost its bewitching, demonic agility; instead we find a somewhat static repose of threatening aloofness and terrific grandeur. The god seems to be withdrawn and absorbed in his own solitary majesty. This heavy, comparatively lifeless style is nearer than the other to perennial, primitive, local handicraft. The weight of matter, the solidity of the stone, and a pious pedantry of detail here assert themselves. The subtle art of the earlier periods * which knew how to convert solid material into a fleeting mirage, a sublime phantasmagoria expressive of the subtle nature of the bodies of the divine apparitions, has here evanesced, and we find asserting itself again the solid tangible matter of the primitive idol and the primitive fetish.

The striking motif of the Dancing God who forces the Elephant Demon to dance with him until he falls down dead, stricken by no weapon, afflicted by no deadly wound, reminds one of the Western motif of "The Dance of the Quick and the Dead." A company of bony specters invite blooming Youth, in

---

* Gupta art, Chālukya Art, the art of Bādāmī, Rāshtrakūta art, the art of Elūrā and of Elephanta, Pallava art, and the art of Māmallapuram.

174

the form of the maiden with rosy cheeks or the young soldier full
of vigor, to dance, and the thin, emaciated apparitions continue,
on and on, until their victim falls exhausted. The finite, limited
individual is no match for the eternal forces of destruction. But
on the other hand, destruction—Shiva—is only the negative aspect of unending life.

6.

The Face of Glory

THERE was once a great titan king called Jalandhara. By virtue
of extraordinary austerities he had accumulated to himself irresistible powers. Equipped with these, he had gone forth against
the gods of all the created spheres, and, unseating them, had
established his new order. His humiliating government was tyrannical, wasteful, careless of the traditional laws of the universe,
wicked and utterly selfish. In a tremendous and ultimate excess
of pride, Jalandhara sent a messenger-demon to challenge and
humble the High God himself, Shiva the creator, sustainer, and
destroyer of the world.

Now the messenger of Jalandhara was Rāhu, a monster whose
function is the eclipsing of the moon.* The moon—this gentle
luminary of the night, streaming with the cool milk that refreshes
the vegetable and animal worlds after their vital fluids have
been extracted by the scorching sun of the day—is a representative of the life-giving principle; the moon is the effulgent cup

---

* [This is a very complex subject. See, for example, Willy Hartner, "The Pseudo-
planetary Nodes of the Moon's Orbit in Hindu and Islamic Iconographies" in *Ars
Islamica* V, 1938; and my *Yakṣas,* II, Washington, 1931, Ch. 4, The Makara. The
Kīrttimukha as the terrible Face of God, who as the Sun and Death both generates
and devours his children, is analogous to the Greek Gorgoneion and the Chinese
T'ao t'ieh, the "Glutton."—AKC.]

from which the gods drink the Amrita, the elixir of immortality. Rāhu's relationship to the boon-bestowing orb was established in the remotest periods of prehistoric time, when the gods and titans, in the first days of the world, churned the cosmic Milky Ocean to extract from it the Amrita, the elixir of immortal life. Rāhu stole a first sip of the liquor, but was immediately beheaded by a stroke of Vishnu. The drink having passed through his mouth and neck, these were rendered immortal, but the severed body succumbed to the forces of decay. The head, ravenous for another taste, has been chasing the cup of the elixir, the moon, ever since. Eclipses come when he catches and swallows it; but the vessel only passes through the mouth and neck (there being no stomach any more to retain it) and reappears. Whereupon the chase is immediately resumed.

This Rāhu, then, was the demon sent by Jalandhara to humiliate the High God. At that time Shiva was on the point of abandoning his aloof and self-contemplative ascetic life to marry. The Goddess, his immortal Shakti, after a period of separation from him, had been recently reborn under the name and form of Pārvatī, the beautiful, moon-like daughter of the mountain king, Himālaya. Fine-featured, with long lotus-eyes, supple-waisted but with abundant hips, and with perfectly rounded breasts that crowded against each other ("she was bowed by the weight of the twin-spheres of the breasts, like a heavily laden fruit tree") the Lady of the Universe had assumed this human birth in order to be reunited with the person of the God, her eternal Lord, and to bring forth in the created world a son, Skanda, who was to become the God of War. The challenge brought by the messenger, Rāhu, was that Shiva should give up his shining jewel of a bride, "The Fairest Maiden of All the Worlds," and without further ado turn her over to the new master of existence, the titan tyrant, Jalandhara.

From the standpoint of the brahmin-theologian who committed the story to writing and handed it down, this impudent demand appears to be a sign of demonic blindness, sheer megalomania. How should it seem otherwise to the orthodox devotee who knows that whereas the demon-titan is only a powerful creature, no higher in rank than those secondary divinities who form part of the web of Māyā and represent specialized inflections of the energies of the world organism, Shiva is *īśvara*, "The Lord," the personalization of the Absolute? From another viewpoint, however, a viewpoint sanctioned by a great tradition of heroic myth and practice, the demand of Jalandhara, the "usurper" (who is actually the temporary lord of the realm of Māyā) is strictly legitimate, even utterly necessary, and should have been anticipated as a matter of course. For of what avail the conquest of the universe, if the crown-jewel, namely Woman, is not won too? *

When a country or town is conquered, it is looted, and the prize objects of booty are "women and gold." Without taking possession of the representatives of the female principle of the conquered realm—the principle that embodies Mother Earth, the very fertility of the soil that has been conquered—the victor would hardly feel himself victorious. He must inseminate sacrimentally the womb of the conquered country; that is the act, according to mythical thought, that puts the seal on the military conquest. So it was that when Persia was subdued by Alexander the Great and the last of the Achaemenids overcome, the young conqueror married the queens and daughters of the king, while the grandees of his suite and army took the daughters of the

---

* [It is thus, indeed, that Indra himself is often represented as seducing the Gandharva's wife Vāc, upon whose possession the victory depends and for whom the gods and titans are therefore always contending. She represents the kingdom, the power and the glory; but her seduction is a violation, and as is emphasized in well known hymns of the Rig Veda and Atharva Veda, "the Brahman's wife" must be restored, i.e., by the Regnum to the Sacerdotium, by an act of submission which recognizes that it is only as the agent and viceroy of the Sacerdotium that the King's *fiat* can be legitimately enunciated. Jalandhara's is, as Dr. Zimmer says, a "*tyrant*-claim," and it is as the would-be tyrant, and not as king, that Jalandhara's satanic claims to the lordship of the universe are condemned.—AKC.]

nobility. The victory was sealed with an earthly re-enactment of the formula of the myth. Oedipus, after he had unknowingly done away with the elderly and inefficient king of Thebes, Laios, his father, and then liberated the city from the curse of the monstrous Sphinx, succeeded to the throne by marrying the queen-widow, Jocasta, who chanced to be his mother. And this he did as a matter of course, that is to say, as a matter of established ritual. There was no call for any love affair, no need for the passionate or tender involvement on which the Freudians interminably dote. Oedipus simply would not have been the real lord of Thebes had he not taken full possession of the royal woman who was the personification of the soil and realm. In the same way, Jalandhara could have been no real overlord of the universe without conquering, marrying, and mastering "The Fairest Female of the Three Worlds" (*tripura-sundarī*). The possession of her, the cosmic Shakti, the living embodiment of the principle of beauty and youth eternal, is the ultimate quest, the very highest prize. She it is who is ever desired, won, and lost again in the endlessly revolving strife for world dominion between the demon-giants and the gods.*

But the myths of the Purānas come down to us reshaped by a definitely post-heroic, anti-tragic age of Indian religion and philosophy. The stories themselves are of immense antiquity. Before receiving their present form the wonderful adventures were told and retold through many centuries. The civilization of India passed, meanwhile, through prodigious transformations: heroic ages of feudal barons, periods of vigorous spiritual search, golden eras of princely munificence and the most sophisticated artistry, catastrophes of invasion—the Huns, the swordsmen of Islam, the armies of the West—disintegrations and reintegrations of the ageless, life-tenacious, primal heritage of the rich

---

* Compare the Eddic-Wagnerian contest of the gods and the giants for the possession of Freya, The Fairest Maiden of the World, bloom and youth, guardian of the golden apples of eternal life.

land. The more recent ages—those that have left to us the bulk of our materials and have stood, so to speak, as censor and redactor of the great heritage of the past—are characterized by a devout and distinctly anti-heroic quality of soul. The old tales have been edited, commentated, and revised, by sectarian theologians, zealous worshipers not so much of the "Ubiquitous Unknown" as of this or that divine personification of the Absolute—Vishnu, Shiva, the Goddess: and these devotees have been not only solicitous for their special god's prestige, but radically suspicious of the joys and agonies of unregenerate, secular man. Their versions of the ancient tales dwell dismally long on the blindness, infatuation, and megalomania of the demon-tyrants, ridden by the active and terrific energies of life, who labored and failed in their warrior-quest of "women and gold." Adventures which in Greek or Nordic mythology and drama would have appeared as tragedies (and which in their now forgotten, earlier Indian forms must have been fired by at least a spark of the tragic pity and terror) stand transformed by these pious hands into sectarian mystery plays "to the greater glory of the god," *ad majorem dei gloriam.* The Tragic Hero appears here, on a cosmic scale, as the Giant Fool.*

We are expected, therefore, to feel little sympathy—only a cosmic disdain—for Jalandhara, the world-conquering tyrant-demon, when he broaches his claim to the highest trophy of all life. We are not to experience the claim as a counterpart of our own highest human hope and effort. On the contrary, since we are the devotees, children, and beneficiaries of the god, we must needs per-

---

* This leads us to the observation that theologians very rarely produce first rate poetry or art. Their outlook on life's ambiguous and ambivalent features is narrowed by their dogmatism. They lack (this is a result of their training) that cynicism and that perilous innocence, candid and childlike, which are basic requirements for anyone dealing with myths. They lack (and this is their virtue, their duty) that touch of "amorality" which must form at least part of one's intellectual and intuitive pattern, if one is not to fall prey to predetermined bias and be cut off from certain vital, highly ironical, and disturbing insights.

ceive in the tyrant-claim only impudence, brutality, and blasphemy, a ridiculous self-aggrandizement. The next turn of the story is calculated to support us in this wholesome, if unadventurous, attitude, and to recommend to us then a potent talisman or cult-object, "The Face of Glory" (*kīrttimukha*), divinely guaranteed to defend all true believers, our homes and our hearts, from the tyrant-forces of the ravenous world.

The moment Rāhu tendered Jalandhara's demand that the Goddess should be delivered to him—the Shakti of the universe to become the tyrant's principal queen—Shiva countered the colossal challenge. From the spot between his two eyebrows—the spot called "The Lotus of Command" (*ājñā-cakra*), where the center of enlightenment is located and the spiritual eye of the advanced seer is opened—the god let fly a terrific burst of power, which explosion immediately took the physical shape of a horrendous, lion-headed demon. The alarming body of the monster was lean and emaciated, giving notice of insatiable hunger, yet its strength was resilient and obviously irresistible. The apparition's throat roared like thunder; the eyes burnt like fire; the mane, disheveled, spread far and wide into space.* Rāhu was aghast.

Rāhu, the messenger, was adept, however, in the techniques of supernatural power-politics. When the incarnate burst-of-wrath made a rush at him, he replied with the only possible remaining move: he took refuge in the all-protecting fatherhood and benevolence of the Almighty, Shiva himself. This created a new and very difficult situation; for the god immediately bade the monster spare the petitioner, and the half-lion was left with a painful hunger but no proper food on which to feast it. The

---

* There is in the mythology of Vishnu a comparable moment, when a certain demon-king, Golden Garment by name (*hiranya-kaśipu*), challenges the power of the god. Vishnu bursts from a pillar of the king's own palace in a "Half-man, Half-lion" manifestation (*narasiṁha*, the fourth incarnation or avatār of Vishnu), and the blaspheming atheist is torn to tatters in a trice.

creature asked the god to assign some victim on which the torment might be appeased.

In Indian mythology, from the Vedas down, this power-principle is constantly reiterated: whenever a demon, by command of a god, is forced, for one reason or another, to release its legitimate prey, some substitute must be provided. Some new victim has to be offered to assuage and stay the voraciousness of this new power-body at large in the reaches of the world. In the present instance, Shiva was equal to the occasion. Shiva suggested that the monster should feed on the flesh of its own feet and hands. Forthwith, to this incredible banquet that incredible incarnation of blind voraciousness proceeded. Ravished by its congenital hunger, it ate and ate. And having devoured not only its feet and hands, but its arms and legs as well, it was still unable to stop. The teeth went on through its own belly and chest and neck, until only the face remained.

Embodied in that monster was the wrath of the Supreme Being, the destructive power of the Universal God, who, under the form of Shiva-Rudra (*rudra*, "The Howler, The Roarer"; this was the Vedic name of Shiva, and refers to his world-annihilating aspect), periodically annihilates the created universe, the wrath and hunger of the cosmic fire that, at the world's end, reduces everything to ash and then itself is quenched by torrential rain. Hence the fantastic spectacle was a dear sight to the god, and one with which he was in essential agreement. "Thou art my beloved son," he might well have exclaimed with satisfaction, "in whom I am well pleased." He watched silently, but with supreme delight, the bloodcurdling, nightmarish procedure, and then, gratified by the vivid manifestation of the self-consuming power of his own substance, he smiled upon that creature of his wrath—which had reduced its own body, joint by joint, to the nothingness of only a face—and benignantly declared: "You will be known, henceforth, as 'Face of Glory' (*kīrttimukha*), and I

181

ordain that you shall abide forever at my door. Whoever neglects to worship you shall never win my grace." *

Kīrttimukha (Figure 51) first was a special emblem of Shiva himself and a characteristic element on the lintels of Shiva temples. (In our discussion of Figure 34,† we called attention to the "Face of Glory" at the summit of the composition.) Presently, then, the "Face" began to be used indiscriminately on various parts of Hindu shrines as an auspicious device to ward off evil; it is incorporated generally into decorative friezes. Kīrttimukha appears also in Shiva's crown of matted hair—presumably in accordance with another version of the story, where the monster was rewarded by being inserted into Shiva's locks. In this position it developed into an ornamental finial for the upper decoration of images, and came thence to figure at the summit of the aureole (*prabhā-maṇḍala*) the so-called "Gate of Splendor" (*prabhā-toraṇa*), at the back of images. With repetition, Kīrttimukha became conventionalized and presently was combined with a pair of sea monsters (*makara*) that commonly serve the same function as himself. Like the Gorgon head in the tradition of the Greeks (but, as we have seen, with a totally different background of legend), Kīrttimukha serves primarily as an apotropaic demon-mask, a gruesome, awe-inspiring guardian of the threshold. The votary, however—the orthodox devotee—greets the "Face" with confidence and faith; for he knows that Kīrttimukha is an active portion of the substance of the divinity himself, a sign and agent of his protective, fiend-destroying wrath.

Particularly in Javanese art the "Face of Glory" is conspicuous. It figures there side by side with other grotesque and threatening creatures of Shiva's suite—demons armed with clubs (the primitive weapon, the phallic symbol), demons wearing (like their master) serpents as bracelets and instead of the traditional

---

* *Skānda Purāna,* Vol. II, Viṣṇukāṇḍa, Kārttikamāsa Mahātmya, Chapter 17. Cf. *Rūpam* I (Calcutta, Jan. 1920), pp. 11-19.
† Cf. pp. 137-9, *supra.*

"sacred thread." * (Figure 52.) The aboriginal traits in the Javanese people, who became converted to Hinduism in medieval times, delight in these figures, at once awe-inspiring and humorous. Divinities, images, of this kind allow for a kind of jocular intimacy with the powers of destruction. They represent the "other side," the wrathful aspect (*ghora-mūrti*), of the well-known and loved divine powers. When properly propitiated, such presences give support to life and ward away the demons of disease and death.

This ambivalent, wise mode of representation is characteristic of the whole range of the Shivaite pantheon. There is a wonderful life-worthy humor in these forms. Regard, for example, the beloved and immensely popular Ganesha, "Lord of the Hosts," debonair son of Shiva and the Supreme Goddess and captain of the deity's jaunty suite. Figure 53 is a typical representation—a work from India proper, not from Java. In the upper corners are flying two representatives of the suite (*gana*),† and by the pedestal is crouching the divinity's vehicle (*vāhana*), the rat. As the rat makes it way through all obstacles into the security of the granary, there to consume the rice stores of the village household, and as the elephant in the jungle forges mightily ahead, trampling and uprooting the vegetation standing in its way, so Ganesha, "The Lord of Obstacles" (*vighna-īśvara*), breaks a path for the devotee. At the outset of undertakings of every kind, he is invoked. In his left hand he here carries a bowl, full either of rice, on which he feeds, or of jewels, pearls, and corals, which he

---

* The sacred thread (*upavīta*) is worn by all upper caste Hindus. It is a cotton thread of three strands, running from the left shoulder across the body to the right hip. It is first placed on a youth by his guru at his ceremony of initiation, which takes place, usually, when he is between eight and twelve years old.

[As explained in the Jābāla Upanishad, the "sacred thread" is the outward and visible symbol of the Sūtrātman, Thread-spirit, on which all the individual existences in the universe are strung like gems, and by which all are inseparably linked to their source.—AKC.]

† The name *ganeśa*, "Lord of the Hosts," is compounded of *gana* (hosts) and *īśa* (lord). In Sanskrit, *a* and *i* run together to give *e*.

showers on his devotees. Paunchy and well-off, he is the bestower of earthly prosperity and well-being.

Blessed is he who faces this pot-bellied, irresistible son of the Goddess from before, but woe to him on whom the divinity turns its back. Figure 54 shows the rear of a Javanese figure of Ganesha, from the thirteenth century A.D. Whereas the auspicious, benevolent aspect (sundara-mūrti), which greets the votary who approaches from before, is full of humor and genial good will, this reverse of the medal, the terrific-destructive phase (ghora-mūrti), known only to those for whom the ways of life remain closed, is a terrifying, devouring monster, exhibiting carnivorous teeth. This monster is Kīrttimukha, "The Face of Glory," a protection to the holy, but to the impious even such a sign of wrath as it was to Rāhu.

Kīrttimukha is called Vanaspati,* "Lord-Spirit of the Woods, Patron of the Wilderness, King of Vegetation." The forest holds all kinds of dangers and demons, enemies and diseases, in contrast to the safety-zones of the village and home, which are under the protection of the house gods and village gods. On Javanese temples Kīrttimukha is a popular ornament, where it serves as a deterrent and protective symbol. This monster is a match for any evil. The principle symbolized in its eloquent deed, once grasped by the mind and assimilated by the faculties, will protect against both spiritual and physical disaster in the deepest darknesses of the jungle of the world. It represents the presence of the Lord in the moment of disaster; his readiness to take to himself and to comfort with his protection even those who have been his enemies; the paradox of life in death; and the wisdom of self-abandonment to the Lord.

---

* [Originally and properly a name of Agni, with whose devouring, Vārunya aspect that of the Kīrttimukha can be equated.—AKC.]

7.

The Destroyer of the Three Towns

BEFORE turning to the mysteries of Devī, "The Goddess," let us consider one more of the "Festival Aspects" of the great divinity whose "Fixed or Fundamental Figure" is the lingam. Figure 55 is a relief from Elūrā, dating from the eighth century A.D., in which Shiva is exhibited under the guise of Tripurāntaka, "He Who Puts an End to the Three Towns or Fortresses." This is the God as the conqueror and liberator of the entire world.

According to an ancient Vedic conception, the universe comprises three worlds (*triloka*), (1) the earth, (2) the middle space or atmosphere, and (3) the firmament or sky. These are called "The Three Towns" (*tripura*).* Shiva as Tripurāntaka puts an end (*anta*, related to the English, "end") to the Three Towns. The story goes, that, once again in the course of history, the demons, titans, or anti-gods (*asura*), half-brothers and eternal rivals of the proper rulers of the world, had snatched to themselves the reins of government. As usual, they were led by an austere and crafty tyrant, who, like Jalandhara, had acquired special power by dint of years of fierce self-discipline. Maya was this tyrant's name.† And when he had taken to himself the entirety of the created cosmos, he constructed three mighty strongholds, one in the firmament, one on earth, and one in the atmosphere between. By a feat of magic he then amalgamated his three fortresses into one—a single, prodigious center of demon-chaos and world-tyranny, practically unassailable. And through the power of his yoga he brought it about that this mighty keep should never be conquered unless pierced by a single arrow.

---

* Hence, the Supreme Goddess, Devī, she who is the female personification of the total Energy of creation, is termed "The Fairest of the Three Towns" (*tripurasundarī*), i.e., Our Lady of the Universe.
† Not to be confused with Māyā.

There was no bowman, either living or imaginable, who would be capable of discharging a shaft gigantic enough to pierce the amalgamated demon-citadel of the world. Indra, the rain and thunder king, overlord of the gods, Agni the Fire God, Vāyu the Wind God, were all efficient, decent specialists, but no match for such an assignment. None of the great Olympians, the brilliant denizens of Mount Meru, now driven from their paradise into the bitter void of exile, could ever hope to muster the power to rive those defenses.

Shiva, according to the Vedic tradition, was in olden time a huntsman; and he was armed with a bow and arrow. At a very early period, when he was still excluded from the respectable and lofty community of the Olympians—the protectors of the human settlement as distinct from the unsettled jungle—Shiva was regarded as the lord of the forest, the master of the animals of the wilderness.* Wandering among these with his primitive weapon, he stood as their anthropomorphic patron. He was the lord, also, of the ghosts and specters that inhabit and make very dangerous those places beyond the village compound. His retinue was composed of the departed souls, and these passed, howling, in his wake.†

The bow of Shiva had, in the past, accomplished celebrated deeds. For example, when the primeval father of creatures, Prajāpati, had desired to commit incest with his daughter, the lovely maiden, Dawn (an old, old story of the first father and the first daughter), it was Shiva who had been called upon by the gods to intervene and punish the offending progenitor by employing this bow. And so now again it is he who is petitioned

---

* Compare the early relationship of the Greek Dionysos to the lofty community supervised by Zeus. In Alexandrian times the Greeks equated Shiva with Dionysos.
† As Lord of the Deceased, Shiva is akin to the Nordic god, Wode-Wodan, the "Wild Huntsman," who, accompanied by his roaring spirit-host, speeds by on the "Wild Hunt." With the christianization of the European pagans, Wodan's beneficent aspect passed to Saint Nicholas (Santa Claus), who gallops over the roof-tops, at the time of the Winter Solstice, dispensing boons to all his devotees.

to intervene to re-establish the divine order of the universe. His work, this time, is to be the annihilation, with a single shaft, of the universal stronghold of the demons, Tripura.

The Elūrā relief shows the divine archer soaring forward in an aerial chariot drawn by prancing steeds. The left hand lifts the bow; the right, with bent elbow, having drawn the string to the lobe of the right ear and to the full length of the arrow, has just released the powerful missile. The magnificence of the gesture forebodes the magnificent result. Shiva's charioteer is the four-headed Brahmā, dignified and beautiful. With a charming expression of earnest attention and confidence the latter concentrates upon his task. Meanwhile the herculean hero, vigorous and dynamic though devoid of the compactness and heaviness of earthly warriors, dashes forward from the background of the relief, with the lightness and the irresistible power of a lightning flash, in a swift, triumphant gesture, without static substantiality. The magic demon-castle falls and its folk pass again into oblivion; the world, once again, is released from the toils of evil; the round of history swings into its course. The tyrannies of the fearful yet fearsome Ego, brutal with inconsequential ambitions and lusts, are dissolved at a stroke. The energies of universal existence, freely pouring again from the transcendental sources, break through all the worlds, and the cosmos sings with the tingle of regenerated life. Shiva's arrow is the vehicle of his energy no less than the lingam: the two are the same.

Along the walls of his major sanctuaries this great god's heroic deeds are displayed. In both oral and literary tradition they are retold. Priests and sages at the centers of pilgrimage, the shrines and temples, unfold the panorama of the god's career throughout the course of the mythological history of the world. Yet reposeful, blissful, beyond repose and bliss, transcendent, unknown and unknowable, beyond even the Twofold wonder of the God and Goddess, Lingam and Yoni, Arrow and Tripura, dwells the One Without a Second, the Absolute. This is that Brahman-

Atman, which is intended in all the images and tales. This is that Bindu,* which is invisible yet taught through all the visible interdelvings of the triangles. This is that vitality out of which the Phenomenon of the Expanding Form proceeds in irrepressible power. Brahman, the pregnant neuter, is a plenitude—not male or female, good or evil, but male *and* female, good *and* evil. Shiva is its personification. Every flash from the limbs of the whirling Yogī-God, every arrow from Shiva's bow, is quintessentially identical with that divine substance of eternal repose and peace.

---

* Cf. p. 147, *supra.*

CHAPTER FIVE

THE GODDESS

1.

The Origin of the Goddess

THE story of Kīrttimukha shows that the violent emotion of a god can be projected or externalized in the shape of an autonomous monster. Such apparitions abound in the mythological annals of India. Shiva's power of destruction is precipitated all around him in the horde of his wrathful "host": a swarm of diminutive Shivas, known as "Rudras," after the Vedic appellation of the god. The fury of Devī, the Supreme Goddess, may be projected as a ravenous lion or tiger. In Figure 57 she appears in the form of a black demoness, slavering over a battlefield in man-destroying wrath; this is a materialization of the exterminating aspect of the Mother of the World. In the same way, a curse can become personified. According to a celebrated myth, which developed in India under the post-Vedic, brahminical theologians, the king of the gods, Indra, became guilty of a terrible sin when he slew the limbless dragon, Vritra, in order to release from its coils the waters of the cosmos. Reckoning the gods and titans as members of the brahmin caste, the later commentators judged that in destroying Vritra, Indra had become guilty of the most heinous of all possible crimes, namely the slaying of a brahmin. A myth developed, representing the god-hero as pursued by an implacable ogress who personified the curse of his crime.*

---

* [The dismemberment of Vritra, by which the one was made into many, at the first sacrifice which was also the act of creation, is Indra's and the gods' original sin (*kilbiṣa*), because of which the Regnum has ever since been excluded from the

This principle of projection or externalization is invoked to account for the first appearance of the Goddess herself, in a magnificent myth reported in "The Text of the Wondrous Essence of the Goddess" (devī-māhātmya).* She is described as an unconquerable, sublime warrior-maid, who came into being out of the combined wraths of all the gods gathered in council. The occasion of the miracle was one of those dark moments for the gods, when a demon-tyrant was threatening to undo the world. This time, not even Vishnu or Shiva could avail. The titan was a colossal monster named Mahisha, in the shape of a prodigious water-buffalo bull.

The gods, under the leadership of Brahmā, had taken refuge in Vishnu and Shiva. They had described the case of the victorious demon and implored the assistance of the twofold All-Highest. Vishnu and Shiva swelled with wrath. The other divinities also, swelling with the power of their indignation, stood about. And immediately, their intense powers poured forth in fire from their mouths. Vishnu, Shiva, and all the gods sent forth their energies, each according to his nature, in the form of sheets and streams of flame. These fires all rushed together, combining in a flaming cloud which grew and grew, and meanwhile gradually condensed. Eventually it assumed the shape of the Goddess. She was provided with eighteen arms.

Upon beholding this most auspicious personification of the supreme energy of the universe, this miraculous amalgamation of all their powers, the gods rejoiced, and they paid her worship as their general hope. In her, "The Fairest Maid of the Three

---

drinking of "what the Brahmans mean by Soma, of which none tastes on earth," otherwise than by the transubstantiation of an analogous draught; and for which an expiation must be made by an ultimate reintegration of the many into one. Both processes, of evolution and involution, are perpetually reenacted in the Sacrifice, whether as ritually and visibly celebrated or as mentally performed throughout one's life.—AKC.]

* Mārkandeya Purāṇa, 81-93. This Purāna is the most famous of the many myth-collections describing the character and deeds of the Goddess.

Towns" (*tripura-sundarī*), the perennial, primal Female, all the particularized and limited forces of their various personalities were powerfully integrated. Such an overwhelming totalization signified omnipotence. By a gesture of perfect surrender and fully willed self-abdication they had returned their energies to the primeval Shakti, the One Force, the fountain head, whence originally all had stemmed. And the result was now a great renewal of the original state of universal potency. When the cosmos first unfolded into a system of strictly differentiated spheres and forces, Life Energy was parceled out into a multitude of individuated manifestations. But these now had lost their force. The mother of them all, Life Energy itself as the primeval maternal principle, had reabsorbed them, eaten them back into the universal womb. She now was ready to go forth in the fullness of her being.

Figure 56 is an illumination from a late manuscript of the *Devī-Māhātmya*, representing the host of the gods making the cosmically significant gesture of abdicating, willingly abdicating, their various masculine attitudes—royal, valiant, and heroic—in order that the titan-demon may be destroyed. Into the hands of the Supreme Goddess they deliver their various weapons, utensils, ornaments, and emblems, these containing their particularized energies and traits. Into the all-comprehending source out of which they themselves originally evolved, they now merge their disparate natures and disparate powers of action. Shiva, the ascetic, is shown in the upper left hand corner, handing over the trident. Facing him, in the upper right, is the four-headed Brahmā, giving up his alms bowl and the manuscript of the magic wisdom of the Vedas. In the central foreground is Kāla, the God of Time, extending to the Goddess a sword and a shield. At his right stands the legendary father of the Goddess, the mountain king Himālaya, with the lion that she is to ride.

Figure 59 is a representation of "The Goddess slaying the Buffalo-demon" (*devī mahiṣāsura-mārdinī*). It is a seventh century relief from Māmallapuram, in the delicate and spirited Pallava style. The works of this Pallava period, though vigorous, are very gentle; in representing brutal dramatic scenes, such as that of the present battle, they tend to avoid the moment of the climax, and seek to suggest their point with restraint and indirectness. The Goddess is here shown advancing, seated on the lion and accompanied by the exultant gods. The adversary, gigantic and grotesque, is sulkily yielding ground. The final triumph is not depicted. Yet it is obviously beyond question. The brilliant amazon, provided with the weapons of all the gods and stimulated by their hymns of praise, is the representative of all the affirmative forces of the universe. The demon is already hopeless; his massive head and club, suggesting darkness, violence, and resentment, are about to fall.

First annihilating the army of the titan, the Goddess roped the mighty buffalo-form with a noose. The demon escaped, however, emerging from the buffalo body in the form of a lion. Immediately, the Goddess beheaded the lion, whereupon Mahisha, by virtue of his Māyā-energy of self-transformation, escaped again, now in the form of a hero with a sword. Ruthlessly the Goddess riddled this new embodiment with a shower of arrows. But then the demon stood before her as an elephant, and with his trunk reached out and seized her. He dragged her towards him, but she severed the trunk with the stroke of a sword. The demon returned, now, to his favorite shape—that of the giant buffalo shaking the universe with the stamping of its hoofs. But the Goddess scornfully laughed, and again roared with a loud voice of laughter at all his tricks and devices. Pausing a moment, in full wrath, she lifted to her lips, serenely, a bowl filled with the inebriating, invigorating, liquor of the divine life-force, and while she sipped the matchless drink, her eyes turned red. The buffalo-demon, uprooting mountains with his horns, was flinging them against her, shouting defiantly at her the while, but with her arrows she was shattering them to dust. She called out to the shouting monster: "Shout on! Go on shouting one moment more, you fool, while I sip my fill of this delicious brew. The gods soon will be crying out for joy, and you shall lie murdered at my feet."

Even while she spoke, the Goddess leapt into the air, and from above came down on the demon's neck. She dashed him to the earth and sent the trident through his neck. The adversary attempted once again to abandon the buffalo-body, issuing from its mouth in the shape of a hero with a sword; but he had only half emerged when he was caught. He was half inside the buffalo and half outside, when the Goddess, with a swift and terrific stroke, beheaded him, and he died.

This lively series of transformations is an excellent example of the mythological trait of externalization or projection. The buffalo-demon, employing his Māyā-power, projects his vital energy into new forms. His aggressiveness, his ambition, his will to victory, relinquish shape after shape, in order to survive. The character of the projections derives from the nature of the energy in play. Shiva's wrath assumed the form of Kīrttimukha. The wrath of the company of the gods produced the invincible goddess of the many arms. So now, the supranormal energies of the world-tyrant, gathered through years of inhuman austerity and self-mastery, powerful enough to unseat the gods and bring the universe to heel, break swiftly and cleverly into form after form.

Vital energy of body and soul, when aroused, flows forth, becomes externalized, in shapes wrathful or beneficent, demonic or divine, depending upon the nature of the occasion. The battleground of the universe is filled by the gods with such temporary externalizations or projections. Furthermore, the universe itself is at most but such a transformation—a transformation or externalization of the Absolute. In the myths celebrating Shiva, Shakti is the materialization of the vital power of her spouse. According to the Vishnu formula, the Goddess is the anthropomorphic counterpart of the cosmic golden lotus: Vishnu puts forth the lotus-calix and thus begins the evolution, the unfolding of the spheres of the world—these to become peopled, presently, with creatures, who in turn are but energy-transformations. Vishnu, recumbent, by sending space forth from himself and then filling it with the process of the universe, simply projects the powers that he has been harboring in his belly. The world-process is the materialization of Vishnu's dream.

The lesson may be read psychologically, as applying to ourselves, who are not gods but limited beings. The constant projection and externalization of our specific shakti (vital energy) is our "little universe," our restricted sphere and immediate environment, whatever concerns and affects us. We people and color the indifferent, neutral screen with the movie-figures and dramas of the inward dream of our soul, and fall prey then to its dramatic events, delights, and calamities. The world, not as it is in itself but as we perceive it and react upon it, is the product of our own Māyā or delusion. It can be described as our own more or less blind life-energy, producing and projecting demonic and beneficent shapes and appearances. Thus we are the captives of our own Māyā-Shakti and of the motion picture that it incessantly produces. Whenever we are entangled and enmeshed in vital, passionate issues, we are dealing with the projections of our own substance. That is the spell of Māyā. That is the spell of creative, life-engendering, life-maintaining energy. That is the spell of nescience, "not knowing better."

In so far as this is true, the shapes and figures projected by the angered and embattled Hindu gods represent a very revealing psychological insight, in fact they amount to a philosophy and a metaphysic. The Highest Being is the lord and master of Māyā. All the rest of us—the lower gods, the demons, human beings—are the victims of our own individual Māyā. We fall prey to the spell of our own vitality as it infects us with its blindness, passion, and obsessions. Its processes in our psyche are autonomous, beyond our control; our reactions to them are compelled. Our state is, thus, one of serfdom and bondage to the life-supporting, life-rushing spell of Māyā-Shakti. Were this not the case, we should not be *individuals* at all; we should have no history, no biography. The very essence of our personal life is our life-illusion.

Indra was prompted by his personal Māyā to believe in his own magnificence, and felt compelled to build his lordly residence on a plan ever increasing in dimensions. To liberate man from such a spell, the thralldom of his own inherent shakti, the Māyā of the purposes and pursuits of his existence, the glowing tints of desirability and fearsomeness, terror and delight, that color for him the objects of his environment, is the principal aim of all the great Indian philosophies. In contradistinction to the modern philosophies of the West, which are purely intellectual pursuits, clarifying, labeling, describing, and systematizing the contents of human thought, Indian wisdom, based as it is on the thought-transcending experiences of yoga, aims at a total transmutation of human nature and at an altogether new awareness both of oneself and of the world. Indian thought aims to release men from the spellbound acceptance of the projections and externalizations of their own shakti—the productions of their own Māyā, their own subjective, phenomenal, emotional "reality." What it seeks is to change the serf of Māyā into a lord of Māyā, comparable to the Highest Being, to God personified either in Vishnu or in Shiva. Indian philosophy seeks seriously —and with a will to results—to make men divine through yoga and enlightenment; divine, even above those divinities who, like Indra, remain tented under the net of their own Māyā.

Indian symbols of art voice the same truth as Indian philosophy and myth. They are signals along the way of the same pilgrim's progress, directing human energies to the same goal of transmutation. Our task, therefore, as students of Indian myth and symbol, is to understand the abstract conceptions of India's philosophical doctrines as a kind of intellectual commentary on what stands crystallized and unfolded in the figures and patterns of symbolism and art, and, conversely, to read the symbols as the pictorial script of India's ultimately changeless wisdom.

For example, in such a case as that of Figure 58 we must strive to grasp the sense of the peculiar attitude of the Goddess while she slays the buffalo-demon. This is perhaps the most magnificent of the representations of Durgā Mahishāsura-mārdinī. It is a work of classical Javanese art. The classical art of Java of the eighth century A.D. and the centuries following, stems from southern India. Its seeds were planted by immigrants sailing from the Malabar shore. Not only for Javanese art, but also for the early Khmer art of Cambodia, the example is set by the Pallava style of India proper, and the finest of the colonial masterpieces match the achievements of the motherland. Furthermore, the peculiar tendencies of Pallava art are continued in the aims and style of the classical Hindu art of Java. Elements of violence and cruelty are avoided, mitigated, keyed down; the dramatic, climactic element is sublimated into a serene grandeur; sensuality is subtilized into a spiritual charm and gracefulness. The bulky body of such a demon as the fierce buffalo-adversary here shows nothing of threatening fierceness; it is subdued to an almost friendly appearance. The titan is so reduced that he becomes a fine farm-specimen of the docile, phlegmatic, ruminant, bovine species. And the desperate demon-hero who emerges for a last stand from the bull-shape, exhibits, with his elaborate hair-do, a grotesquely feminine loveliness. He is wholly resigned to his doom at the hands of the Goddess.

She has caught the demon by the hair and is about to deal the death-blow, the heroic stroke that is to save the world. But in the features of the great victress there is no trace of wrathful emotion; she is steeped in the serenity of eternal calm. Though the deed in time and space is bound to be accomplished, the expression on the countenance of the Goddess minimizes, indeed annihilates, its importance. For her the whole course of

196

this universe, including her own apparition in the role of its rescuer, is but part of a cosmic dream. It is only a feature of the universal display of Māyā. Though the Goddess, as the supreme divine being, assumes a form and plays a part in the dream-drama of the universe and playfully enacts the leading role at a great climax of the piece, nevertheless, she behaves as someone might who was playing the role of hero in his own dream, fully aware meanwhile that he is only dreaming. Fundamentally and consciously this presence remains totally unconcerned with her own triumphant manifestation. Her splendid countenance, vigorous and graceful, dreamy and far away, is comparable in this respect to the enigmatic mask of the dancing Shiva.

2.

The Island of Jewels

SHIVA and Devī, Shiva and his consort with the many names—Kalī, Durgā, Pārvatī, Chandī, Chāmundā, Umā, Satī, etc.—are regarded as the primeval twofold-personalization of the Absolute. They are the first and primal unfolding of the neuter Brahman into the opposites of the male and the female principles. The literary religious tradition of the Tantra represents an unending dialogue between these two, each alternately teaching and asking questions of the other. Through this dialogue the secret essence of the Brahman is made known to human understanding, and instruction is given in the means for approaching it by ritual and yoga—ritual remaining within and yoga going beyond the natural, inborn limitations of the individualized human consciousness as beclouded by the shakti of Māyā.

There are many representations of the sacred union of the Two-in-One. We have already discussed Figure 34. Figure 60 shows Shiva and his queen-consort sitting in state in their mountain home on Mount Kailāsa. The perfect serenity and timeless harmony of the couple is emphasized in this relief by their response to an attempt of a demon to shake their Olympus from below. The villain of this piece is Rāvana, who in the *Rāmāyana* appears as the antagonist of Rāma; as a great foe of the godly powers, he has been imprisoned in the netherworld and is held down by the towering weight of Shiva's mountain. Here he is shown suddenly trying to break free. He is shaking the mountain and the quivering has been felt. The goddess in a graceful, semi-recumbent posture, turns to Shiva, as if in a sudden access of fear, and grasps his arm. But the great god remains unmoved and by calmly pressing down his foot holds all secure. In spite of Pārvatī's lively gesture of anxiety, an atmosphere of safety prevails, not to be disturbed by the world-shaking demon who rocks the universe with his twenty arms. As evidence of the character of the divine couple we have here not the dramatic triumph of the godly principle through a hero-manifestation in one of the vivid, ever-recurrent battles of the cosmogonic round, but an undramatic, almost anti-dramatic, vision of their unconquerable grandeur. They are beyond every earthly assault —beyond even the superhuman-demonic—absolutely secure. This is an eighth century work from the Kailāsanātha Temple at Elūrā.

In the eighteenth century miniature reproduced in Figure 61 Shiva and Pārvatī are again in their solitary resort: this time we see a honeymoon-idyll. Nāndī, the milk-white bull, Shiva's animal representation and vehicle, is in the foreground. Shiva's staff with the trident is in the background. The god is girded with the typical loin-cloth of the brahmin-ascetic, a black antelope-skin, and wears in his matted hair the crescent; serpents take the place of bracelets and the other usual ornaments. The couch of the lovers is a tiger-skin, the classic seat-cover of the yogī. Not only the opposition of the male and the female but also that of the ascetic and the perfect husband-lover we discover here transcended. All polarities whatsoever stem from the supernal non-dual duality of this timeless, world-central scene of bliss. Kailāsa is the mountain of the heart, wherein the fire of life, the energy of the creator, is quick with the ardor of its eternal source and at the same instant throbbing with the pulse of time. Here God and Creature are consubstantial, Eternity and Life one and the same. This is the mountain—the cave—the bed—of rapture, cosmogonic rapture, the world and all its myriads proceeding from the re-conjuncture of the One who was never Two. The tender atmosphere of this perfect love-idyll is typical of the Hindu God-and-Consort scenes. Shiva and Devī as the primeval pair in close embrace have set the model for countless similar couples. Also we find that from Shiva and Devī was derived the general pattern for the representation of gods and their shaktis in the schools of Shivaite Buddhism and in the Lamaism of Tibet.

Shiva and the Goddess represent the polar aspects of the one essence and therefore cannot be at variance; she expresses his secret nature and unfolds his character. A startling expression of this idea appears in a late Cambodian development of the Shivaite tradition, where the symbol of the lingam opens up at the four sides and discloses, among other figures representative of its power, the Goddess herself. Figure 64 is a good example; here the Goddess has ten arms and five heads, the latter feature being symbolical of Shiva's universal supremacy, since the five heads immediately place him above the four-headed Brahmā. This female figure is the essence, the creative energy, the shakti, of the phallic pillar.

It is possible that this late development may have been inspired by a parallel evolution of the highest Buddhist symbol, the stūpa. For centuries Buddhism and Hinduism flourished and developed side by side, submitting to identical influences, cross-influencing each other, and bringing to expression in their diverse systems of iconography identical ideas. The stūpa is a very different thing from the lingam. It is a relic-shrine, often containing a bone of the Buddha, and symbolizing him who has attained to extinction through enlightenment. An austere, completely anonymous structure crowned by the parasol of universal spiritual emperorship, it is representative of the state of Nirvāna, which is beyond all concepts and forms. Figure 62 shows a chaitya hall, or Buddhist church, at Bedsā, dating from about 175 B.C. This monument is carved into the living rock. It is patterned after wooden structures of the practically undocumented earlier centuries, and consists of a great nave, flanked by aisles and terminating in an apse. The aisles are separated from the nave by pillars (not constructed, but carved from the body of the rock) and are continued round the apse, where they come together. In place of an altar we behold a simple stūpa, austere, severe and serene, magnificent and forbidding. The hall itself is devoid of ornamentation. Here the puritanical severity of the earliest Buddhist regimen is reflected tellingly; the intensity of the concentration on the ideal and experience of Nirvāna renders superfluous, distracting, uninteresting, every suggestion of the play of the worlds of form. Contrast with this the richness of the stūpas of the later periods. Figure 65 shows an early seventh century structure at Ajantā. The negative, forbidding shell of Nirvāna, beyond human conception, beyond all earthly and celestial forms, now discloses its positive kernel—the apparition of the Enlightened One, the transcendent Savior, who is the embodied and personalized substance of the Absolute. Sheer Suchness, That-ness, beyond limiting, qualifying attributes and characteristics, has become reflected in Him who became one with it while yet remaining in the flesh. And even as the apparition of Devī out of the extreme symbol of maleness, the lingam, brought with it a shock of new realization (namely, that the God and Goddess, the Absolute and its reflection in Phenomenal Nature, are ultimately one), so in this stūpa the abrupt bursting of an anthropomorphic Buddha out of Nirvāna, the anonymous void, lets it be known that in the light of final enlightenment, in the thought-transcending experience of the "Wisdom of the Farther Bank" (*prajñā-pāramitā*), the ultimate polarity—that of Nirvāna and Samsāra, Freedom and Bondage—is totally annihilated: Nirvānic serenity and the wild play of the worlds of form are one and the same. Clearly, this is a Buddhistic parallel to the Shivaite realization. Very likely a considerable interaction took place during the centuries of the neighborly common development of the two systems in the rich spiritual soil of medieval India.

There is much to be said for the later symbols, ornate and ambiguous though they may appear to those whose taste has been developed in a sterner tradition. Depths and abundances of meaning and implication come to light through them, as though through a breaking and decay of surfaces. We stand astonished before apparitions emerging from profundities hitherto forbidden to the mind. And a vast reconciliation of the sentiments and powers of judgment with everything that may have hitherto seemed either abominable or absurd unstrings the last resistance of the living ego to the all-inclusive, all-affirmative, all-annihilating death-and-life womb of final peace.

Shiva symbolism delves deeper into the mystery of the Two-in-One than any other Hindu tradition of Shakti worship. That is what makes it particularly interesting and illuminating. The motif of the union of opposites here is orchestrated with piercing harmonies. To grasp fully the implications, however, we cannot simply trust our own resources; we have to study a very recondite Shivaite-Tantric tradition, which is represented in certain miniatures and their corresponding literary texts. Figure 66 is a representation of the so-called "Island of Jewels" (*mani-dvīpa*). It is rich with allegorical meaning in every detail. It reveals the pair of opposites, in union with each other, growing out of each other, supporting and counter-balancing each other. This painting is intended to serve as a model or pattern for the guidance of the inward contemplation of the initiate-devotee. It is a yantra. The devotee should let it unfold to his inner vision and then concentrate upon it. He should become imbued with its meaningful features and realize that they disclose the secret essence, the truth, the esoteric reality of the nature of both the universe and his own being.

First, there are the deep-blue, tranquil waters of the ocean of life-substance. Their melody is voiced in the prelude of Wagner's *Rheingold,* and in the soothing passage of the next to last bars of the *Götterdämmerung,* where the waters engulf the universal conflagration. This is the ocean of eternal life in its primal state. And just as in the Vishnu mythology the ocean, as represented by the cosmic serpent and recumbent Vishnu, brings forth the lotus of the cosmos which floats upon its waves, so here, the vast sea of infinite life-energy, this ocean of nectar, this elixir of immortality (*amṛita-ārṇava*), discloses in its center a mystical isle.

The ocean represents the "Alogical Immense." It is an expanse, dormant in itself, and full of all potentialities. It contains the germs of all conflicting opposites, all the energies and features of all the pairs of co-operating antagonisms. And these energies concentrate and evolve here at the center, in the Island. Out of the dormant, quiescent state they move here to creation.

The ocean, standing for universal consciousness, is comparable to the ubiquitous, subtle element of the ether (*ākāśa*), which constitutes, substantially, all space, and supplies the stage for all subsequent evolution and development. The Island, in contradistinction to this surrounding fluid, is regarded as the metaphysical Point of Power. It is called "The Drop" (*bindu*) the first drop, which spreads, unfolds, expands, and becomes transmuted into the tangible realm of our limited consciousness and the universe.

The Island is represented as a golden, circular figure. The shores are made of powdered gems (*maṇi*)—hence the name of the Island, Mani-dvīpa. It is forested with blooming, fragrant trees, and in the center stands a palace made of the precious stone that grants all desires (*cintāmaṇi*), a kind of *lapis philosophorum*. Within the palace is a jeweled awning (*maṇḍapa*), under which, on a jeweled and golden throne, is seated the Universal Mother (*jagad-ambā, mātar*), "The Fairest One of the Three Worlds or Towns" (*tripura-sundarī*). She is the deity, the energy of the Bindu, which in turn was the first, concentrated Drop of the dynamic force of universal divine substance. Out of the Goddess there come into being the three world-spheres of the heavens, the earth, and the space between.

The Goddess is red in color, for here she is creative. Red is the active color. She is the primordial energy, planning and producing the evolution of the universe. She is called *vimarsa-śakti; vimarṣa* meaning "deliberation, reasoning, planning"; *śakti,* "energy." The Goddess is our familiar Māyā: *mā* is "to measure out, to plan (after the manner of the carpenter and housebuilder)." She is the potentiality and maternal measure of the world. Regarded from the standpoint of the all-containing divine Essence, she is a mere "This"; she is indeed the first-born "This" emerging from indiscriminate, latent totality; the quintessence of "This," the first, pure object-of-experience known to the supreme, divine Self-experience, out of which she herself has emerged. What man, later on (as a late product and link in the chain of evolution), is to call "matter," divine Consciousness first experienced as a mere "This," or "Other," which yet was identical with the Supreme Self. Gradually, by the operation of Māyā, this "This" became experienced by Mind as separate from, and different from, and outside of Itself; it was experienced as total "otherness." This experience was identical with the creation of the world.

In the throne-hall of the Island of Jewels, the Goddess holds in her hands four familiar weapons or instruments, familiar from her representations as the warlike, demon-slaying divinity. Here they have a psychological meaning, and are to be understood on the spiritual level. The Goddess carries, namely, the bow and arrow, the noose, and the goad. The bow and arrow denote the power of will. The noose—the lasso that catches wild animals and fetters the enemy, in sudden assault on the battle-field—denotes knowledge, the master-force of the intellect, which seizes and fixes with a firm hold on its objects. The goad, for the urging on of the mount or beast of burden, denotes action.*

Within the throne-hall of the Island of Jewels the goddess of the red hue sits upon two inert, more or less corpse-like, male figures, who are lying one upon the other on the six-sided throne. Both represent Shiva as the Absolute. The upper figure is called Sakala Shiva. *Sakala* is the compound, *sa-kala; kalā* meaning "a small part of anything, a bit, a jot, an atom," especially, "a digit of the moon"; *sa* meaning "with." The digits of the moon are sixteen in number: *sakala* is the moon possessed of all its digits, "whole, entire, complete, all"—the Full Moon. The opposite of *sakala* is *niṣkala*, "devoid of digits or of constituent parts"; the New Moon, which, though virtually existent, is imperceptible, intangible, apparently non-existent. The upper figure, then, is Sakala Shiva; the figure beneath is Nishkala Shiva: i.e., the figure above is the Absolute in its full actuality, the lower one is the Absolute in its transcendent, dormant, quiescent state—mere potentiality.

Read in psychological terms, the upper Shiva is all-containing, omniscient supra-consciousness; the lower is deepest unconsciousness, all-containing also, but apparently void, in the state of com-

---

* There is another allegorical reading of the bow and arrows. The bow denotes the mind; it dispatches the five arrows—the five sense faculties. Each of these is sent forth to find its corresponding object of sound, touch, light, taste, and smell. The senses and their respective objects are composed of identical elements, to wit: ether (hearing-sound), air (touch-tangibility), fire (vision-light), water (tasting-taste), and earth (smell-fragrance). As resident in the five sense-faculties these elements are said to be in the state of "subtle matter" (*sūkṣma*), whereas as encountered in the material, tangible sphere, they are in the state of "gross matter" (*sthūla*). It is through this substantial affinity and common origin that each of the faculties is capable of grasping its proper objects.

plete quiescence. The two are antagonistic, yet equally valid aspects of the Absolute, which contains and reflects all and everything, and in which all distinctions and oppositions vanish and come to rest. The Absolute is both plenitude and voidness, everything and nought. It is the source and receptacle of every energy, but at the same time utter inertia, the slumber of all slumbers, deep and quiet.

Sakala Shiva, the uppermost of the two, is in the state of actualization because he is in bodily contact with his own universal energy, the Shakti, the Goddess, the feminine active principle, the efficient and material cause of the universe, the Māyā that evolves the differentiated elements and beings. Sakala Shiva bears on his head the crescent of the moon. This moon, this tiny sickle of the crescent, is here to be understood as symbolizing the first utterance of sound, that is to say, the first manifestation of the element that is perceived through the quality of sound: ether, space, the most subtle and first-born of the five. As the primary element of sense-perception, associated with the pristine ether, this "sound" (*nāda*) represents the State of Power. It is experienced by the yogī when he plunges deep into himself. It is made manifest in the heartbeat. And since the microcosm is finally identical with the macrocosm, when the yogī hears the Nāda, this Sound of Power, he is listening to the heartbeat of the Absolute; this is the universal Life Power as made manifest within his own ephemeral frame. He is coming very near to the final experience of the Absolute itself.

Every detail of the Island of Jewels is meant to be visualized, and to be understood as an aspect of the innermost recess of the heart. Sakala Shiva throbs with the resounding Sound of Power because he is in immediate contact with the active, creative, feminine principle. Since he is pure consciousness, spontaneous Self-Illumination (*sva-prakāśa*), he is white. The Goddess above him, his own energy (*śakti*), helps him to display himself as the universe, which is both being and becoming. He is the immaculate spirituality of the Self, shining forth of itself; she is the former of forms. It is he who illuminates the forms that she has evolved.

But now, beneath this Sakala Shiva lies another, Nishkala Shiva, his twin or double. The eyes are closed, and this figure is not so much radiant white as colorless. *Niṣkala* means "without parts." When applied to a man, its meaning is "worn out, decrepit, old." When applied to a woman, it means "unable to bring forth children, sterile." As applied now to Shiva, it denotes the Absolute in that state in which nothing comes to pass. Nishkala Shiva is the unchanging, sterile Absolute, devoid of every urge of energy towards procreation and cosmogonic transmutation. This is the Absolute as sublime lifelessness, primary and ultimate inertia, the supreme void; here nothing whatsoever throbs or stirs.

Nishkala Shiva is called "the dead body, the corpse" (*śava*). In Sanskrit there is a meaningful play implied in this juxtaposition of the two names, Shava and Shiva. The pun is based on a peculiarity of the Sanskrit mode of writing, and when grasped supplies a very neat formulation of the sense of these three symbolic personages of the Island of Jewels. In the classical Devanāgarī script, the basic signs represent consonants *plus* the vowel *a*. For example, श = *śa*, व = *va*. To convert the *a* into an *i*, the element ि is added: शि = *śi*, वि = *vi*. Hence Shiva is written शिव and Shava शव; that is to say, if the sign ि is omitted from the written name of Shiva, there is left the script equivalent for Shava. Without this ि or *i*, Shiva is but a corpse, a Shava. Who or what, then, is this enlivening vowel-sign, or *i*, if not the Goddess, Shakti, the supreme representative of movement and life? The Absolute (*brahman*) regarded in and by itself, devoid of this activating, vitalizing energy, this sign of its procreative, cosmogonic impulse (*māyā*), is but a corpse. The German philosopher, Hegel, in the closing, crowning paragraph of his great work, "The Phenomenology of the Universal Spiritual Principle" (*Die Phaenomenologie des Geistes*) refers to this same

Ultimate as *das leblose Einsame,* "the lifeless Solitary One." Shiva thus regarded as Shava, Brahman destitute of Māyā, can do nothing (so far as Manifestation is concerned); he is nothing; he is the purest Nought.

In the picture of the throne-hall of the Island of Jewels, Nishkala Shiva is dissociated from the red energy of life, in contrast to Sakala Shiva, who is in bodily contact with the upper, feminine figure. It is because he is separated from her that he is Shiva without the *i,* Shava, a corpse. This point is emphasized in the picture and in its doctrine. The emphasis gives stress to the dignity and supreme virtue of the Goddess. She is the Māyā that produces the world; she is the mother of our individual, swiftly transitory lives. The meaning is, that, though these lives of ours are caught in the whirligig of rebirth where everything fails of its end, and are fraught with sufferings and guilt, shortcomings, cruelties, and absurd infatuations, nevertheless they are the unique manifestation of divine energy. Through the processes of universal life, the divine has become phenomenal actuality. Whatever we may perceive or experience, and no matter how we may perceive it—whether brightly or darkly—everything, both ourselves and our world, is a revelation of the virtual infinity of divine energy. Hence: the supreme sanctity of Māyā—whatever she may signify, or be.

Distressed though we inevitably are, in all our deficiencies, we constitute, nevertheless, particles of the abundant display. We are emanations, children, of the Absolute: we are of its fold; we are in its lap; we cannot be lost. Individually we pass through all kinds of disaster, and suffer, in the end, destruction. Individually, at the same time, we are refractions of the Image of God. We have no need to go in quest of the Absolute in and by itself, the Absolute dormant in its first and ultimate inertia, lying prostrate like a corpse; for the very life essence, the Energy, of the Absolute is manifest in everything around us, it is everywhere before our eyes, by virtue of the transforming power of the Goddess, Shakti, the Mother. All things pour frantically into the oblivion of death; she pours new life again from her inexhaustible womb. Philosophers have quibbled with existence; the ascetics have insulted and abandoned it, to go in titanic quest of the Corpse: and yet, the very Absolute, but under its dynamic aspect, as playful, relentless energy, is our life, has become transformed into us and the effects of our bewildered thoughts and deeds. When we pay worship to the Goddess, as devout children of the world, we are no further from the Divine than are the yogīs. They realize the Absolute in their innermost Self, in a state of unruffled inactivity, supreme quietude, transcendent peace. But we are the Absolute inasmuch as we are children of Māyā, the World.

This lesson of the Island of Jewels will at first flatter us with its apparent vindication of our unspiritual propensities; but a second thought, and we shall perceive that in its attitude of total acceptance this profoundly dionysiac, trans-moral, wholesale Yea is finally quite as wild, quite as stern, as the total life-negation of the ascetic. In India the pendulum of thought swings between extremes, inhuman extremes, implying inhuman attitudes and pointing to extra-human goals. On the one hand we find a pessimistic criticism of life in doctrines and practices of the severest ascetic character, wherein the dream of life is regarded as a frightful nightmare to be shattered by an awakening. Human existence is but a springboard to be left behind in a sublime leap to the supra-human, supra-divine, extra-cosmic sphere of being, which is beyond the spell and veil of the world. But here, on the other hand, in this symbolism of the Tantra, the same Māyā, screening the true, divine reality, screening the Self under the mirage of individual personality and under the display of the perishable universe, is somehow that Self, that very Absolute—pure spirit, pure bliss. Māyā is simply the dynamic aspect of the Absolute. Hence, all and everything is a revelation, a manifestation, a particularization of the one and sole divine essence.

This amounts to such a wholesale, indiscriminate sanctification of all and everything on the earthly plane, that there is no need any more for yoga, for sublimation through asceticism. The children of the world are in immediate contact with the divine, *if* they can only look upon and deal with *everything* as part and parcel of its everchanging-everlasting self-revelation. In symbols such as this one produced by the Shivaite Tantra philosophy, the old "accursed Māyā of somber and woeful appearance," as Vishnu himself styled her when letting Nārada experience her spell, the Māyā whose power is so difficult even for fervent and advanced saints to overcome, assumes a surprising aspect: she becomes suddenly the revelation, the very incarnation of the divine energy of the Absolute. Life with all its features and experiences, the universe in its decline and strife, though screening the divine Self within us, is holy and divine. Just beneath the veil of Māyā, the magic mirage of the universe, dwells the Absolute. And the energy of Māyā is precisely the energy of that Absolute, under its dynamic aspect. Shakti, the Goddess, emerges from Nishkala Shiva, so that he may show forth the totality of his potentialities, as the moon its total orb.

The three figures—Nishkala Shiva, Sakala Shiva, and Shakti-Māyā—superimposed as they are, one upon the other, can be read either upward or downward as, respectively, the evolution and the involution of the Absolute in its unfolding and reabsorption of the universe. Nishkala Shiva is the Absolute, the divine essence in and by itself, beyond event and change, inactive, dormant, void. Sakala Shiva is the state in which the Absolute shows its infinite potentiality for differentiation into the universe. Shakti-Māyā is the energy of the Absolute making itself manifest, its static repose transmuted into procreative energy. Thus reading the picture from bottom to top, the Absolute evolves through three aspects or gradations, passing from the pole of inertia, complete inactivity and voidness, to that of infinite activity and dynamic differentiation, the universe teeming with its creatures and abundant in its variety of forms. Reading from top to bottom, on the other hand, the three figures express in abbreviation the progress of the yogī-initiate from normal consciousness to the realization of the Self. They outline the way back from the experiences of the senses, the awareness of the intellect, first to the plenitude of supra-individual consciousness, the radiant and pure essence of Sakala Shiva, and then finally to a complete self-absorption in the utter Void, Nishkala Shiva, unconscious of itself in supreme quiet.

The symbolic pattern is meant to guide the initiate in a process of introvert regression to the state beyond all attributes, limitations, and characterizations. This psychological process occurs in time and space. Time and space, however, are but categories of our individual, limited consciousness, the most elementary limitations or frames of our human perception and conception, they do not apply to the transcendent Absolute. What appears to the human mind of the adept yogī as a sequence or gradation of antagonistic states—proceeding from the Māyā of normal individual consciousness (the Shakti at the top) to the experience of the highest Self (Shava beneath)—is not a sequence at all, from the standpoint of the Absolute. The three are only aspects of a single, unique and eternal essence. The truth is voidness *and* plenitude, everything *and* nought. Through concentrating on this truth, the initiate should ultimately come to realize *the basic identity of the individual personality with the universal Self.* What is mortal in himself and what is imperishable he should know to be one. What is changing and what is above change he should discover to be coincident. Thus he should learn at last to accept the Māyā of his transient, frail existence as a dynamic radiation of the Self-Eternal.

In the picture of the Island of Jewels, Shakti, the divine energy, sits in the attitude of Brahmā, the demiurgic creator, who unfolds the universe according to the dictates of the sacred wisdom of the Vedas, the manuscript of which he holds in his hands. The

210

Goddess, thus, shows here a very positive, extremely benevolent, purely creative aspect of the supreme energy of life. She is the so-called "Deliberating Shakti" (*vimarśa-śakti*), reasoning out and planning the gradual evolution of the universe. But the energy of life is finally no less destructive than creative: so too the Goddess. Life feeds on life. In the end, every creature becomes food for another. The aging and dying generation is to be replaced by the younger, pressing on its heels. What the Goddess bestows benignantly upon the one, she has taken ruthlessly from the other. Studying the rich and meaningful symbol of this Mani-dvīpa pattern, this Goddess of the Jewel Island, one might be tempted to say that there is something missing—at least, from the standpoint of the Absolute; for the Goddess in the Brahmā-like, Vimarsha-aspect is all too benign, beneficent, and bright. She exhibits only the positive aspect of the Shakti-Māyā life-force. We have now to see how the opposite side of the coin is represented in the fearless world of Indian myth and art.

It might be said that the Goddess represents clearly enough by her feminine nature the life-bearing, life-nourishing, maternal principle; this, her positive aspect, hardly needs to be further emphasized. But the counter-balancing, negative aspect, her ever-destructive function, which takes back and swallows again the creatures brought forth, requires a shock of vivid horror, if it is to be duly expressed. To this end she is represented as Kālī, the Black One. *Kālī:* that is the feminine form of the word *kāla*, meaning "Time"—Time, the all-producing, all-annihilating principle, in the onflow of which everything that comes into existence again vanishes after the expiration of the brief spell of its allotted life.

There is a celebrated hymn to Kālī, the Goddess, composed by the famous Shankarāchārya, the great philosopher and divine who flourished about A.D. 800, the Thomas Aquinas of orthodox Vedāntic non-dualism. He was a fervent devotee of the Goddess. In this hymn he first addresses her in the classic manner, celebrating the plenitude of her essence, as "She who takes up her abode in all perishable beings under the form of energy." * Whereupon the Goddess states of herself:

> *"Whosoever eats food, eats food by me;*
> *Whosoever looks forth from his eyes,*
> *And whosoever breathes,*
> *Yea verily, whosoever listens to whatever is said,*
> *Does so by me."*

She is "abundant with food, possessed of the plenitude of edible stuff" (*anna-pūrṇa*). She holds in her right hand a golden ladle † adorned with rare jewels, and in her left the vessel of abundance, from which she deals to all her children in the universe sweet milk-rice, "the best of all food" (*parama-anna*). But now, in the very next stanza, Shankarāchārya describes this Goddess according to her other aspect: with four hands that hold the symbols not of abundance but of death, renunciation, and the spiritual path of devotion. These are the noose (the lasso that catches and strangles the victim), the iron hook (which drags the victim to his doom), the rosary, and the textbook of prayer. Shankarāchārya addresses her:

> *"Who art thou, O Fairest One! Auspicious One!*
> *You whose hands hold both: delight and pain?*
> *Both: the shade of death and the elixir of immortality,*
> *Are thy grace, O Mother!"*

That is to say: the creative principle and the destructive are one and the same. Both are at unison in the divine cosmic energy that becomes manifest in the process of the biography and history of the universe.

Innumerable representations of the devouring Black Kālī de-

---

* *Yā devī sarvabhūteṣu śakti-rūpena saṃsthitā.*
† Gold, the non-corroding metal, is the symbol of life, light, immortality, truth.

pict this wholly negative aspect of the Universal Mother, Alma
Mater, "The Shade of Death." In Figure 68 she appears as an
emaciated, gruesome hag of bony fingers, protruding teeth, un-
quenchable hunger—cold-blooded, self-centered, ungenerous old
age, sturdy decrepitude, and obsessive voraciousness. The hunger for life, which impels all of us throughout the length of our
days—makes the adorable suckling cry and seize upon its mother's nipples to drink her sweet milky heart blood—here shows itself in its most loathsome transformation, hideous, and yet as
spontaneous, "natural" and innocent as the tender infant's en-
dearing gesture. The Goddess feeds upon the entrails of her
victim. And who among beings born is not her victim? She
cleaves the belly and draws out and gobbles the intestines—that
is what she is fond of—steaming with the last breath of expiring
life. And she is encompassed by the halo of flames, the aureole
of the Dancing Shiva: these are the tongues of the universal conflagration that reduces everything to ashes at the termination
of a world-period (*kalpa*). But these tongues, furthermore, lick
incessantly: for life feeds on life. With every newborn creature's
entrance into the world, there is another turning back to clay.

Just as the Creatrix is visualized as surrounded and supported
by an ocean, so also this negative, annihilating aspect of the
Mother Shakti. There is a vivid description in the Tantra texts
particularizing the details of the form in which she is to be known.
She is standing in a boat that floats upon an ocean of blood. The
blood is the lifeblood of the world of children that she is bringing forth, sustaining, and eating back. She stands there and sips
the intoxicating warm blood-drink from a cranial bowl that she
lifts to her insatiable lips. This is the "other aspect" of the red
mistress of the Island of Jewels and of the crystal-clear blue
waters.

Whenever the totality, rather than a single aspect, of the
essence of the Goddess forms the subject of a representation,
it is imperative that her ambivalent character should be made

manifest in her form. That is to say, the negative, deadly features must be emphasized; for the motherly, positive, attractive side is evident in her very femininity. As the "Fairest of the Three Spheres of the Universe," the one and only "she," this majestic, wonderful figure is the embodiment of man's desires and delights, the archetypal object of all longings and all thought. In order that she may represent the *full* significance of Shakti-Māyā, this alluring, ever-charming Eternal Female of our Soul has to be painted black, has to be clad with the symbols of destruction and death as well as the symbols of life.

In a Tantric representation of Kālī standing on Shiva-Shava, shown in Figure 67, this total aspect of the Goddess is to be seen. We have as before the hexagonal platform, but this time no Island of Jewels, no crystal Ocean of Inexhaustible Life. Instead, bones and skulls are scattered around, beasts of prey are feeding on the remains, deer of the wilderness move about. A group of divinities of the Hindu Olympus, at the left, in the background, are clustered in terror, gazing in awe at this apparition of the Dark Lady of the World. She is black entirely. In place of a garland of flowers, she wears a wreath of severed heads that dangles from her neck to her knees. In one right hand she carries the sword, the symbol of physical extermination and spiritual decision; this sword cuts through error and ignorance, the veil of individual consciousness. The other right hand holds an unusual symbol, the pair of scissors that severs the thread of life. But in her two left hands she exhibits the bowl that yields abundance of food and the lotus symbol of eternal generation.

Beneath the feet of this goddess are the two Shivas again. The lowermost is represented as a bearded naked ascetic, lifeless and dormant because he is out of touch with Shakti, the life-giving and life-taking energy. This is Shava, the Plenitude of the Absolute as Total Void, utterly "dead for immortality" (*tot vor Unsterblichkeit*), to quote a formula of Nietzsche in his *Thus Spake Zarathustra*. Lying above him is his beautiful, youthful

214

double, stirring slightly, as if in a dream, as if about to awake. This living Shiva raises his head and begins to lift his left arm, animated by his contact with the feet of the Goddess who is the embodiment of his very essence, and who, as such, reveals herself to be the Destroyer. She is destruction incarnate—the destruction unending, wrought by the generating, life-bearing, *Ewig-Weibliche, le charme éternel.*

One of the most popular symbols of the perennial, loving union of the God and his Spouse is that of the Goddess, Kālī, the Black One, adorned with the blood-dripping hands and heads of her victims, treading on the prostrate, corpse-like body of her Lord. (Figure 69.) The Goddess is the feminine partner of the Two-in-One, the faithful spouse, the ideal wife-consort of Hindu myth and civilization, yet she treads on the inanimate body of her beloved and only mate. She is black with death and her tongue is out to lick up the world; her teeth are hideous fangs. Her body is lithe and beautiful, and her breasts are big with milk. Paradoxical and gruesome, she is today the most cherished and widespread of the personalizations of Indian cult. To us of the West—brought up under the shadow of the Gothic Cathedral, where the benign figure of the Blessed Mother, immaculate, is uncontaminated by the darker principle, the poison-brood of the serpent whose head she has come to crush, the hell-brood and the gargoyle-brood that swarms over the outer walls and up the spires—India's Mother, eternal India's horrific-beautiful, caressing-murdering symbolization of the totality of the worldcreating-destroying eating-eaten one, seems more than difficult to love. Nevertheless, we may learn from her Tantric philosophy and art, which unfold the rich Hegelian implications of her dialectic. Through these utterly disillusioned and yet world-affirming, profoundly living productions of the last great period of Indian creative thought, the Goddess in the fullness of her terrible beauty stands revealed to us. In the illuminations supplementary to the texts, and intended, as yantras, for the guidance of yoga-visualizations, channeling the initiatory experiences of the Tantric devotee, we too may discover—if we will pause—something that will speak to us of a wonder beyond beauty-and-ugliness, a peace balancing the terms of birth and death.

The extreme symbol of the Goddess treading down her Lord is counterbalanced by another sign of their interrelation, "The Shiva Half Female" (*śiva ardha-nārī*). (Figure 70.) Here the antagonistic principles unite to constitute a single organism, a paradox, representative of the intrinsically twofold nature of the onefold universe and its inhabitant, man.

CHAPTER SIX

CONCLUSION

I SHOULD like to conclude this brief and fragmentary discussion of myths and symbols in Indian art and civilization with a general remark and then a little parable which has been among my favorites since I came to know it some ten years ago.

As for the general remark: It is well known that our Christian Western tradition has long refused to accept the wisdom of the pagans on an equal footing with the body of revelation that it cherishes and worships as its own. The books that it accepts as divinely inspired are the Four Gospels, penned by four members of the early Christian community, the pamphlets addressed by St. Paul to certain small, ex-Jewish, heretical communities in Salonika and Cappadocia, and in the oriental quarters of Rome and Corinth, a few minor letters to other communities composed by other apostles (as it were, mere typewritten or mimeographed sheets, quite inconspicuous and unknown at the time, yet destined to outlive and outshine all the marketable best-sellers of the period), and then together with these the cryptic, somewhat delirious Book of Revelation; added to this Christian corpus are the very different tribal records of the legendary history of the Chosen People (including a biography of their jealous, wrathful God) as shaped and colored by Jewish leaders back from exile. These and only these have we deigned to accept as the all-comprehensive source of guidance for the human soul. And yet, there has been a semi-liberal, timid, and guarded acknowledgment that in pagan tradition also there may be found some light, the "natural light," a kind of bedimmed reflex of the truth of revelation.

The most enlightened, virtuous, and pious souls of Antiquity, even though pagan and deprived of both baptism and the Lord's gospel, are not inmates of the hell-pit proper. Dante, touring the circles of the underworld, encountered them in a sort of idyllic, Elysian lobby, near the entrance to, yet set quite apart from, the frightening inner apartments of the satanic Inferno. He recognized in that outer circle Socrates and Plato, Democritus, Diogenes, Anaxagoras and Thales, Empedocles, Heraclitus, Zeno, Dioscorides, Orpheus, Cicero, Livy, Seneca, Euclid, Ptolemy, Hippocrates and Galen, together with the Muslim authorities on Hellenistic philosophy and science, Avicenna and Averroes, and then, along with these, Noah and Moses, Abraham, Abel, King David, Jacob and his sons, Rachel, and even the wise Muslim ruler, Saladin; furthermore, many heroic and pious figures of Greek mythology were there: Hector of Troy, Aeneas and Caesar, Penthesilea, Electra, Lucretia, and many others.*

The fact that there are virtue, wisdom, and inspiration to be found even among the historical enemies of Christianity, the Jews who hung the Savior on the tree, the Romans who persecuted the martyrs, the Muslims who battled the Crusaders, was ever acknowledged by the broad-minded, orthodox doctrine of medieval Christianity, and is to this day upheld by the Roman Catholic Church—though it was rejected by certain Protestant denominations of narrow-minded, fanatical, Calvinistic extraction. During the Renaissance, there was even a moment (represented strikingly in the figure of Pico della Mirandola) when the last walls of orthodox exclusiveness seemed about to yield, and Ovid, Homer, the Kabbalah, the Koran, were being found to be in essential concord with the sacred pamphlets of the Chris-

* *Inferno*, Canto IV.

tian movement. Behind the variety of symbols, a universally constant, vastly sophisticated, tradition of human wisdom was joyfully recognized, and was on the point, even, of being officially conceded by the guardians of the "One True Faith." *

There is a humorous Jewish parable in the tradition of the Hassidim (this is the text on which I wish to close) that brings into an eloquent image the final sense to the individual of a broad-minded, fearless adventure into the worlds of "gentile" faith and life. When I first read this tale,† some ten years ago, I realized that I had been living and acting along its lines for over a decade—ever since that moment when the millenary, spiritual, treasure of Hindu myth and symbol had begun to reveal itself to me through my academic studies of Indian sacred diagrams and Mandalas, in conjunction with research in the Tantras and Purānas. It is a brief story, told of the Rabbi Eisik, son of Rabbi Jekel, who lived in the ghetto of Cracow, the capital of Poland. He had remained unbroken in his faith, through years of affliction, and was a pious servant of the Lord his God.

---

* [*Extra ecclesiam nulla salus* is an admittedly difficult Christian doctrine, not to be taken *au pied de la lettre*. It must not be overlooked that "All that is true, by whomsoever it has been said, is from the Holy Ghost" (St. Ambrose on I Cor. 12. 3, endorsed by St. Thomas Aquinas, *Sum. Theol.* I-II. 109. 1 and 1); accordingly, even St. Thomas could speak of the doctrines of the pagan philosophers as affording "extrinsic and probable proofs" of the truths of Christianity; and the same would apply to the teachings of Indian and Chinese metaphysicians of whom there was no knowledge in those days. All fundamental theological propositions, the doctrine, for example, of the "single essence and two natures" (respectively impassible and passible), after which also "there are two in us" (respectively immortal and mortal), are common to all orthodox traditions. "*All* Scripture cries aloud for freedom from self." Religions (subject to the fallibility of human interpretation) necessarily differ in emphasis and modality, but the infallible truth of which all are expressions is one; and the time is coming when a Summa of the Philosophia Perennis (et Universalis), based on all orthodox sources whatever, not excluding those of "folklore," will have to be written. Aldous Huxley's *Philosophia Perennis* represents a step in this direction; a step, that is to say, towards the "reunion of the churches" in a far wider sense than that in which this phrase is commonly taken.—AKC.]

† Martin Buber, *Die Chassidischen Bücher* (Hegner, Hellerau, 1928), pp. 532-3.

One night, as this pious and faithful Rabbi Eisik slept, he had a dream; the dream enjoined him to proceed, afar, to the Bohemian capital, Prague, where he should discover a hidden treasure, buried beneath the principal bridge leading to the castle of the Bohemian kings. The Rabbi was surprised, and put off his going. But the dream recurred twice again. After the third call, he bravely girded his loins and set forth on the quest.

Arriving at the city of his destiny, Rabbi Eisik discovered sentries at the bridge, and these guarded it day and night; so that he did not venture to dig. He only returned every morning and loitered around until dusk, looking at the bridge, watching the sentries, studying unostentatiously the masonry and the soil. At length, the captain of the guards, struck by the old man's persistence, approached, and gently inquired whether he had lost something or perhaps was waiting for someone to arrive. Rabbi Eisik recounted, simply and confidently, the dream that he had had, and the officer stood back and laughed.

"Really, you poor fellow!" the captain said; "Have you worn your shoes out wandering all this way only because of a dream? What sensible person would trust a dream? Why look, if I had been one to go trusting dreams, I should this very minute be doing just the opposite. I should have made just such a pilgrimage as this silly one of yours, only in the opposite direction, but no doubt with the same result. Let me tell you my dream."

He was a sympathetic officer, for all of his fierce mustache, and the Rabbi felt his heart warm to him. "I dreamt of a voice," said the Bohemian, Christian officer of the guard, "and it spoke to me of Cracow, commanding me to go thither and to search there for a great treasure in the house of a Jewish rabbi whose name would be Eisik son of Jekel. The treasure was to have been discovered buried in the dirty corner behind the stove. Eisik son of Jekel!" the captain laughed again, with brilliant eyes. "Fancy going to Cracow and pulling down the walls of every house in the ghetto, where half of the men are called Eisik and the other half Jekel! Eisik son of Jekel, indeed!" And he laughed, and he laughed again at the wonderful joke.

The unostentatious Rabbi listened eagerly, and then, having bowed deeply and thanked his stranger-friend, he hurried straightway back to his distant home, dug in the neglected corner of his house and discovered the treasure which put an end to all his misery. With a portion of the money he erected a prayer-house that bears his name to this day.

Now the real treasure, to end our misery and trials, is never far away; it is not to be sought in any distant region; it lies buried in the innermost recess of our own home, that is to say, our own being. And it lies behind the stove, the life-and-warmth giving center of the structure of our existence, our heart of hearts—if we could only dig. But there is the odd and persistent fact that it is only after a faithful journey to a distant region, a foreign country, a strange land, that the meaning of the inner voice that is to guide our quest can be revealed to us. And together with this odd and persistent fact there goes another, namely, that the one who reveals to us the meaning of our cryptic inner message, must be a stranger, of another creed and a foreign race.

The Bohemian captain at the bridge does not believe in inner voices or in dreams, yet he opens to the stranger from afar the very thing that terminates his troubles and brings to fulfillment his quest. Nor does he do this wonderful thing by intention; on the contrary, quite inadvertently his epochal message is delivered while he is making a special point of his own. Hindu myths and symbols, and other signs of wisdom from afar, in just such a way will speak to us of the treasure which is our own. And we then must dig it up from the forgotten recesses of our own being. And at last it will end for us our troubles and permit us to erect for the benefit of all around us a temple of the living spirit.

INDEX

Abhramū, 105, 106
Absolute, The:
  beyond differentiating qualities of
    sex, 123
  Buddha as personification of, 64,
    146
  Buddha's quest for, 162
  differentiation of, 76, 137, 147-8,
    197, 209
  heartbeat of, 205
  in art, 148, 150, 156
  manifestations of, 142, 144, 193
  ourselves as emanations of, 207-8
  productive energy of, 152, 209
  quiescence of, 136, 155
  reality of, 145
  Shiva as personification of, 124-5,
    135, 167, 204-5
  substance of, 200
  transcendence of, 188, 210
  union with, 153
  Vajradhara-Vajrasattva as symbol
    of, 146
  Vishnu and Shiva as personifica-
    tions of, 65, 78
  waters as creative aspect of, 90
  Yab-Yum as symbol of, 146
    See also Bindu; Brahman-At-
      man; Essence, divine; Self;
      Self, universal; Substance,
      eternal; Void; Waters, cos-
      mic
Adi-Buddha. See Buddha, universal
Aeschylus, 41
Agastya, 113-4

Agni (god of fire), 90 (footnote),
  124, 184, 186
Air, 51, 204 (footnote)
  See also Vāyu
Airāvata:
  ancestor of earthly elephants, 53
  as vehicle of Indra, 57, 61, 107
  origin of, 104-5
    See also Ocean, Churning of
      Milky
Ajantā, 200
Alā-ud-dēn, 54
Alexander the Great, 177
Alkmene, 73
Allahabad, 109
Alphabets:
  Hebrew, 71, 72
  Indian, 72, 106
  Phoenician, 71
Amrita:
  etymology of, 60 (footnote)
    See also Immortality, elixir of
Ananta (Shesha, the cosmic ser-
  pent):
  ancestor of earthly serpents, 62
  as manifestation of Vishnu, 88
  as representative of cosmic wa-
    ters, 76, 202
  as vehicle of Vishnu, 37, 61, 76
  in art, 60
  incarnate in Balarāma, 89
Andrae, Walter, 169 (footnote)
Annales du Musée de Guimet, 128
  (footnote)

Apasmara-Purusha (demon of forgetfulness), 153
Aphrodite, 74
Apollo, 86, 87
Apsarases, 163 (and footnote), 164
Aristotle, 19
Arjuna, 61, 62 (footnote), 68
Arrow:
  emblem of Goddess, The, 204 (and footnote)
  emblem of Shiva, 186-8
Art:
  Bengalese, 110-1
  Buddhist:
    basically one with Hindu, 63
    Buddha harmonized with serpent in, 66, 68
    Buddha symbolic of Absolute in, 64
    elephant in, 102-3
    former existence of the Buddha in, 107-8
    Indra (Sakka) in, 53, 161
    Lotus Goddess in, 96, 102
    popular divinities in, 63, 64, 164, 165, 196, 199
  Cambodian, 66, 68, 76, 164, 165, 196, 199
  Chalcolithic, 92
  Chalukya, 131
  Chinese-Buddhist, 158
  Gandhāra, 76 (footnote)
  Gupta, 60, 62, 77
  Hellenistic-Buddhist, 76 (footnote)
  Indian:
    concept of time in, 13
    continued in Cambodia and Siam, 66
    continued in Ceylon, 65
    earliest extant monuments of, 64-5, 71, 103
    God and Goddess in, 139

later symbols in, 201
Mesopotamian patterns in, 70-1, 79
monism in, 119
popular divinities in, 63, 65
prosaic realism in, 56-7
relationship to mythology and philosophy, 195-6
vāhana in, 70-1
visionary forms in, 53, 57
  See also Phenomenon of expanding form; Shiva, Dance of
Jaina, 56
Japanese-Buddhist, 97
Javanese, 101, 164, 182-4
Maurya, 64
Mesopotamian, 72, 79, 93-4
  See also Seals, ancient
Pala, 88
Pallava, 112, 117, 192, 196
pre-Aryan, See Art, Chalcolithic; Harappa; Mohenjo-Daro
Sena, 110
Sumerian, 73
Tibetan, 146
Asceticism, 42 (and footnote), 48, 114 (and footnote), 115, 117, 118, 172, 209
  Buddha as master of, 69
  of Jaina sect, 54-5, 57, 166
  of Shiva, 115, 125, 191
  of titan-demons, 158, 193
  See also Dance; Hair
Ascetics. See Agastya; Bhagīratha; Hermits; Man, Old Wise; Nārada; Mārkandeya; Shiva; Sutapas; Vyāsa
Ashoka, King, 64, 65
Ashoka (tree), 69
Ashramas (Four Stages of Life), 42 (footnote)
Ashva-chikitsita, 107 (footnote)
Ashva-vaidyaka, 107 (footnote)

Brahmā: *Cont.*
four heads of, 52, 199
in the lingam, 130
mythology of, 125 (footnote)
night of, 6, 16, 19, 37, 38
on gander, 48
on lotus, 61, 96
plurality of, 6, 9
relationship to Shiva and Vishnu, 6, 80, 125 (footnote), 128-30, 190
relationship to Vishnu, 4, 5, 47, 81, 125 (footnote)
son of (Marīchi), 5
transformed into gander, 129-30
years of, 19
Brahman, gender of, 123 (and footnote), 188, 197
See also Self, universal
Brahman-Ātman, 101, 142 (and footnote), 143 (and footnote), 151, 154, 156, 188, 210
See also Absolute
Brahmāna, 116, 157 (footnote)
Brāhmī. See Alphabets, Indian
Breath, vital (prāna), 35, 47, 49, 50, 134
See also Yogīs, breathing exercises of
Brihaspati, 10, 22, 125 (footnote), 138
Brindaban, 82
Brother-pairs, 81
Buber, Martin, 219
Buddha:
-Bodhisattva relationship, 96, 98-9, 102
historical. See Gautama Siddhārtha
images of:
in association with serpent-genii, 65-6
of the Great Departure, 162-6

significance of, 144-6
types of:
lotus-seat, 146
Muchalinda, 67-8
Vajradhara-vajrasattva, 146
Yab-Yum, 146
yantra, 144
universal (Ādi-Buddha), 99-102, 144
See also Prajnā-Pāramitā
Buddhahood. See Enlightenment
Buddhism:
Hīnayāna, 68 (and footnote)
historical development of, 64, 199
in Cambodian and Siamese art-forms, 66
in Tibet, 100 (footnote), 116 (footnote), 144, 146, 199
Mahāyāna, 68 (and footnote), 96-7
Padmapāni in Far East, 97
Prajnā-Pāramitā in, 100 (foot-note)
relationship to Hinduism, 63-4, 99, 199, 201
Vajrayāna, 145
Buffalo-demon, 191-3, 196
Bull (Nandī), 48, 61, 70, 138, 196, 198

Cambodia, 101. See also Art, Cambodian
Ceylon, 65, 66, 160
Chalukya. See Art, Chalukya
Channa, 161, 162
Chaos. See Night, cosmic
Child, Divine, 4-10, 22, 26, 43-7, 82-6
Christ, 18, 89, 171
Christian nativity, 128 (footnote)
Christianity, 64 (footnote), 217-9 (and footnote)

226

Club:
emblem of demons, 182
emblem of Vāyu, 62
emblem of Vishnu, 88
Consciousness:
divine, 203
ego-, 34, 89
individual, 24, 39, 42, 78, 98, 143,
150, 197, 202, 210, 214
restricted in Māyā, 26
Sakala-Shiva as supra-individual,
210, 215
Shiva as supra-individual, 204
states of, 145
time-, 20, 23
universal, 202
unlimited, 50
Consecration figures. See Figures,
consecration
Coomaraswamy, Dr. Ananda K., 14
(footnote), 63 (footnote), 64 (footnote), 68 (footnote), 76 (footnote),
128 (footnote), 137 (footnote)
Cosmic night. See Night, cosmic
Cosmogony. See Cycle, universal
Cosmology, 6, 45 (footnote), 52,
62, 185
See also Heavens; Hell; Purgatory; "Three Towns"; Underworld; Universe; Waters, terrestrial; World, axis of; Worlds,
three
Cosmos. See Cosmology; Cycle, universal
Cow, sacred, 13, 14, 80
Cowell, E. B., 107 (footnote)
Creation. See Cycle, universal; Boar,
creation by the
Creator. See under Brahmā; Shiva;
Vishnu
Cycle:
individual:
and law of action (Karma), 7-8

basic to Indian thought, 13
experienced as Māyā, 24-5
identified with vital breath of
cosmic gander, 49
in Jaina doctrine, 56 (footnote)
parallels universal cycle, 11 ff
proceeding from cosmic waters,
34
release by Bodhisattva from, 99
release by Prajnā-Pāramitā
from, 100-1
symbolized by Aum, 154
symbolized in Dance of Shiva,
153
symbolized in Island of Jewels,
207, 210
symbolized in yantra, 143, 215,
216
transcended by Buddha, 67
Jaina, 55 (and footnote), 56 (and
footnote)
universal:
as biological process, 20
basic to Indian thought, 13
duration of, 19
experienced as Māyā, 24-5
impersonality of, 59
proceeding from cosmic gander, 48-50
proceeding from Goddess, The,
191, 212
proceeding from Shiva, 128,
135
proceeding from Vishnu, 47,
124
relation to yugas, 16
repeating infinitely, 5, 6, 12
repeating without variation, 17
symbolized by Aum, 154
symbolized in Dance of Shiva,
152-5
symbolized in Island of Jewels,
209-10

229

Mansions, celestial. See Gods, mansions of
Mantra, 72, 140, 141 (footnote)
Manu, 16
Manu Vaivasvata, 16 (footnote), 114
Manvantara, 16, 17, 18
Marīchi, 5
Mārkandeya, 35, 38, 41-50, 59
Marriage, Sacred, 127, 137-9, 144, 147, 176, 197-9
   See also Island of Jewels; Opposites; Polarity; Shiva-Shakti; Yantra
Marshall, Sir John, 93, 94 (footnote), 168 (footnote)
Mask, demon. See Kīrttimukha
Mātangalīlā, 103 (footnote), 106 (footnote)
Matter, cosmic, 135
Maturā, 82
Maya (titan-demon), 185 (and footnote)
Māyā:
  and problem of reality, 39
  as phychological term, 45 (footnote)
  basic conception of, 54
  concealing True Being, 154
  contrasted with Jaina belief, 54, 55 (footnote), 56
  definition and etymology of, 24 (and footnote), 25
  dynamism of, 131, 208
  energy of, 136, 192, 193
  generative forces of, 166
  Goddess as, 203, 205, 207
  impalpability of, 57, 150
  in art, 53, 119
  is differentiation, 102
  is identity of opposites, 46
  is nescience, 159 (footnote)
  opposed to Brahman-Ātman, 156

  ourselves the product of, 208
  -Shakti, 25-6, 142 (footnote), 194-5, 209, 211, 214
  spell of, 100, 120, 195
  symbolism of, 35
  toils of, 64, 82
  veil of, 209
  world as, 151, 208
Māyā-Shakti-Devī, 26, 151
  See also Māyā; Shakti; The Goddess (Devī)
Mediterranean Sea, 92
Megha, 109
Mendicancy, 9, 42 (footnote)
Mendicants, 48, 64, 162
Meru (also Sumeru), 4, 52, 80, 81, 186
Mesopotamia, 70-4, 92-5
  See also Art, Mesopotamian
Metaphysics, Hindu, 194
  See also Philosophy, Hindu
Mitra, 113, 123
Mohammedanism, 54
Mohammedans, 64
Mohenjo-Daro, 93-6, 103, 126, 168, 170
Moksha. See under Enlightenment
Mon-Khmer, 18, 164, 196
Monasticism. See Asceticism
Monism. See Brahman,Ātman. See under Philosophy, Hindu
Monotheism, 135
Monster, composite, 71, 73
Monsters. See Buffalo-demon; Kīrttimukha; Rāhu; Titan-demons
Monsters, sea (makara), 17, 111, 175 (footnote), 182
Moon, 60, 71, 175
  as emblem of Sakala-Shiva, 205
  eclipse of, 176
  full, 204
  sound symbolized by new, 205
  See also Shishu

Nārada (Sage), 27, 30-4, 45, 50, 209
Narāyana (Cosmic Man). See under Vishnu, archetypal manifestations of
Natarāja, temple. See Perur
See also under Shiva
Neminātha, 54
Neolithic period, 126
Nerval, Gérard de, 149
Nicholas, Saint, 186 (footnote)
Nietzsche, Friedrich, 74, 76, 214
Night, cosmic:
as interval of non-manifestation, 33-6
Māyā suspended during, 25
universe reincubated during, 20
visited by Mārkandeya, 38-9, 46
Nile, 93, 168
Nirvāna, 37, 64, 68, 98, 145, 146, 200, 201
Nishkala Shiva. See under Shiva
Noah, 16
Non-existence, Waters of, 35 ff
Noose:
emblem of Goddess, The, 192, 204, 212
emblem of Shiva, 133, 172

Ocean:
cosmic. See Waters, cosmic
Churning of the Milky, 17, 105 176
Oceans, four, 47, 52
Oedipus, 178
Om, 154
Opposites:
blending of, 89, 127, 136, 173, 174, 201
co-operative antagonism of, 137
identity of, 46
liberation from pairs of, 136 (footnote)

See also Island of Jewels; Marriage, Sacred; Polarity; Shiva-Shakti; Yantra

Padmā. See Lotus Goddess
Padmapāni, 96, 97
Pāli Canon, 160 (and footnote)
Pāndava. See under Myths and tales
Pantheon:
Buddhist, 99
Hindu:
adopted by Jains, 56
Buddha and the, 63
divinities personifying the Absolute in, 124
major figures of, 61
Shivaite, 183
Vedic, 91, 169
Parents, archetypal, 127
Paris, 130, 164, 165
Parshvanātha, 54
Pārvatī, 140, 197-8
Peacock, 48, 72
Persia, 16 (footnote)
Perūr, 172
Phallic symbol, 162
See also Lingam
Phenomenon of expanding form, 130-2, 134, 140, 188
Philo, 116 (footnote)
Philosopher's stone, 203
Philosophy:
Buddhist, 100 (footnote)
Hindu:
aims of, 26, 39, 136, 195
and reality, 24, 39
concept of divinity in, 35
concept of universe in, 20, 132
contrasted with western thought, 12, 13, 18, 19, 21, 41, 75, 195
embodied in battle of the gods, 194

monistic, 119, 135-6
perennial, 20, 26
related to art and mythology, 39, 40, 119, 132, 195, 196
synthesizing temporal and spiritual wisdom, 47
Tantric development of. See Tradition, Tantric
See also Thought, Indian
Plato, 19, 142 (footnote)
Pleiades, 71
Poetry. See Atharva Veda; Epics; Hymns; Rig Veda
Poets. See Shankarāchārya; Vyāsa
Polarity, 199
  male and female, 147, 148, 149, 155, 197
  Nirvāna-Samsāra, 146, 201
  See also Island of Jewels; Marriage, Sacred; Opposites; Shiva-Shakti; Yantra
Polyandry, 62 (footnote)
Ponds, 72
Prajāpati, 123, 186
Prajñā-Pāramitā, 97-102, 201
Prāna. See Breath, vital
Principle:
  female, 25, 148-9, 177-8, 205
  male, 26
  and female, 208
  See also under Polarity
Projection, 180, 189, 190, 193, 194
Psychology, 45 (footnote), 57, 194, 203, 204, 210
Psyche, 76 (footnote)
Purānas, 15, 18 (footnote), 21, 27, 60, 110, 128, 178
  Bhāgavata, 77 (footnote), 112 (footnote)
  Brahmavaivarta, 110 (footnote)
  Mārkandeya, 128 (footnote), 190 (footnote)

Matsya, 35 (footnote), 105 (footnote)
Shivaite, 134
Skānda, 182 (footnote)
Vishnu, 77 (footnote), 79 (footnote)
Purgatory, 99
Puri, 75

Rāhu. 175, 176, 180, 184
Rainbow, emblem of Indra, 104
Rajasa Anurva-Bhumi, 102
Rāma (brother of Krishna). See Balarāma
Rāma (hero of Rāmāyana). See under Vishnu, avatārs of
Ramakrishna, 32
Rao, T. A. G., 134 (footnote)
Rat, 70, 183
Rāvana, 198
Ravenna, 198
Reality:
  as aim of Indian thought, 26
  manifested by Shiva, 167
  of the Absolute, 145
  subjectivity of, 39, 195
  "suchness" of, 146
  unification of opposing views of, 50, 98-9
Redeemer. See Savior
Redemption, 64
Reincarnation. See Samsāra
Rheingold, das, 202
Rhetoric, Hindu system of, 173
Rhine, 159, 202
Rig Veda, 34 (footnote), 60 (footnote), 68 (footnote), 91, 92, 96, 138 (footnote), 157 (footnote), 172 (footnote), 177 (footnote)
Ring (Nibelungen) der, 158, 159
Rishabhanātha, 54
Ritual, 42 (and footnote), 72, 108, 197

attending Ananta, 89
Buddha and the, 67-8
conquered by Krishna (Vishnu), 77-90
eagle and, 72, 73, 74-6
female (nāginī), 63
in Buddhist art, 69
in "Descent of the Ganges" relief, 117, 121
in devotional attitudes, 69
in Indian art, 65-6
instructed by Buddha, 68
-pair, 72, 73, 74, 76
symbolism of, 37, 59-62, 63, 69, 74, 75, 88-9
Western symbolism of, 66, 69, 75
See also Ananta (Shesha); Kāliya; Muchalinda
-hoods, 62, 67, 70, 73, 117
-ornaments, as emblems of Shiva, 182, 198
Sex, symbolism of, 123 (footnote)
See also Island of Jewels; Lingam; Marriage, Sacred; Opposites; Polarity; Shiva-Shakti; Yantra; Yoni
Shachi (Indrānī), 10, 62 (footnote), 161
Shakti:
as consort of Indra, 161
as consort of Shiva, 147
as eternal feminine, 26
as goal of conquest, 177-8 (and footnote), 180
as power of the lingam, 199
destructive aspect of, 213-4
etymology of, 25
our individual, 194-5
personified in goddesses, 139-40, 146-7
relationship to Shiva. See Shiva-Shakti

summation of godly powers, 190-1
symbolized in triangles, 147-8
worship of, 201
Shankarāchārya, 211-2
Shastri, T. Ganapati (editor), 103 (footnote)
Shava, 206-7, 210, 214
Shelley, 41
Shesha. See Ananta
Shield, emblem of Shiva, 133
Shishu, 167
Shiva:
abode of, 52
and Jalandhara, 175-6, 180-1
as arch-ascetic, 115, 125, 133, 191
as Creator, Maintainer, Destroyer, 154, 155
as Destroyer, 130, 135, 154, 167, 175, 181, 187, 189
as goal of devotee, 7, 29, 111
as Natarāja. See Shiva, Dance of
as personalization of the Absolute, 65, 124, 135, 167, 177, 188, 190, 204
as supreme teacher, 9
baffled by Vishnu's Māyā, 31
conjured up by saint, 116
Dance of:
as slayer of elephant, 172-4
benign and wrathful phases of, 171-2
symbolism of, 131, 151-7, 166-8. See also Dance
emblems of:
arrow, 188
arrow and lingam, 187
bow, 186, 188
bowl, 173
drum, 152, 172
hook, 172
lingam with lotus petals, 138
noose, 133, 172

Tibet, 100 (footnote), 116 (footnote), 144, 146, 199
Ti'en, 128
Tiger:
  as manifestation of Goddess, The, 189
  -skin, 198
Tigris-Euphrates basin. See Mesopotamia
Time:
  a category of individual consciousness, 210
  -consciousness, 20, 23
  cyclic, 20-22
  does not apply to the Absolute, 210
  god of (Kāla), 155, 191
  in Indian art (publication), 137 (footnote)
  Indian conceptions of, 12, 20-1
  linear, 19
  personified in Kāla and Kālī, 211
  personified in Shakti of universal Buddha, 146
  symbolized in Dance of Shiva, 155-6
  symbolized in yantra, 140, 142
  transcended by universal cycle, 142
    See also Brahmā, century of; Brahmā, day of; Brahmā, night of; Brahmā, year of; Cycle, individual; Cycle, universal; Kalpa; Manvantara; Night, cosmic; Samsāra; Years, heavenly; Yuga
Titan-demons:
  asceticism of, 155
  conquered by Goddess, The, 190
  conquered by Shiva, 187-198
  conquered by Vishnu, 17, 79 ff, 105

conquered with help of Brihaspati, 10
  See also Jalandhara; Serpent-dragon
Titian, 163 (footnote)
Tonsure. See Hair
Tortoise Man. See Kashyapa
"Towns, Three." See "Three Towns."
Tradition:
  Buddhist. See Buddhism
  Lamaistic, 144, 199
  pre-Aryan (non-Vedic):
    continuity of, 166, 170
    lotus and Lotus Goddess in, 90-1
    Mesopotamian continuity in, 73, 92
    Mother Goddess in, 92, 96
    serpent-pair in, 73
    surviving in Buddhist and Hindu folklore, 70
    surviving in Jainism, 54
    Vishnu and Shiva in, 125 (footnote)
  Tantric:
    influence on Buddhism, 99
    Māyā revaluated in, 208-9
    relationship to modern Hinduism, 125 (footnote), 137
    revealed in yantras, 215-6
    Shiva-Shakti dialogues in, 197
    term for frame of yantra in, 143
    value of esoteric texts in, 201
  Vedic:
    Brahmā in, 125 (footnote)
    Brihaspati in, 125 (footnote)
    fate of The Goddess in, 96
    legend of Agastya in, 113
    lotus and Lotus Goddess in, 90 (and footnote), 91
    Shiva in, 186
    sun-god in, 16 (footnote)
    "Three Towns" in, 185

244

PLATES

1. Indra (Bhājā), c. 200 B.C.

2. Indra (Elūrā), c. 800 A.D.

3. Vishnu on Ananta (Deogarh), c. 600 A.D.

4. Nāga (Nālandā), c. 600 A.D.

5. Nāga (Ceylon), V–VIII cent. A.D.

6. Krishna (Bengal),
c. 825 A.D.

7. Buddha (Cambodia),
XIV cent. A.D.

8. Nāgakals (Mysore), XVII–XVIII cent. A.D.

9. Garudas and Nāgas (Siam), XII–XIV cent. A.D.

10. Assur (Assyria),
c. VII cent. B.C.

11. Sacrificial goblet (Sumer),
c. 2600 B.C.

12. *Vishnu's Boar Avatār*
   (Gwalior), 440 A.D.

13. *Deliverance of the Elephant*
   (Deogarh), IV–VI cent. A.D.

14. *Krishna conquering Kāliya (Kāngrā), XVIII cent. A.D.*

15. *Padmā (Bhārhut),*
II–I cent. B.C.

16. *Winged Goddess (Basārh),*
III cent. B.C.

17. *Gangā (Bengal),*
XII cent. A.D.

18. *Padmapāni (Nepāl),*
IX cent. A.D.

19. *Tree Goddess (Bhār-*
hut), II–I cent. B.C.

20. Prajñā-Pāramitā (Java), c. 1225 A.D.

21–25. Seals, Nude Goddess, and Lingam (Indus Civilization), 3000–2000 B.C.

26. Elephant-caryatids (Elūrā), VIII cent. A.D.

27. *The Descent of the Ganges (Māmallapuram), early VII century A.D.*

28. *Bhagīratha at Gokarna; detail from above.*

29. *Sanctuary of the Lingam
(Elephanta), VIII cent. A.D.*

30. *Origin of the Lingam (South
India), XIII cent. A.D.*

31. *Growth of the Cosmic Pigmy
(Badāmī), VI cent. A.D.*

32. *Shiva-Trinity and Host
(Parel), c. 600 A.D.*

33. The Great Lord (Elephanta), VIII century A.D.

34. *Shiva-Shakti (Bengal), X century A.D.*

35. Yab-Yum (Tibet), XVIII century A.D.

36. Shrī-Yantra

37. The Cosmic Lotus (Tibet), late XVIII century A.D.

38. *Lord of the Dance (South India), XII–XIV centuries A.D.*

39. *Slayer of the Elephant (Perŭr), XVII cent. A.D.*

40. *Slayer of the Elephant (Madura), XVII cent. A.D.*

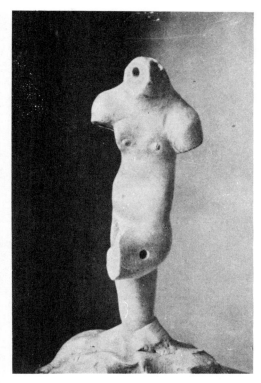

42. *Divinity (Mohenjo-Daro),*
3000–2000 B.C.

41. *Dancer (Harappa), 3000–2000 B.C.*

43. *Jointed Toy (Mohenjo-Daro), 3000–2000 B.C*

44. *Severing the Hair-Tuft*
(Burma), XI cent. A.D.

45. *Miracle of the Hair-Tuft*
(Burma), XI cent. A.D.

46. *Festival of the Hair-Tuft*
(Bhārhut), c. 175 B.C.

47. *Vajra (Cambodia),*
XII–XIV cent. A.D.

48. Buddha (Cambodia), XI–XII cent. A.D.

49. Lohan (China),
Tang Period.

50. Buddha (Cambodia),
XI–XII cent. A.D.

51. Kīrttimukha (Java), XIII cent. A.D.

52. Member of Siva's Host (Java), c. 875 A.D.

53. Ganesha (India), c. XVII cent. A.D.

54. Ganesha, rear view with Kīrtti-mukha (Java), XIII cent. A.D.

55. *Shiva-Tripurāntaka (Elūrā), VIII century A.D.*

56. Origin of the Goddess (MS. illumination), c. 1800 A.D.

57. Wrath of the Goddess (Rājput), XVII cent. A.D.

*58. The Goddess slaying the monster buffalo
(Java), VIII cent. A.D.*

*59. The Goddess slaying the monster buffalo
(Māmallapuram), VII cent. A.D.*

60. Shiva and Pārvatī on Mt. Kailāsa, Ravana imprisoned beneath (Elūrā), VIII cent. A.D.

61. Shiva and Pārvatī (Rājput), c. 1800 A.D.

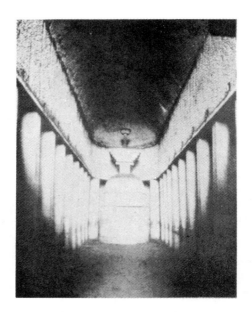

62. Chaitya hall (Bedsā), c. 175 B.C.

63. The Great Stūpa (Sāñchī), III–I cent. B.C.

*64. Lingam revealing the Goddess
(Cambodia), XIV cent. A.D.*

*65. Stūpa revealing the Buddha
(Ajantā), VII cent. A.D.*

66. The Island of Jewels (Rājput), c. 1800 A.D.

67. Kālī on Shiva-Shava (Kāngrā), c. 1800 A.D.

68. The Devouring Kālī (North India), XVII–XVIII cent. A.D.

69. Kālī dancing on Shiva (Modern Period)

70. Shiva-Ardhanārī (Kāngrā), early XIX century A.D.